SPIRITUAL EXERCISE
Simplified Version of the Basic Lessons
on Practical Christian Living

D1568766

WATCHMAN NEE

CHRISTIAN FELLOWSHIP PUBLISHERS, INC.
NEW YORK

SPIRITUAL EXERCISE

*A Simplified Version of the Basic Lessons
on Practical Christian Living*

Copyright © 2007
Christian Fellowship Publishers, Inc.
New York
All Rights Reserved.

ISBN 13: 978-0-935008-87-6
ISBN 10: 0-935008-87-X

Available from the Publishers at:

11515 Allecingie Parkway
Richmond, Virginia 23235
www.c-f-p.com

Printed in the United States of America

SPIRITUAL EXERCISE
A Simplified Version of the Basic Lessons on Practical Christian Living

ii

FOREWORD

"Exercise thyself unto godliness: for bodily exercise is profitable for a little; but godliness is profitable for all things, having promise of the life which now is, and of that which is to come. Faithful is the saying, and worthy of all acceptation" (1 Tim. 4. 7b-9). How very true is the above word and how worthy it is to be followed. Everybody knows that *physical* exercise is good and necessary to bodily health and many are doing it. But how few of God's children know the exceedingly great importance of performing *spiritual* exercise, and even fewer are those who are doing it. No wonder there is much to be desired in spiritual growth among Christians.

In view of such lack in spiritual exercise, brother Watchman Nee–in the course of conducting training sessions for church workers held in 1948 in China–gave a series of basic lessons on practical Christian living, with the hope that these lessons would be given successively once a week throughout the year in order to encourage God's children to exercise themselves unto godliness. However, when these talks were originally given, he had the Christian workers, not the latter's potential hearers, in mind. He wanted to help workers by supplying them with abundant materials on these subjects, from which they could then select according to the requirements of their particular audiences. Hence, when these lessons were published, they may have appeared to be too complicated for the average reader to grasp. We have therefore come to see the need of simplifying these messages to suit the need of the readers, especially young believers. By making these lessons more concise, we hope the readers will be able to have a firmer grasp of these basic principles on practical Christian living and can thus receive help in exercising themselves unto godliness. May the Holy Spirit lead us into all truth.

Scripture quotations are from the
American Standard Version of the Bible
(1901), unless otherwise indicated.

Contents

BOOK FOUR: NOT I BUT CHRIST

BOOK FIVE: DO ALL TO THE GLORY OF GOD

BOOK SIX: LOVE ONE ANOTHER

BOOK ONE:
A Living Sacrifice

Baptism

Scripture to Memorize:
*He that believeth and is baptized shall be saved;
but he that disbelieveth shall be condemned.*

Mark 16.16

Realizing the comprehensiveness of baptism in the Bible, we shall focus our consideration on just two of its aspects which, we are convinced, every new believer must know. These two aspects are: (1) What can baptism do for a person? and (2) What is the real meaning of baptism? Before the believer is baptized, he should look ahead and ask: Now that I am going into the water, what will baptism do for me? This is viewing baptism in advance. But after baptism, the believer needs to cast a backward look and ask the second question: What is the meaning of this which I have undergone? The first is foresight, an understanding before baptism; the second is hindsight, an ascertaining following baptism.

What Can Baptism Do for a Person?

*"He that believeth and is baptized shall be saved;
but he that disbelieveth shall be condemned."*

Mk. 16.16

Now let us be clear as to the meaning of the word "salvation" in the Bible. What is the objective of salvation? This may not be easily understood by new believers because they lack an accurate knowledge of what salvation is. According to the Bible, salvation is related to the world,

3

not to hell. The opposite of eternal life is perdition (perishing), while the opposite of salvation is the world. We are to be saved out of the world. As long as we belong to the world, we are in the state of perdition.

Let us notice the four cardinal facts concerning the world as shown in the Bible: (a) The world is condemned or judged before God, (b) the world lies in the evil one, (c) the world crucified the Lord Jesus, and (d) the world is an enemy to God. Please note that the world not only sins, but has also crucified the Lord Jesus. It is therefore God's enemy. These are the four cardinal facts of the world as God sees it. All who are in the world, irrespective of their personal conduct, are already judged and thus in perdition.

What is wrong with people in this world is far more than personal unrighteous acts of behavior. Their very position is wrong before God. How can a person forsake the world if he is still keenly aware of its loveliness? But one day he is made to see the wrong position of the world before God. However lovely the world may be, it has to be forsaken. So salvation deals with deliverance from an improper relationship with, and position in, the world.

What is meant by salvation then? To be saved is to be released from that fraternity, that position, and that relationship of, in and with the world. In other words, I come out of the world. People are usually most concerned with their personal justification, but they need to be reminded of the place from which they have been saved. Salvation is to be saved out of the world, not only out of hell, for the world is under the judgment of God.

BAPTISM FOLLOWS BELIEVING

There is not the slightest doubt that whosoever believes in the Lord Jesus has eternal life. We have preached this glad news for many years. As soon as one believes in the Lord Jesus, whoever he may be, he receives eternal life and is thereby forever favored by God. But let us remember: believing without being baptized is not yet salvation. Indeed, you have believed; indeed, you have eternal life; but you are not yet reckoned as a saved person in the eyes of the world. As long as you are not baptized, you will not be recognized as saved. Why? Because no one knows your difference from the rest of the world. You must rise up and be baptized, declaring the termination of your relationship with the world; then and only then are you saved.

What is baptism? It is your emancipation from the world. It frees you from the fraternity to which you once belonged. The world knew that you were one with it, but the moment you are baptized, it immediately becomes aware of the fact that you are finished with it. The friendship which you had maintained so many years has now come to an end. You were buried in the tomb, you terminated your course in the world. Before baptism, you knew you had eternal life; after baptism, you know you are saved. Everybody recognizes that you are the Lord's, for you belong to Him.

"He that believeth and is baptized shall be saved." Why? Because having believed and been baptized, it is now an open fact where one stands. Were there no faith, there would not be that inward fact which alone makes things real. But with that inward reality, baptism puts one outside of the world and terminates the former relationship with the world. Baptism, therefore, is separation.

NO BAPTISM, NO TESTIMONY

"But he that disbelieveth shall be condemned." Disbelief alone is enough for condemnation. As long as one belongs to the world fraternity, his disbelief seals his condemnation. In contrast, he who believes must be baptized, for as long as he is not baptized, he has not come out of the world in outward testimony.

What Is the Real Meaning of Baptism?

Now that the Christian is baptized, he needs to look back and assess the real meaning of baptism. "Are ye ignorant that all we who were baptized into Christ Jesus were baptized into his death?" (Rom. 6.3). "Having been buried with him in baptism, wherein ye were also raised with him through faith in the working of God, who raised him from the dead" (Col. 2.12). This is a looking backward, not forward.

Romans 6 stresses death and burial, though in addition it touches upon resurrection. Colossians 2, however, emphasizes burial and resurrection. It is therefore a step further, for its focal point is resurrection. The water serves as a tomb. What is buried must be dead, but what emerges must be alive in resurrection. Romans describes the first part of the truth and Colossians the last part of the same truth.

Therefore, beloved, when you step into the water of baptism or when you look back to your baptism after the lapse of many years, you need to remember that you are one already dead. You ask people to bury you because you believe you are dead. You would no doubt vigorously object if anyone should want to bury you before your death. Even if you were too weak to voice your objection, you would certainly resist being buried before you had breathed your last breath. Death is therefore *the* prerequisite of burial.

New believers should be instructed that at the time of the crucifixion of the Lord Jesus they too were crucified. It is on this basis that they request to be buried in water. But just as the Lord Jesus was raised from among the dead, they too shall be raised through the working of the same power of resurrection within them. In coming out of the water, they become resurrected ones; they are no longer their former selves.

This is something which they ought often to look back upon. Having believed that they were dead, they asked to be buried. Now having emerged from the water, they thus shall walk in newness of life. They are now on the resurrection side.

Concluding the Past

Scripture to Memorize:

Wherefore if any man is in Christ, he is a new creature: the old things are passed away; behold, they are become new.

2 Corinthians 5.17

After one believes in the Lord, he invariably has a number of things from the past that await termination. The question before us is: how should he conclude them?

The Teaching of the Bible

In the Bible, especially in the New Testament, God does not seem to stress much on the things which one did before he trusted in the Lord. Try to find some passages anywhere between Matthew and Revelation which deal with the concluding of the past. If you do try, you will have to concede that it is extremely difficult to find such passages. True, the epistles do recount our past improper manner of life; they also reveal to us what our future actions should be. But they do not recommend what to do about our past. For instance, in both the letter to the Ephesians and that to the Colossians our past is mentioned, but neither of them tells us how we ought to conclude it. They only deal with what we should do hereafter. The same is true in the letters to the Thessalonians. They too recall the past without specifying how to conclude it, for the emphasis again is on the future, as if the past were no longer a problem. However, there is no doubt that the past needs to be properly concluded.

9

Due to some mistaken concepts concerning the gospel, dealing with the past is sometimes stressed to such an excess that it puts people into bondage. We are not suggesting that the past needs no dealing, for there are a few things which do require such dealing. However, we have to maintain that this is not foundational. God tells us that all our past sins are under the blood. We are completely forgiven because the Lord Jesus has died for us. We are saved through Christ our Substitute, not on the ground of our dealing with the past. No one is saved by his past good conduct, nor is anyone saved because of repentance for his past evil. We are saved through the redemption accomplished by the Lord Jesus on the cross. This alone is the foundation on which we firmly stand.

What Needs to Be Dealt with

What, then, should we do about the past? After searching the New Testament carefully, we find a few places where this matter of concluding the past is mentioned. But all these cases are examples, none of them is a teaching. Our Lord has thus left us a few examples for our guidance in solving the past.

1. THINGS OF IDOLS MUST BE CONCLUDED

". . . Ye turned unto God from idols" (I Thess. 1.9). Things pertaining to idols are not as simple as many think. Remember, we are the temple of the Holy Spirit. What agreement has the temple of God with idols? Even the apostle John, in writing to the believers, exhorts, "My little children, guard yourselves from idols" (I John 5.21).

We must understand the way Scripture views idolatry. God forbids the making of any graven image or any likeness of anything that is in heaven above or in the earth beneath or in the water; He also prohibits the entertaining of any thought that these images are alive. As soon as such a thought is cherished, these images become idols. The images in themselves are nothing, but if they are reckoned as alive, they turn diabolic. Hence the worship of these images is strictly forbidden; no heart is allowed to turn towards them. One of the ten commandments bans the making of images (see Deut. 5.8).

". . . Inquire not after their gods, saying, How do these nations serve their gods?" (Deut. 12.30b). Do not inquire after other gods through curiosity. Do not ask how the nations serve their gods. God forbids us to make such investigations for this will only lead to following the ways of the nations.

Starting from the very first day of his life of faith in Christ, a believer must be separated from idols and things pertaining to idolatry. He must not any more mention the names of idols, nor consult with fortunetellers. He should keep himself away from heathen temples, from entertaining any thought of worshipping images. He should not inquire into how other religions worship. The past must be totally concluded. Any idolatrous objects he may have should be smashed, not sold; they should be destroyed. This is very serious, for God is extremely jealous of idols.

2. CERTAIN THINGS REQUIRE A CONCLUSION

"And not a few of them that practised magical arts brought their books together and burned them in the sight of all; and they counted the price of them, and found it fifty thousand pieces of silver" (Acts 19.19). This, too, is something a new believer must bring to a conclusion. Though there is no command nor teaching, yet such dealing is clearly the result of the Holy Spirit's working. The Holy Spirit so works in believers that they bring forth those things which ought not to be in their possession and burn them. The books mentioned in Acts 19 were worth fifty

11

thousand pieces of silver—a lot of money. But they were not sold so that the church might use the proceeds; rather, they were burned. If Judas had been present, he certainly would have objected to that burning for the value of the books was worth far more than thirty pieces of silver; the money could have been used to aid the poor. The Lord, however, was pleased to have the books burned.

There are several things that need to be brought to a conclusion. Images are one, books on magic are another. The principle is clear: all images must be rejected and all doubtful things must be dealt with. We have the scriptural example that things that have a definite connection with sin, such as gambling instruments or obscene books, must be burned.

How about things which are unbecoming to the saints? In an unbeliever's home, it would be quite natural to find things connected with sin and things not befitting the saint. Thus, after one has believed in the Lord, he should go home and look over his belongings. Things connected with sin should be destroyed, not sold. Things unbefitting the saint may be altered where possible, as with clothing, or may be sold.

3. ALL INDEBTEDNESS MUST BE REIMBURSED

"And Zacchaeus stood, and said unto the Lord, Behold, Lord, the half of my goods I give to the poor; and if I have wrongfully exacted aught of any man, I restore fourfold" (Lk. 19.8). Zacchaeus sets us a good example. Strangely, there is no teaching on this subject but each believer acts as he is moved by the Holy Spirit. Hence a little more here and a little less there, each doing as he is led by the Holy Spirit. If this were something merely of doctrine or teaching, then all would be done uniformly.

If a new believer has in the past extorted or cheated anybody or has stolen or taken possession of anything

unrighteously, we believe he should deal with these things
as the Lord works in him. Financially he may be unable to
clear up what he has defrauded. Though this will not affect
his being forgiven by God, it will have a definite bearing on
his testimony. As a new believer, one needs to ask himself if he has
wronged or defrauded anybody, if he has taken home things
which do not belong to him or things which he has obtained
unrighteously. If so, he could make a clean sweep of them
by dealing with each one. Christian repentance includes the
confession of past faults. It is not like ordinary repentance
which simply involves a change of conduct. For example:
if, as a worldling I often lost my temper in the past, it
would be enough for me to show my repentance by not
repeating it. But as a Christian, in addition to the change in
conduct, I must also confess that losing my temper was
wrong. I must not only control my temper before God but
also I must confess to men my former fault of losing my
temper. Thus shall this matter be concluded.

Selling All

Scripture to Memorize:

No man can serve two masters: for either he will hate the one, and love the other; or else he will hold to one, and despise the other. Ye cannot serve God and mammon.

Matthew 6.24

Let us start with the example of the young ruler in Luke 18. He was a man of good conduct, not a bad person before God. He had kept all the commandments and had shown due respect to the Lord Jesus by calling Him a good teacher. And the Lord Jesus considered him quite precious, for to meet such a person was rare. Looking upon him, Jesus loved him.

However, the Lord laid down one requirement. If anyone desires to serve Him, he must be perfect. Notice what the Lord said: "If thou wouldst be perfect, . . . One thing thou lackest yet" (Matt. 19.21; Lk. 18.22). In other words, the Lord wants those who follow Him to follow Him perfectly, not lacking in anything. People cannot follow God if they have solved ninety and nine of their problems but have yet one problem unsolved. To follow God demands the whole being. It must be all or not at all. Indeed, this young ruler had kept the commandments from his youth up. He habitually feared God. Yet he lacked one thing. He needed to sell all his property and distribute the proceeds to the poor; then the way would be clear for him to come and follow the Lord.

This exacting demand must be clearly understood. According to the record of the Bible, when the young man

15

heard the saying, he went away sorrowful, for he was one who had great possessions. Having come so near to the Lord and having seen so clearly too, he yet kept his sorrow even as he determined to keep his wealth. "The love of money . . . some [have] reach[ed] after...and have pierced themselves through with many sorrows" (I Tim. 6.10). Men may hoard wealth but they cannot hoard happiness. As they accumulate wealth, they also accumulate trouble. In gathering wealth, they gather sorrows and problems. Here was a young man who kept his wealth but was unable to follow the Lord. If wealth is what you want, then you need not think of following the Lord. To keep wealth is also to keep your sorrow, for wealth and sorrow always go together. He who gives up his wealth is a happy man, whereas he who is reluctant to part with it is a sad person. This statement is always true. Those who are greedy of material things dwell in sorrows. May the newly saved Christian seek happiness by laying aside all and following the Lord.

The Lord Jesus answered with one sentence, and in this one sentence is the crux of the whole problem. Let us, too, hold onto this word: "The things which are impossible with men are possible with God." (Luke 18.27). It is quite clear that such a thing as abandoning all to enter into the kingdom of God is unheard of in this world. The Lord acknowledges this as humanly impossible. What was wrong with the young ruler was not his inability to sell all, but rather his sorrowful departure. God knows it is impossible for *men* to sell and distribute all to the poor. But when the young man sadly left, he seemed to conclude that this was also impossible with *God*. Of course it is wrong for me not to forsake my all, but does not the Lord know all about it? Therefore the Lord declares: what is impossible with men is possible with God. How can anyone get a camel through a needle's eye? Impossible. Similarly, people on this earth all love wealth and to ask them to sell all is to ask for the impossible. But if I go away with sorrow, then I am truly wrong, for I have limited the power of God.

The Lesson of Zacchaeus (Luke 19.1-10)

Zacchaeus was a Jew, but he worked for the Roman government. From the Jewish standpoint, he was a traitor, because he cooperated with the Roman Empire. He helped the Roman Empire collect taxes from his own people. Furthermore, he was a sinner. He did not have a good character like the young ruler who kept the commandments from his youth. Like other tax collectors, he was greedy and extorted as much as he could. He certainly had earned his poor reputation. Yet, the Lord Jesus passed by. Great is His power to attract people to Him. "No man can come to me, except the Father that sent me draw him" (John 6.44). So this tax collector was drawn by God to His Son. Due to his short stature, Zacchaeus climbed a tree to see Jesus. The Lord looked at him but did not preach a sermon to him. He did not say, "You must repent and confess your sins," nor did He reproach him for extortion and greediness; neither did He require him to sell all, give to the poor, and follow Him. No sermon was preached, just a few simple words were said: "Zacchaeus, make haste, and come down; for to-day I must abide at thy house." Not a single word of exhortation. It was just a personal contact, a private encounter. A heart which desired the Lord was met by the Lord who chose him. Zacchaeus knew nothing at all of any doctrine.

Take note of the point of emphasis here. The Lord did not preach any doctrine, but simply said, "I must abide at thy house." That simple word, however, was sufficient. Actually, He had not yet come to Zacchaeus' house; He merely suggested His coming. But this was enough, for wherever the Lord is, there the love of money departs.

When He comes, all those problems are solved. His desiring to go to Zacchaeus' house was as powerful as if He were already there. Just that simple statement, "I must abide at thy house," made Zacchaeus bankrupt, for he stood and declared, "Behold, Lord, the half of my goods I give to the poor; and if I have wrongfully exacted aught of any man, I restore fourfold."

The young ruler was exhorted by the Lord, but he failed to obey; Zacchaeus was not even persuaded and yet he fully followed the Lord's wish. Both were rich, and generally speaking, the older a person is the more he loves money. But here it was the older one who let go his money. The young ruler represents "impossible with men," whereas Zacchaeus represents "possible with God." To sell all and follow the Lord is not a small matter. To do so is not easy, for who would be willing to forsake his wealth? Unless he had gone mad, no man would part with all his possessions at once. But the story of Zacchaeus demonstrates to us that what is impossible for man is possible for God. Zacchaeus did what the Lord wished without hearing or accepting any teaching. This illustrates how easily it can be done.

God's Way for Today

Take note of these two chapters, Luke 18 and 19: in the one the young ruler was charged by the Lord to sell all, but went away sadly; in the other Zacchaeus abandoned all without even being asked. In His days on this earth our Lord required people to forsake all and follow Him. Likewise the church, shortly after its founding, did the same thing. In Acts 2 and 4 we find that at the beginning of the church all things are held in common; that is, not one of the believers said that any of the things he possessed was his own. In other words, the hand of the Lord was upon all those who were saved. Once they had gained eternal life, their possessions began to lose their grip, and, in quite a natural way, they sold their houses and properties.

Applying this principle to those of * us today who come to follow the Lord, it should also be quite natural to us that our many possessions be touched by Him. Our attitude should be turned so that we no longer regard these things as our own. No one then will say that this or that thing belongs to me. No one will claim anything as peculiarly his own.

God or Mammon

Let us return to Matthew 6 where it says we can only serve one master. We cannot serve God and mammon. Mammon (or riches) is an idol which many have served over the past years. Such service gets a firm grip on the heart. Now, though, if we are going to serve God, we must choose whom to serve—God or mammon. We cannot serve both. What does the Lord say? "For where thy treasure is, there will thy heart be also" (Matt. 6.21). Once a brother told me: "My treasure is on earth but my heart is in heaven." Such a brother should be exhibited in a Christian museum as a rarity! The Lord says it cannot be, but this person invents a "can be". Is it not greater than a miracle? However, the word of the Lord is candid and sure: one's heart always follows the treasure; there is no escape from it. No matter how one reasons, his heart goes after his treasure.

* Note: To be a follower of Christ, one must forsake all and follow Him. This principle applies to all followers, though its practice may differ in each one, according to the leading of the Holy Spirit.— *Translator*

19

"Lay not up for yourselves treasures upon the earth" (Matt. 6.19). If you do, you will end up serving mammon and not God. You cannot serve both God and mammon. You must choose either one or the other. How detrimental it would be to choose mammon, for such treasure is subject to moth and rust and thieves. Let us therefore learn to serve God. Let us give all that we have to God and maintain the simplest kind of life here on this earth.

Consecration

Scripture to Memorize:

I beseech you therefore, brethren, by the mercies of God, to present your bodies a living sacrifice, holy, acceptable to God, which is your spiritual service.

Romans 12.1

In order to build up a new believer, the first problem to solve is the matter of consecration. But whether or not he can take in this lesson depends largely on how well he has been saved. If the gospel has not been well presented, the one who comes to the Lord Jesus may consider himself as doing God a great favor. For a person like him to become a Christian adds much glory to Christianity! Under such an illusion how can anyone speak to him about consecration? Even a queen has to be brought to the place where she gladly lays her crown at the Lord's feet. We all need to realize that it is we who are favored by the Lord in being loved and saved. Only then can we willingly lay down everything.

The Bases of Consecration

Let us search the New Testament first. There we find how the children of God are constrained by love to live unto the Lord who died and rose again for them (2 Cor. 5.14). The word "constrained" means to be tightly held or to be surrounded so that one cannot escape. When a person is moved by love, he will experience such a sensation. Love will bind him and thus he is helpless.

Love, therefore, is the basis of consecration. No one can consecrate himself without sensing the love of the Lord. He has to see the Lord's love before he can ever consecrate his life. It is futile to talk about consecration if the love of the Lord is not seen. Having seen the Lord's love, consecration will be the inevitable consequence.

However, consecration is also based on right or divine prerogative. This is the truth we find in 1 Corinthians 6.19-20. "Know ye not that your body is a temple of the Holy Spirit which is in you, which ye have from God? and ye are not your own; for ye were bought with a price: glorify God therefore in your body." Today among Christians this matter of being bought with a price may not be clearly understood. But to the Corinthians at the time of the Roman Empire, it was perfectly clear. Why? Because at that time they had human markets. Just as one could go to the market to buy chicken or duck, so one could buy human beings in the human market. The only difference was that whereas food prices were more or less established, in the human market the price of each soul was established by bidding at auction. Whoever bid the highest price got the man, and whoever owned the slave had absolute power over him. Paul uses this metaphor to show us what our Lord has done for us and how He gave His life as the ransom to purchase us back to God. The Lord paid a great price—even His own life. And today, because of this work of redemption, we give up our rights and forfeit our sovereignty. We are no longer our own, for we belong to the Lord; therefore, we must glorify God in our bodies. We are bought with a price, even the blood of the cross. Since we are bought, we become His by right, by divine prerogative.

On the one hand, for the sake of love we choose to serve Him; and on the other hand, by right we are not our own, we must follow Him; we cannot do otherwise. According to the right of redemption, we are His; and according to the love which redemption generates in us, we

22

must live for Him. One basis for consecration is legal right and the other basis is responsive love. Consecration is thus based on the love which surpasses human feeling as well as on right according to law. For these two reasons, we cannot but belong to the Lord.

The Real Meaning of Consecration

We should know that being constrained by love is not yet consecration; nor is seeing the Lord's right yet true consecration. After one has been constrained by love and has seen the Lord's prerogative, he needs to do something additional. This extra step puts him in the position of consecration. Being constrained by the Lord's love and knowing that he has been purchased, he quietly sets himself apart from everything in order to be wholly the Lord's. This is the consecration depicted in the Old Testament. It is the acceptance of a holy office, the office of serving the Lord. "O Lord, being loved, what else can I do than to separate myself from everything that I may serve You? Hereafter no one may use my hands or feet or mouth or ears, for these my two hands are to do Your works, my two feet to walk in Your way, my mouth to sing Your praise, and my ears to listen to Your voice." This is consecration.

Suppose you purchase a slave and bring him home. At the door of your house, the man kneels and does you homage, saying, "Master, you have bought me. Today I gladly hearken to your words." For you to have purchased him is one thing, but his kneeling before you and proclaiming his desire to serve you is something else. Because you have purchased him, he acknowledges your right. But because you have loved him even though he is such a man, he proclaims himself wholly yours. This alone is consecration. Consecration is more than love, more than purchasing; *it is the action which follows love and purchasing.* Henceforth the one who consecrates himself is separated from everything in this world, from all his former masters. Hereafter he will do nothing but what his Master commands. He restricts himself to doing only the things of that one Master. This is what consecration really means.

The Aim of Consecration

Consecration aims not at preaching or working for God, but in serving God. The word "service" in the original bears the sense of "waiting on," that is, waiting on God in order to serve Him. Consecration does not necessarily involve incessant labor, for its aim is to wait upon God. If He wishes us to stand, we stand; if He wants us to wait, we wait; and if He desires us to run, we run. This is the true meaning of "waiting on" Him.

What God requires of us is to present our bodies to Him, not for the purpose of ascending the pulpit or of evangelizing far distant lands, but of waiting upon Him. Some may indeed have to accept the pulpit, because they are sent there by God. Some may be constrained to go to distant lands, for they are commissioned by God to go. The work itself varies but the time consumed remains the same—our lifetime. We need to learn to wait on God. We offer our bodies that we may be those who serve.

Once we become Christians, we must serve God for life. As soon as a medical doctor becomes a Christian, medicine recedes from being his vocation to being his avocation. So will it be for the engineer. The Lord's demand occupies the first priority; serving God becomes the major job. Should the Lord permit, I can do some medical or engineering work to maintain a living, but I will not be able to make either of them my life work. Some of the early disciples were fishermen, but after they followed the Lord they did not hope anymore to be great and successful fishermen. They might be allowed to fish occasionally, but their destiny was altered.

May God be gracious to us, especially to young believers, that we may all see how our vocation has been changed. Let all the professors, doctors, nurses, engineers, and industrialists see that their vocation is now to serve God. Their past vocations have receded to avocations. They should not be too ambitious in their special fields, though the Lord may still give some of them special positions. We who serve God cannot expect to be prosperous in the world, for these two are contradictory. Hereafter we are to serve God alone; we have no other way or destiny.

In consecration, our prayer is: "O Lord, You have given me the opportunity and privilege to come before You and serve You. Lord, I am Yours. Henceforth my ears, hands and feet, being bought by the blood, are exclusively Yours. The world can no longer use them, nor will I use them either." What, then, is the result? The result will be holiness, for the fruit of consecration is holiness. In Exodus 28 we have consecration on the one hand and holiness to the Lord on the other. We need to be brought to see that after we become Christians, we are spoiled for everything else. This does not mean we will be less faithful in our secular jobs. No, we must be subject to authorities and faithfully fulfill our tasks. But we have seen before God that our life must be spent in the way of serving God; all other jobs are side lines.

Studying the Bible

Scripture to Memorize:

Every scripture inspired of God is also profitable for teaching, for reproof, for correction, for instruction which is in righteousness: that the man of God may be complete, furnished completely unto every good work.

2 Timothy 3.16,17

No good Christian should be ignorant of the word of God, for God's way of speaking to men today is to reiterate the words He has already spoken. It is extremely rare to find God speaking to anyone with words that are not found in the Bible. Although at times God does speak directly to some who have gone on far with the Lord, yet even these utterances are largely words which He has already set forth in the Scriptures. God's speaking, then, is His repeating what He has said before. Young believers, if unfamiliar with what God has already spoken, create a problem for God in that they do not have the foundation for God to speak to them.

The Bible is the word of God. It reveals to us all that God has done for us in the past. It also shows us in what ways God has led men to know Him in days gone by. In order to know the richness and fullness of God's provision for us, we must study the Bible. And to understand by what steps God will lead us to Himself, we also need to study the Bible.

Furthermore, when God desires to use us to speak for Him, He usually uses the words He already has spoken. Should we be ignorant of these words, it is difficult for God

27

to speak through us. We then will be useless persons before Him. Thus we need to store the word of Christ richly in our hearts that we may hear those words which God wants to speak to us now and also that we may know how God has walked in the past.

The Bible is a big book and a serious one. If we were to spend the whole of our life in the study of it, we would but touch its fringes. How can any believer know the word without spending time on it? It is absolutely impossible. Thus young people especially ought to be diligent in studying God's word so that as they reach middle age and then old age, they will have a rich supply of the word for the needs both of themselves and of others.

Whoever wishes to know God must study God's word well. Every new believer needs to recognize the importance of studying God's word at the very start of his Christian life.

How to Study the Bible

How, then, should we study the Bible? Four basic principles are:

(a) Find or discover facts

(b) Memorize the word

(c) Analyze, deduce and compare the word

(d) Receive enlightenment from God

However varied may be the external methods, the basic principles of studying the word remain unchanged. And the order given above should also be kept: first fact finding, next memorizing, then analyzing, and finally receiving enlightenment.

The Bible contains many spiritual facts which to the spiritually blind are hidden. If one discovers any fact in the Bible, he already has half the light and hence has fulfilled

28

half of the study purpose. It is therefore absolutely necessary to find facts; otherwise we will not be able to receive God's enlightenment, for the light of God shines only on the facts in His word. Why does God speak in this way or in that way? Through analysis, comparison and deduction we are open to enlightenment. Thus shall we be fed and thus shall we be able to feed others. If we study the Bible carelessly, God's word will leak away and we will not know what is in it.

It is a matter of great importance to be able to discover cardinal facts in the Bible. For example, what the Bible says and what it does not say are deeply significant. Why does it say things differently in different places? God has forbidden that a single word of the original Bible be changed. Why then in some instances is the singular number used whereas in other instances it is the plural? Why sometimes are years clearly mentioned and other times many years just skipped over? All these are facts to be noticed.

For the above reasons, one who studies the Bible must be a careful person before God. He cannot afford to be inattentive. He must be a single-minded individual, for the word of God is pure. As soon as he hears God's word, he should know where the emphasis lies. But many Christians read the word without hearing anything. They find neither its facts nor its keys.

Practical Hints in Studying the Bible

Finally, the Bible must be read daily and consecutively. It is best if the Old and the New Testaments are read together. The reading should not be too fast but rather daily and systematically.

Before his death, George Muller thanked God for enabling him to read the Bible one hundred times. Young believers should remember the number of times they have read through the Bible. Begin with Matthew in the New Testament and Genesis in the Old Testament, and read through both Testaments. Mark down the number of times in your Bible. We hope every believer will be able to read through one hundred times. If a person lives to be a Christian for fifty years, he should have read the Bible at least twice each year for him to reach one hundred times.

In studying the Bible, two different times should be set apart and two Bibles should be used. The morning time of reading should be accompanied by prayer. It is for the purpose of building up one's own spiritual life. Only three or four verses each morning are enough. Prayers with meditation should be mixed with the reading. The afternoon time is devoted to knowing more of God's word; therefore, a longer time may be spent in the reading. This is also the time to find out facts in the Bible. If possible, use two Bibles: one for the morning and one for the afternoon. In the morning Bible, nothing should be written inside except a record of the dates in which one has had special dealings with God while reading a particular passage. The afternoon Bible should record the light received in the reading; hence everything of value can be written in, and circles, straight lines, or colored lines can be drawn all over the pages.

By reading the word over and over again, gradually our knowledge of the Bible will be increased. If possible, try to memorize one or two verses each day. This may be difficult in the beginning, but it will be a great help later on.

Prayer

Scripture to Memorize:
Ask, and it shall be given you; seek, and ye shall find; knock, and it shall be opened unto you.

Matthew 7.7

Learning to pray follows studying the Bible. Prayer is both the most profound and the simplest of all Christian exercises. A person newly saved can pray. Yet, many of God's children—even on their deathbeds—confess that they have not yet mastered the art of prayer.

Answered prayer is one of the basic privileges or rights of a Christian. A Christian is given by God the right of having his prayers heard. If one has been a Christian for three to five years and has not had one prayer answered, his Christian life must be quite questionable. For a child of God not to have his prayers answered is wrong. A Christian's prayers ought to be answered.

"Hitherto have ye asked nothing in my name: ask, and ye shall receive, that your joy may be made full" (John 16.24). He who prays often and has his prayers answered often will be a happy Christian. This is a fundamental experience that every believer must have. One may be careless in other spiritual matters, but in this matter of answered prayer a Christian cannot afford to deceive himself. It is either yes or no. He must seek to have prayers answered.

The Conditions for Answered Prayer

A number of conditions for answered prayer may be found in the Bible, but we will pick out a few which we believe are quite sufficient for beginners. These few may well cover over half of the requirements learned by advanced Christians.

1. ASK

To pray one must really ask. "Ye have not, because ye ask not" (Jas. 4.2). "And I say unto you, Ask, and it shall be given you; seek, and ye shall find; knock, and it shall be opened unto you. For every one that asketh receiveth; and he that seeketh findeth; and to him that knocketh it shall be opened" (Lk. 11.9-10).

When I was newly saved, I professed that I prayed daily. One day a sister in the Lord asked me, "Have your prayers been answered by God?" I was surprised because to me prayer was simply praying and nothing more. I prayed but I never thought of whether or not I was heard. Since that time, however, I have prayed to be heard. After she asked me, I first examined my prayers to see how many God had answered. I discovered that I had not prayed many prayers of the type that required answers. My prayers were mostly general, so the answers really did not matter too much. It was like asking God for the sun to rise tomorrow; it would rise whether one prayed or not! After having been a Christian for a whole year, I could not find a single instance of answered prayer. Yes, I had knelt before God and uttered many words, but I had not really asked for anything.

2. DO NOT ASK AMISS

Men ought to ask of God. Scripture, however, lays down a second condition: do not ask amiss. "Ye ask, and receive not, because ye ask amiss" (Jas. 4.3a). Men may ask God for their needs, but they are not supposed to ask unreasonably or beyond their measure. It requires a few years of learning before anyone can pray so-called "big prayers" before God.

In the early days of our spiritual life, it is rather difficult for us to differentiate between big prayers and praying amiss. It is best for us at the beginning not to ask according to our desires or pleasures nor to ask lustfully for what we are not in need of. (see Jas. 4.3b). God will only supply our need and give us that which is necessary. Many times, though, God does grant us exceedingly abundantly above all that we ask. But if the young ask wrongly they will not be heard.

What is meant by asking amiss? It means asking beyond your measure, beyond your need, beyond your actual want. For instance, I have a certain need and I ask God to supply it. I ask according to the amount of my need. If I ask beyond my need, I will be asking amiss. If my need is great, I can ask God to supply that great need. But I should not ask for more, for God has no delight in hearing flippant prayer. Prayer ought to be measured by need; it should not be offered recklessly.

3. SIN MUST BE DEALT WITH

It may be that men have asked and have not asked wrongly, yet still are not heard. Why? Perhaps it is because there is a basic hindrance—sin standing between God and man.

"If I regard iniquity in my heart, the Lord will not hear" (Ps. 66.18). If anyone has a known sin in his heart and his heart clings to it, he shall not be heard. What is meant by regarding iniquity in the heart? It simply means there is a sin which one in his heart will not give up. Though a person may have great weaknesses, God will forgive them.

But if one has a sin of which he is aware and yet still desires it in his heart, then it is more than a weakness in outward conduct; it is regarding iniquity in his heart.

"He that covereth his transgressions shall not prosper; but whoso confesseth and forsaketh them shall obtain mercy" (Prov. 28.13). Sin must be confessed. After it is confessed, the Lord will forgive and forget. One should go to the Lord saying: "Here is a sin which my heart does regard and finds hard to give up, but now I ask for your forgiveness. I am willing to forsake it; I ask you to deliver me from it that it may not remain with me. I do not want it and I resist it." The Lord will pass over your sin if you so confess before Him. Then your prayer will be heard. This is a matter that should not be overlooked.

4. MUST BELIEVE

There is yet a positive condition that must be fulfilled, and that is, one must believe. Otherwise prayer will not be effectual. The incident in Mark 11.12-24 shows us clearly the necessity of faith in prayer. The Lord with His disciples came out from Bethany. He hungered on the way. Seeing a fig tree afar off, He approached that He might find some figs, but He found nothing except leaves. So He cursed the tree, saying, "No man eat fruit from thee henceforward for ever." The next morning they passed by and saw the fig tree withered away from the roots. The disciples were astonished. And the Lord answered, "Have faith in God. Verily I say unto you, Whosoever shall say unto this mountain, Be thou taken up and cast into the sea; and shall not doubt in his heart, but shall believe that what he saith cometh to pass; he shall have it. Therefore I say unto you, All things whatsoever ye pray and ask for, believe that ye receive them, and ye shall have them."

One must believe when he is praying, because if he believes then he shall receive. What is faith? Faith is believing that he receives what he prays for.

5. KEEP ON PRAYING

There is another side of prayer which may seem contradictory to what we have just said but which is equally real; which is, that men "ought always to pray, and not to faint" (Lk. 18.1). The Lord shows us that some prayers require persistency. We must keep on praying till the Lord is worn out, as it were, by our continual coming. This is not a sign of unbelief, rather, it is just another kind of faith: "Nevertheless, when the Son of man cometh, shall he find faith on the earth?" says the Lord. (Luke 18.8b). This is the kind of faith which believes that by praying persistently God will eventually answer, with or without a previous promise.

Prayer Has Two Ends

Prayer has two ends: one end is in the person who prays and the other end is the thing or person prayed for. Oftentimes the first end needs to undergo transformation before the other end can be changed. It is futile just to hope for the other end to change. We must learn to pray: "O Lord, where do I need to be changed? Is there yet sin that has not been dealt with? Is there any selfish desire which needs to be purified? Is there any practical lesson of faith that I must learn? Or is there anything that I need to forsake?" If there is need on our side for change, then let it be changed first. Too many of God's children hope the prayed—for end may be realized, while they themselves refuse to be changed.

If young brothers and sisters learn the lesson of prayer from the outset as well as learn the lesson of studying the Bible, the church will be greatly strengthened. God will grant a glorious future which will far surpass our past.

Early Rising

Scripture to Memorize:

O God, thou art my God; early will I seek thee.
My soul thirsteth for thee, my flesh languisheth for
thee, in a dry and weary land without water.

Psalm 63.1 (Darby)

Why Must We Rise Early?

That which we wish to lay before new believers now is extremely simple: we must rise early from our bed each day.

Let me quote the words of Miss Groves, a co-worker of Miss M. E. Barber, who has helped us greatly. She stated that the first choice giving evidence of one's love towards the Lord is the choice between one's bed and the Lord. If one chooses to love his bed more, he sleeps longer; but if he chooses to love his Lord more, he will rise up a little earlier. She spoke these words to me in 1921, but I still sense the freshness of them even today. Yes, a man has to choose between the bed and the Lord. If you love your bed more, sleep on longer; but if you love the Lord more, you must rise up earlier.

Many of God's servants in the Bible had the habit of early rising. Manna has to be gathered before the sun rises. Anyone who wishes to eat the food God has promised for him must rise up early. As the sun gets hot the manna melts, and then there will be none. Every young believer needs to know that to receive spiritual nourishment before God, to obtain spiritual food, to be spiritually uplifted and to enjoy spiritual communion, he has to rise up a little earlier. If he rises too late, he will lose his food. The sickly Christian life which prevails among God's children today is less due to any serious spiritual problem than it is to rising up too late in the morning. Do not, therefore, count this a small matter. The spiritual problem of many actually lies in their failure to rise up early in the morning.

It is as if in the early morning before or just as the day begins to dawn, God dispenses His provision of spiritual food and holy communion to His children. Whoever rises late will miss it. Many of God's children do not lack in consecration, zeal and love, and yet they fail to be good Christians because of getting up too late. Rising early has much to do with spiritual life. I have never met a prayer warrior who rises late, nor have I known anyone close to the Lord who gets up late. All who know God at the very least go to God early in the morning.

"As the door turneth upon its hinges, so doth the sluggard upon his bed" (Prov. 26.14). How does the sluggard act on his bed? He is like a door turning upon its hinges. The slothful person will turn in his bed, but will never leave it. He will turn this way and that way but yet remain in bed. Many people simply cling to their beds. Turning to one side, they find the bed lovely; turning to the other side, they find it still lovely! They love to sleep, to sleep a little longer, and to linger more in bed. Let brothers and sisters notice, however, that if they desire to serve God they must daily rise early.

Whoever purposes before God to rise early will soon experience manifold spiritual profit. His prayer at other times of the day cannot be compared with his early morning prayer. His Bible study at other hours cannot equal that of the morning hour; and his communion with the Lord is never as sweet at other moments as at daybreak. Remember well that the early morning is the best time of the day. We ought to present our best time to God, not to men or to the affairs of the world. He is a fool who spends his whole day in the world and then in the evening, when he is dog-tired, kneels down to pray and read the Bible before retiring to bed. Who can wonder that his prayer, his Bible study and his communion with the Lord are defective? His problem is one of getting up too late in the morning.

What to Do after Rising Early

Our aim is not just to get people out of bed in the early morning. We are seeking for spiritual value and spiritual content. So here are a few things which people should do after rising:

1. COMMUNE WITH GOD

Men rise early in the morning that they may commune with the Lord. "Let us get up early . . . There will I give thee my love" (S.S. 7.12). Being the best time of the day, it should be spent in holding fellowship with God, in waiting quietly before God, in meditating in God's presence, in receiving guidance and impressions from God, and in allowing God to speak to us, our spirits being open to Him. Communion means having one's spirit opened to God. As the spirit is opened to God, so is one's mind opened. This gives God opportunity to confer light, to supply a word, to grant an impression, and to render a living touch; it also gives the soul the privilege of learning to touch God, to meditate and contemplate, and to draw nigh in heart to God. This, in short, is communion with God.

2. SING AND PRAISE

The morning hour is the best hour to sing praises unto the Lord. We may send forth our highest praises at the morning hour.

3. SEEK BEFORE GOD FOR FOOD

This is the time to gather our manna. What is our manna? (Of course, manna points to Christ, but this is not our emphasis here.) It is the word of God which we daily enjoy and through which we receive strength to walk in the wilderness. Manna is food in the wilderness and has to be collected in the early morning. How can one be satisfied and nourished if he spends the early morning in attending to other affairs?

Let there be communion, praise, manna and prayer in the early morning. "O God, thou art my God; early will I seek thee" (Ps. 63.1 Darby). "And returned and sought early after God" (Ps. 78.34 Darby). In both psalms we find the word "early" in the original. Early in the morning is the time for prayer. After having communed with God and fed on manna, one is strengthened to lay all things before God and to carefully pray over them. It takes strength to pray; the weak cannot pray. With the new strength gathered from communion and from feeding on the manna, one is able to pray—for himself, for the church and for the whole world.

So every new believer needs to know the four things he ought to attentively do before God each morning: communion, praise, Bible reading and prayer. If he neglects these four, the day will declare it. Even a person like George Muller confessed that whether or not he was fully fed before God in the morning determined his spiritual condition for the whole day. His early morning foretold the day. Many Christians find their days hard because their mornings are ill spent. (I acknowledge that a person would not be easily affected by outward circumstances if he knew the separation of spirit and soul and thus the brokenness of the outward man. This, however, is a totally different aspect.) To new believers, the exhortation must be directed towards early rising, for once they become careless about this, they will be careless about almost everything else. The

40

difference it makes in the day—whether one has had nourishment in the morning or has gone hungry—is exceedingly great.

BOOK TWO:
The Good Confession

Public Confession

Scripture to Memorize:
For with the heart man believeth unto righteousness; and with the mouth confession is made unto salvation.

Romans 10.10

The matter of confession ought to be brought to the attention of new believers as soon as possible. Once a person has trusted in the Lord, he must confess the Lord before men. He should not hide his faith but should publicly confess it. The importance of such confession is both laid down in the Bible and borne out by our experience.

Suppose a baby makes no sound after one, two, or even three years of age. What would you think? If the child never talks in childhood, most probably he will be dumb for the rest of his life. If he cannot call "Papa," "Mama," as a child, he very likely never will. Likewise, one who believes in the Lord must confess Him immediately, or else he may be spiritually dumb throughout his life.

"For with the heart man believeth unto righteousness; and with the mouth confession is made unto salvation." The first half has to do with God while the second half has to do with men. No one can see whether you have believed or not; but if you come to God really believing, you will be justified before Him. Nevertheless, if you believe in your heart but never confess with your mouth, though justified before God, you will not be delivered from the world. The people of this world will not acknowledge you as a saved person. They will still reckon you as one of them, for they have not witnessed any difference between you and them. On this account the Bible emphatically states that besides believing with the heart there must also be confessing with the mouth.

The Advantages of Public Confession

One distinct advantage of publicly confessing the Lord lies in saving the new believer from many, many future troubles. If he does not open his mouth and say that he has followed the Lord Jesus and is now the Lord's, he will always be considered by those of the world to be one of them. Consequently, whenever they decide to engage in social, sinful, or carnal affairs, they will count him in. For example, when they want to play cards or go to the theater, they will ask the believer to join them. Why? Because they number him among them. He may sense in his heart that since he is a Christian he should not mix with them, yet he cannot refuse for he desires to please them. Even should he refuse once, undoubtedly he will be asked the second time. Each time he may think of some excuse; yet the problem remains unsettled. How much better it would be if the newborn Christian unfurled the flag on the very first day and confessed that he is a believer. After confessing once or twice, the inroads of the world will be cut.

If a new believer fails to open his mouth and confess the Lord, as a secret Christian he will have ten times as many troubles as an open Christian. His temptations will also be ten times more. He will not be able to free himself from the bondage of human affection and past relationships. He cannot excuse himself every time something comes up by saying he has a headache or is busy. It would be absurd to offer an excuse every time. But if he were to show the flag on the very first day, declaring that formerly he was a sinner but that now he has received the Lord Jesus, all his colleagues, schoolmates, friends and relatives would realize what kind of person he now is and would not bother him anymore. To confess the Lord saves one from many troubles.

Changed Life and Confession

Many new believers, especially those who come from Christian families, have a mistaken idea. They maintain that to confess with their mouths is not essential; what really matters is to shine with good conduct. In other words, their theology is that one's life must change, one's conduct must change; whether his mouth has changed or not does not really matter. We agree with them that should the life remain unchanged, it is futile for the mouth to speak. But we maintain that a changed life without a corresponding confession of the mouth is also useless. Change in conduct is no substitute for confession of the mouth.

New believers should seize the first opportunity to stand up and confess, "I have believed in the Lord Jesus." We must confess with our mouths. If we do not, the world may imagine many things about us. Some may think we have simply been disappointed and hence have taken a pessimistic attitude towards life. Others may consider us as just having had enough of the world; they explain us philosophically without ever touching upon the Lord Jesus. We must therefore stand up and tell them the real reason. Good conduct cannot take the place of confession with the mouth. Good conduct is necessary, but confession is also indispensable. No matter how good one's conduct is, if he has not spoken out for the Lord, his standing is dubious; sooner or later he will be drawn into the whirlpool of this world.

Some are afraid to confess the Lord for fear that they may not be able to persevere to the end. They are afraid they will become laughingstocks if after three or four years they quit being Christians. Therefore, they would rather wait for a few years; only then, after they have proved themselves worthy, will they finally confess the Lord. To such ones we say: if you dare not confess the Lord for fear of falling, you surely will fall. Why? Because you have left your back door open; you have already prepared for the day of your fall. It is far better if you stand up and confess that you are the Lord's, for this will shut the back door and make it harder for you to back out. You will then have a better chance to advance rather than to retreat. You can expect to go forward.

Should one wait for better conduct before he confesses the Lord, most probably he will never in his life open his mouth. He will be dumb even after his conduct is good. It is most difficult to open one's mouth if one does not do so at the very beginning.

One fact should comfort us, and that is, God is the God who keeps us as well as the God who saves us. What is it to be saved? It is like purchasing something. What is it to be kept? It is like keeping the thing in hand. Who would ever buy something in order to throw it away? If you buy a watch for yourself, it is because you are thinking of using it. You do not buy it that you may throw it out. Likewise, when God purchases us, it is to keep us. God redeems us in order to keep us. He will keep us until that day. He so loves us as to give up His Son for us. Had He not meant to keep us, He would never have paid such an immense price. Keeping is God's purpose; keeping is God's plan. Do not, therefore, be afraid to rise up and confess. You do not need to worry about tomorrow, for God will worry for you. All you need to do is to stand up and confess in simplicity that you belong to God. Just cast yourself into His hands. He knows when you need succor and He will comfort and preserve you. We have the greatest confidence in proclaiming that God keeps those whom He has saved.

Separated from the World

Scripture to Memorize:

Come ye out from among them, and be ye separate, saith the Lord, and touch no unclean thing; and I will receive you.

2 Corinthians 6.17

There are many commands, examples, and teachings in the Bible concerning the matter of separation. Since the world has so many facets to it, our separation needs to be full and complete. There are four different places in the Bible used to typify the world: Egypt represents the pleasures of the world; Ur of Chaldea, the religion of the world; Babylon, the confusion of the world; and Sodom, the sins of the world. From all of these we need to be separated.

When the Israelites were in the hand of the destroyer, how did God deliver them? It was by the Passover lamb. At the time the angel of God went through the land of Egypt to smite the firstborn, he passed over those houses which had blood on them. If there were no blood on the door, he went in and smote the firstborn. Thus, the whole question of salvation does not depend on whether or not the door is good, the doorposts are special, the household is commendable, or the firstborn is obedient. It rather hinges on whether there is blood. The difference between salvation and perdition is determined by acceptance or rejection of the blood. The basis for your salvation is not in what you or your family are, but in the blood.

We who are saved by grace are redeemed by the blood. Let us remember, however, that once we have been

51

redeemed by the blood, we must start to make our exit. The Israelites killed the lamb before midnight and, after they had put the blood on the doorposts and the lintel, they hurriedly ate their meal. As they ate, they had their loins girded, their shoes on their feet and their staves in their hands, for they were ready to go out of Egypt.

The first effect of redemption, therefore, is separation. God never redeems anyone and leaves him in the world to live on as before. Every regenerated person, as soon as he is saved, needs to take his staff in his hand and start to make his exit. As soon as the angel of destruction separates between those who are saved and those who are perishing, the saved souls must go out. This is most clearly typified in Exodus. A staff is used for journeying; no one uses it as a pillow for lying down. All the redeemed, both big and small, must take their staves and move out that very same night. Whenever souls are redeemed by the blood, they become pilgrims and strangers in this world. The moment they are redeemed, they leave Egypt and are separated from the world. They ought not continue to abide there.

Principles Governing Separation

Some probably will ask: from what should we come out? What are the things of the world? Wherein must we be separated from the world? We shall suggest five principles of separation. But before going into these principles, there is one thing needed first: we need to have our heart and spirit released from the world first. If anyone still desires to be in the world, these principles will be of no avail to him. Even if he separates himself from a hundred things, he is yet in the world. Separation of the person with his heart and his spirit must precede the separation of things.

The man must completely come out of Egypt and be separated from the world. Do not be afraid to be called peculiar. There are things we have to deal with and there are ways in which we ought to be different from the world, even though we desire to be at peace with all men. In our homes, in the office, or wherever we may be, we do not contend. We are not belligerent towards anyone. But still there are a few things from which we must be separated.

1. THINGS THE WORLD CONSIDERS UNWORTHY OF A CHRISTIAN

We must be separated from anything the world considers unworthy of a Christian. We start our Christian life before the world and the world sets up certain standards for Christians. If we cannot measure up to their standards, where will our testimony be? Of the things which we do, we should never permit non-believers to raise their eyebrows saying, "Do Christians do such things too?" Under such an accusation, our testimony before them is finished. For example: Suppose you visit a certain place and meet a non-Christian there. He murmurs, "Do you Christians visit this place?" There are many places non-believers may frequent and be quite able to defend their action when questioned. But if a Christian should go to those same places, immediately they will raise an objection. They may sin, but you cannot. They may do it without any problem, but if you do the same thing you will be criticized. Consequently, whatever the world condemns as unworthy of a Christian, we must not do. This is a minimum requirement.

2. THINGS WHICH ARE INCONSISTENT TO OUR RELATIONSHIP WITH THE LORD

Anything which is inconsistent to our relationship with the Lord must be rejected. Our Lord was humiliated on earth; can we seek for glory? He was crucified as a robber; can we court the favor of this world? He was slandered as being possessed of a demon; can we look for praise from men that we are most clever and rational? Such conditions reveal their inconsistency with our relationship with the Lord. They make us different from the Lord, even contrary to Him. All the ways which He has gone we also must walk through. For this reason we must eradicate everything that is inconsistent to our relationship with the Lord.

"A disciple is not above his teacher, nor a servant above his lord" (Matt. 10.24), says the Lord. This refers to our relationship with the world, showing how we must suffer slander and reproach. If they treated our Lord that way, can we expect to be treated differently? If this is the way they dealt with our Teacher, can we hope for anything different? If we are treated differently, something must be drastically wrong in our relationship with the Lord. Let us be careful that along with other children of God, we walk together in the way of the Lord. Whatever conditions our Lord faced on this earth, we must also face.

What is the world? What is not the world? You will know when you come to the Lord. You need only ask one question: how is this thing which now confronts you related to the Lord Jesus while He was on earth? What was the relationship of the Lord to the people of the world? If your relationship is not different from Christ's, it is good. But if your position differs from His, it is wrong. We are followers of the Lamb who has been slain. We follow the Lamb wherever He goes (see Rev. 14.4). We stand together with the Lamb in His slain position. Whatever does not stand in that position, whatever is contrary to the Lord's position, is the world from which we must be separated.

3. THINGS WHICH QUENCH SPIRITUAL LIFE

Again we ask, "What is the world?" Each and everything which tends to quench our spiritual life before the Lord is the world. How impossible it is to tell new believers what things are permissible and what things are not permissible. If we tell them ten things, they have the eleventh thing to ask. But if they understand but one principle, they can apply it to numberless things. Whatsoever thing makes you lose zeal for prayer or for Bible reading or causes you to lose courage to testify is the world.

The world creates a kind of atmosphere which cools our love to the Lord. It withers our spiritual life; it chills our zeal; it freezes our longing for God. Hence it must be rejected.

Can things which are not sinful be reckoned as things of the world? Many things rate highly in human estimation; but the question is, do they help us draw nearer to the Lord? Or will they quench our spiritual life? Indeed, they may be good things, yet in doing them several times, our inner fire begins to dwindle; if we continue in them, the fire soon becomes cold. We find ourselves unable to confess our sins, to pray and to read the Bible. Though these worldly things may not have occupied our time, they surely have occupied our conscience. They have weakened our conscience before God and given us an unspeakable sense of being wrong. Our conscience cannot rise above that feeling. It takes away our taste for the Bible. It makes us feel empty when we wish to testify. It swallows up our words. No matter how sinless these things are, how very right they may be, they still must be labeled as the world. All which quenches our spiritual life belongs to the world.

4. Social Affairs Which Hinder the Testimony

Another principle to be mentioned is concerned with social relationships. Whatever social gatherings or feasts or good times together cause our lamp to be covered under a bushel are of the world. These should be rejected. How can Christians continue in social intercourse if they cannot confess that they are the Lord's and if they have to pretend to be polite by listening to and smiling with unbelievers? How can we suppress our inward feeling and put on a smiling face? How can we inwardly sense the world, yet show sympathy outwardly? How can we judge anything sinful, if we externally agree with it? Many of God's children have been gradually drawn back into the world because they failed to differentiate in their social life.

Come Out from the World

"Wherefore come ye out from among them, and be ye separate, saith the Lord, and touch no unclean thing; and I will receive you, and will be to you a Father, and ye shall be to me sons and daughters, saith the Lord Almighty" (2 Cor. 6.17-18). This is the first time in the New Testament where the name "the Lord Almighty" is used. We shall find it later in the book of Revelation. In Hebrew, it is "El Shaddai." "El" means God, "Shaddai" has its root in the word which means a woman's breast or milk. Hence, this name should be translated as the All-Sufficient God. What a child needs is milk, and this milk comes from the mother's breast. So the mother's breast supplies all the needs of a child. So does our God.

The Lord as the All-Sufficient God calls us to come out from the world and touch not the unclean things that He may receive us as sons and daughters. These are not mere words, for they are supported by the All-Sufficient God. If we leave all, we shall be empty-handed, but He will receive us.

The Elimination of Distinctions

Scripture to Memorize:

Where there cannot be Greek and Jew, circumcision and uncircumcision, barbarian, Scythian, bondman, freeman; but Christ is all, and in all.

Colossians 3.11

After having confessed the Lord before men and having been separated from the world, new believers should be shown that all believers are one in the body of Christ. We may call this the elimination of distinctions.

"For in one Spirit were we all baptized into one body whether Jews or Greeks, whether bond or free; and were all made to drink of one Spirit" (1 Cor. 12.13). The word "whether" implies that all distinctions have been eliminated. In the body of Christ, there can be no earthly discriminations. We are all baptized in one Spirit to be one body, and then we are all made to drink of one Spirit.

"For as many of you as were baptized into Christ did put on Christ. There can be neither Jew nor Greek, there can be neither bond nor free, there can be no male and female; for ye all are one in Christ Jesus" (Gal. 3.27-28). Those in Christ are those who have clothed themselves with Christ. The natural distinctions of Jew and Greek, bond and free, male and female have been abolished.

"And have put on the new man that is being renewed unto knowledge after the image of him that created him: where there cannot be Greek and Jew, circumcision and uncircumcision, barbarian, Scythian, bondman, freeman; but Christ is all, and in all" (Col. 3.10-11). Again, it tells us that natural distinctions no longer exist among believers, for we have become one new man who is created after the image of God. In this new man, all the differences of Greek and Jew, circumcision and uncircumcision, barbarian and Scythian, bondman and freeman have disappeared, for Christ is all and in all.

Having read these three passages of the Bible, we can readily see that all believers are one in Christ. Each and every natural distinction is abrogated. This is a foundational matter for the building up of the church. If we were to bring all these worldly distinctions into the church, we would find that the relationship among brothers and sisters could never be properly adjusted and that the church could not be established before God.

Of the distinctions mentioned in these passages, there are five contrasts; namely, Greek and Jew, bond and free, male and female, barbarian and Scythian, and circumcision and uncircumcision. However, the apostle tells us that in Christ we are one.

The world pays great attention to personal status—to what race do I belong, what background do I have, and so forth. I must maintain my honor; I must protect my status. But once we become Christians, we should exclude all such discriminations. No one should bring his personal status or position into Christ and the church—the one new man; to do so would be to bring in the old man. Nothing that belongs to the old man should ever be carried over into the church.

The Abolishment of National Distinctions

May God graciously open the eyes of young believers to see that no matter whether they were originally Jews or Gentiles, they are now one in Christ. All their national limitations have been broken; national distinctions simply no longer exist. Whether some are American believers, some English believers, some Indian believers, some Japanese believers, or some Chinese believers, they are all brothers and sisters in the Lord. No one can divide them as God's children. We cannot have American Christianity; if we insist on having America, we cannot have Christ. These two are contrary to each other. In Christ, we are all brothers and sisters. It is but natural that in Christ no national boundary can exist. The body of Christ is the one new man, completely one, without any national distinctions. Even strong nationalism, such as the Jews had, must be broken in Christ.

Whenever we meet a person in Christ, we should no longer label him as a Chinese or an American, for we are all one in Christ. It is a mistake of the gravest consequence to try to establish a Chinese church or to set up an American testimony. In Christ there is neither Jew nor Gentile. To attempt to bring outside things such as national differences into the church will completely destroy the things within. In Christ all are coordinated together without any discrimination. The moment distinctions are brought in, the body of Christ is changed into a carnal institution.

The Elimination of Class Differences

Class identity presents another difficulty in relation to the body of Christ. We do not come across national differences until we meet an alien, but we are confronted with class relationships every day. The apostle mentions that the bond and the free are also eliminated in Christ.

Assume that you belong to the servant class or that you are an employee or subordinate. In the home or in the office you should keep your place and learn to listen and obey. But when you and your master or employer or boss come together before God, you do not need to listen to him on the basis of his being your superior. In spiritual matters such class differences do not enter in.

This elimination of class differences is only possible among Christians. Only Christians can thoroughly carry this out. We Christians can shake one another's hand and declare that we are brothers. We have the love that overcomes differences. In the world, one class of people tries to overthrow another, thus raising themselves to a higher class. But we who are in Christ are able to eliminate class discrimination completely. That hard-to-be-broken class difference between freeman and slave must be totally shattered. We fellowship with other brothers and sisters on the sole ground of what the Lord has given to us—His life. Thus shall we receive great blessing from God. Such a church will be full of the love of Christ, and we will be those who minister Christ to one another.

When anyone becomes a Christian, he must leave his national characteristics outside the church for there is no such thing in the church. Today there are problems in many churches caused by the intrusion of national peculiarities. Those who are talkative group together; so do those who dislike talking. The cool gather together and the warm do likewise. Thus there exist many differences among God's children.

Please remember: national characteristics have no place in the church, in the new man, in Christ. Do not judge others because they have a different temperament. They will judge you in the same way if you do. You may wonder why they are so cold when you talk to them so warmly. Perhaps at the same time, though, they are suffering with your peculiarity.

Many who come into the church affirm that they are such-and-such naturally. They say it rather proudly. But they should be told that the church does not need their natural selves. They ought not to bring their old selves to the church, for it is not in Christ and it tends to divide.

Consequently, we must reject everything that belongs to the old man. Only thus can we go on with all the children of God.

The Dismissal of Cultural Divergences

There is a contrast in Colossians 3.11, that of barbarian and Scythian, which puzzles commentators. A barbarian is a man in a rude, uncivilized state; sometimes specifically one in a state between savagery and civilization (Webster). But what a Scythian is, is a mystery. Some consider him as more barbarous than the barbarian, for the savageness of the Scythians is proverbial (J.B. Lightfoot); while others, such as B.F.Wescott, reflect that since in the classics the Scythians are often mentioned together with the Galatians, they must be a very respectable people. Whatever interpretation we may personally accept, the point is that certain places are known for their specific qualities.

As a matter of fact, cultural divergence does cause lots of trouble, but we must remember that this too has been deleted in Christ. We who are in Christ are big men and women. We alone of all people can endure what the world cannot stand. We make no distinction among brethren. We as individuals do not set ourselves up as being the standard and judge everyone else accordingly. Such a situation simply does not exist in Christ, in the church, in the one new man. Some brothers may come from India, some from Africa. Their cultures are greatly different from ours, but we ask only one question: are they in the Lord? Yet they too ask the same question concerning us. If all are in the Lord, everything is settled. We maintain our contact in the Lord; we love one another in the Lord. We can endure everything else and refuse to allow anything to divide us as children of God.

Could we gather all the sophisticated brethren and form a church with them? Or gather all the simple brethren and form another church? No, neither of these would be the church. It is true that the conflict of culture is a very hard matter to endure. Yet it is equally true that this cultural divergence does not belong in the church. It is something outside the body of Christ. Never bring it into the church. Never allow it to become an issue.

No Show of Piety in the Flesh

Another contrast is "circumcision and uncircumcision." This speaks of the distinctions in outward signs of piety in the flesh. We all know that Jews receive circumcision in their flesh. They have the sign upon them. They profess that they belong to God, that they are God-fearing, and that they deny the flesh. By this sign in the flesh, they are confident of having part in God's covenant.

The Jews lay much stress on circumcision. This is a characteristic of Judaism. He who is circumcised is included in the covenant of God; he who is uncircumcised is excluded from God's covenant. No one is allowed to marry the uncircumcised. In Acts 15 circumcision was the focus of discussion, for some of the Jewish believers would have liked to force circumcision on the Gentiles. The whole book of Galatians deals with this matter of circumcision. Paul declares that if he were to preach circumcision, the salvation of the cross would no longer exist, for people would simply depend on an outward show of piety in the flesh.

Paul makes it quite clear that circumcision does not take away the defilement of the flesh; it is only aimed at curtailing the activities of the flesh. What is important is the inward, not the outward things. If the inward vision is the same, though the outward expression may be slightly different, no division would be made.

The Suspension of Gender Disparity

The last distinction to be suspended in Christ is the matter of gender. In church government, male and female have their respective positions. When the church meets, the man functions differently from the woman. In the family, husband and wife hold different responsibilities. But *in Christ*, there can be no male and female. Neither the man nor the woman has any peculiar position. Why? Because Christ is all and is in all. Notice the word "all" used twice. Christ is both all and in all. Hence, in spiritual life there is absolutely no way to differentiate between male and female.

No doubt in the realm of service, the sisters sometimes have a different ministry from that of the brothers. This is due to the arrangement in the order of authority of this present age; but when we come to the future age, the arrangement will be different. However, even today, there can be no difference in Christ. Both the brother and the sister are saved by the life of the Son of God. Both become children of God. The word "children" (Greek, "teknon") makes no distinction between male or female (though according to its root it is masculine in form).

We are all brothers and sisters. We are each a new creation in Christ. We are members of the one body. All natural distinctions have been annulled in Christ. We therefore must shut out of our hearts any party spirit, any divisive spirit. So shall we advance one step further.

Witnessing

Scripture to Memorize:

For thou shalt be a witness for him unto all men of what thou hast seen and heard.

Acts 22.15

New believers must learn to witness for the Lord; otherwise the gospel will terminate with them. You are already saved; you have life and your light is kindled. But if you do not ignite others before you are all burned up, then you are really finished. You should bring many to the Lord lest you see Him empty-handed.

"For thou shalt be a witness for him unto all men of what thou hast seen and heard." The Lord spoke these words to Paul through Ananias. Whatever you have seen and heard, you shall witness to all men. So the first foundation of witnessing is seeing and hearing. You cannot testify what you have not seen or heard. The advantage Paul had was that unlike other people he personally had heard and seen the Lord. He witnessed to that which he had seen and heard.

"And we have beheld and bear witness that the Father hath sent the Son to be the Saviour of the world" (1 John 4.14). This tells us what witnessing is. We witness to what we have seen. Thank God, you have recently believed in the Lord. You have met Him, believed in Him, and received Him. You are now redeemed. Having been set free from sin and having received forgiveness, you have peace in you. You know how happy you are after you have believed—a happiness which you never knew before. Formerly the load of sin weighed heavily upon you, but

65

today, thank God, this load has been rolled away. So you are a person who has seen and heard. What should you do now? You should send forth your testimony. This does not mean you are to be a preacher or to leave your job and be a full-time worker. It simply means you are to witness to your friends and relatives and acquaintances of that which you have seen and heard. You should try to bring souls to the Lord.

How to Witness

The above two Scripture passages form a set on the meaning of witnessing. Now we will turn to another set, a set of four passages which will tell us very simply what witnessing is.

1. SPEAK IN THE CITY—THE SAMARITAN WOMAN

In John 4 the Samaritan woman met the Lord who then asked her for water. But after asking, the Lord turned around and offered her the living water without which no one could really live and be satisfied. He who drinks of the water of the well will thirst again. There will at least be as many times of thirstiness as there are times of drinking. You will never be satisfied, so you have to drink again and again. What the world can offer may satisfy for a time but sooner or later thirstiness will return. Only the fountain that springs up from within can satisfy forever. This inward satisfaction alone can deliver people from the demand of the world.

After the Lord Jesus showed the Samaritan woman who He was, the woman left her waterpot—until then something most important to her—and went into the city and said, "Come, see a man, who told me all things that ever I did; can this be the Christ?" (v. 29). Here we have a real example of witnessing.

What did she testify? She said, "Here is a man who told me everything that I ever did" (see v. 39). She had done lots of things; some known to the public but some unknown. She was afraid to tell people all that she had done; yet now the Lord had done just that. So she testified that here was a man who told everything that she ever had done, things which she herself alone knew. Could this man be the Christ? Let me tell you: as soon as she saw the Lord, she opened her mouth. The Bible says, "And from that city many of the Samaritans believed on him because of the word of the woman, who testified" (v. 39).

From this we may see one thing: everyone has the need to testify, to tell his own story. Since the Lord has saved such a big sinner as you, can you shut your mouth and not testify? The Savior has saved me; I cannot but open my mouth and confess Him. Though I cannot explain why, at least I see that this is God, this is Christ, this is God's Son, this is God's appointed Savior. I can also see that I am a sinner saved by grace. All that is required of me is to express my feeling. I may not be able to tell what has happened, but you all can see how greatly I am changed. I do not know how it happened—I, who formerly considered myself a good man, today see myself as a sinner. What I did not regard as sin, the Lord has pointed out to me to be sinful. Now I know what sort of person I am. I did many things in the past without anyone's knowledge; sometimes even I myself was not aware of what I did. I sinned greatly but I was not conscious of being sinful. Yet here came a Man who told me all things that I ever did. He told me that which I did not know as well as that which I did know. I have to confess that I have touched the Savior. This One must be Christ who alone can save.

2. WITNESS AT HOME—THE DEMONIAC

In Mark 5.1-20, we find a man who was terribly possessed by an unclean spirit. He cut himself with stones, and no man had strength to tame him. He rent the chains that bound him, and broke the fetters in pieces. He dwelt in the tombs, and people dared not pass that place. But the Lord cast the unclean spirit out of that man. He wanted to follow the Lord, but the Lord bade him, "Go to thy house unto thy friends, and tell them how great things the Lord hath done for thee, and how he had mercy on thee" (v. 19). To tell what great things the Lord has done for you is witnessing for the Lord.

When you receive grace, you ought to let your family, your neighbors, and your relatives know that you are now a saved person. Tell them what great things the Lord has done for you as well as how you have believed in Him. Tell them the fact and truthfully witness to them. Thus you will ignite other people and let the salvation of the Lord continue on.

3. PROCLAIM IN THE SYNAGOGUES—SAUL

"And he was certain days with the disciples that were at Damascus. And straightway in the synagogues he proclaimed Jesus, that he is the Son of God. And all that heard him were amazed, and said, Is not this he that in Jerusalem made havoc of them that called on this name? and he had come hither for this intent, that he might bring them bound before the chief priests" (Acts 9.19b-21). The word "straightway" (immediately) is quite emphatic in the Greek.

So the first thing a person should do after receiving the Lord is to witness for the Lord. As soon as Saul's eyes were healed, he seized the first opportunity to testify that Jesus is the Son of God. Let me tell you: each and everyone who believes in the Lord Jesus should do just that.

Can a person get saved and sit quietly as if nothing has happened? Can he believe on the Lord Jesus and not feel amazingly surprised? I doubt that anyone can do that, for he has made a tremendous discovery, the most special of all: Jesus of Nazareth is the Son of God! I would not at all be surprised if he knocked on the door of his friend's house after midnight. Indeed, he ought to climb to the mountaintop to shout the news or go to the seashore to proclaim that Jesus of Nazareth is the Son of God! No other discovery is anywhere near the magnitude of this one. Even putting all the world's discoveries together would fall far behind this one. Indeed, we have discovered the Son of God. What a tremendous thing this is!

4. PERSONAL WITNESSING

> *One of the two that heard John speak, and followed him, was Andrew, Simon Peter's brother. He findeth first his own brother Simon, and saith unto him, We have found the Messiah (which is, being interpreted, Christ). He brought him unto Jesus. Jesus looked upon him, and said, Thou art Simon the son of John: thou shalt be called Cephas (which is by interpretation, Peter).*
> *On the morrow he was minded to go forth into Galilee, and he findeth Philip: and Jesus saith unto him, Follow me. Now Philip was from Bethsaida, of the city of Andrew and Peter. Philip findeth Nathanael, and saith unto him, We have found him, of whom Moses in the law, and the prophets, wrote, Jesus of Nazareth, the son of Joseph.*

John 1.40-45

In this fourth passage we find how Andrew sought out Simon, and Philip sought out Nathaniel. From this we learn

69

that after we believe in the Lord we should not only witness in the city, at home, and in the synagogues but also should witness person to person.

The Believer's Secret of Happiness

In every believer's life there are two big days, two days of special rejoicing. The first happy day is the day when he believes in the Lord. The second happy day is the day when he for the first time leads someone to Christ. To many, the joy of leading a person to the Lord for the very first time even exceeds the joy of their own salvation. But many believers are not happy, for they have never uttered a word for the Lord nor ever led a soul to Christ. Do not let this be your condition; do not degenerate to the point of having no joy.

The Bible says, "And he that is wise winneth souls" (Prov. 11.30b). New believers should learn to bring souls to salvation from the start of their Christian life. They must learn to be wise so as to be useful in the church of God. The spiritual understanding of many believers has never been opened because they do not know how to win souls. We do not encourage people to preach in the pulpit, but we do persuade them to save souls. Many can preach but cannot save souls. If you bring people to them, they do not know how to deal with these souls. Only those who know how to deal with souls and lead them to Christ are useful in the church. May new believers learn this early in their Christian life.

How to Lead People to Christ

Scripture to Memorize:

He that is wise winneth souls.

Proverbs 11.30b

Let us look at the matter of how to lead people to the Lord from two sides: first, approaching God on behalf of sinners; and second, approaching sinners on behalf of God and the technique of how to lead people to the Lord.

Approach God on Behalf of Sinners

1. PRAYER IS THE BASIC WORK IN SAVING SOULS

There is a basic principle in the saving of souls, and that is, before you speak to a person you must first pray to God. First ask the Lord and then speak to him. It is absolutely necessary for you to speak to God on behalf of the person to whom you will later speak. If you speak to him first, you will not be able to accomplish anything.

Hence, the first thing to do is to ask God for a few souls. "All that which the Father giveth me shall come unto me" (John 6.37), said the Lord Jesus. And we also remember how God added to the church day by day those that were saved (Acts 2.47). We must ask God for souls. We need to pray: "O God, give souls to the Lord Jesus, add people to the church." People are given by the asking. Human hearts are so subtle that they are not easily turned. For this reason, we must pray faithfully for a person before we speak fully to him. How important is prayer. Pray by name for those people whom you wish to lead to Christ, believe that God will save them, and then lead them to the Lord.

2. THE GREATEST HINDRANCE TO PRAYER IS SIN

Special attention should be paid by new believers to reject all known sins. We must learn to live a holy life before God. If anyone is lax in the matter of sin, his prayer will definitely be hindered. Sin is a big problem. Many cannot pray because they tolerate sin in their lives. Sin will not only obstruct our prayers, it will also wreck our conscience.

New believers ought to see that the sin question must be solved if they desire to be skillful in prayer. Thus, they should note especially the preciousness of the blood. They have lived in sin so long that they will not be able to be completely freed from sin if they are even slightly lenient toward it. They need to confess their sins one by one before God, put them one after another under the blood, reject each one of them, and be freed of them. Thus shall their conscience be restored. By the cleansing of the blood, the conscience is instantly restored. With the washing of the blood, conscience no longer accuses and one may naturally see God's face. Never let yourself fall into the place whereby you become weak before God, for you will not then be able to intercede for others. Thus this question of sin is the first thing to which you must attend daily. Deal well with sin; then you can pray well before God and lead people to Christ. If you daily remember people before the Lord with faith, you will soon win them to Christ.

3. PRAY IN FAITH

Once believers have dealt thoroughly with their sins and maintained a strong conscience before God, they need to be further helped to see the importance of faith.

Actually the prayer life of new believers is mainly involved with conscience and faith. Though prayer is rather profound, to new believers it is only a matter of conscience and faith. If their conscience before God is without offense, their faith can easily be strong. And if their faith is sufficiently strong, their prayer will easily be answered. Therefore, it is necessary for them to have faith.

What is faith? It is not doubting in prayer. It is God who constrains us to pray. It is God who promises that we may pray to Him. He cannot but answer if we pray. He says: "Knock and it shall be opened unto you." How can I knock and He refuse to open? He says: "Seek and ye shall find." Can I seek and not find? He says: "Ask and it shall be given you." It is absolutely impossible for me to ask and not be given. Who do we think our God is? We ought to see how faithful and dependable are the promises of God.

Faith comes by the word of God. For God's word is like cash that can be taken and used. God's promise is God's work. Promise tells us what God's work is, and work manifests to us the promise of God. If we believe the word of God and do not doubt, we will abide in faith and see how trustworthy is all that God has said. Our prayers shall be answered.

Approach Sinners on Behalf of God

It is not enough just to pray for sinners and to approach God on behalf of sinners. We must also approach sinners on behalf of God. We need to tell them what God is like. Many people dare to speak to God but have no courage to speak to men. Young people should be trained to be bold to speak to others. They must not only pray but also seek opportunities to talk.

In talking with people, there are a few things which should be especially observed.

1. NEVER ARGUE UNNECESSARILY

In speaking to people, we need a little technique. First of all, we must not enter into unnecessary arguments. This does not mean that we should never argue, because in Acts we find several instances where they argued; even the apostle Paul argued. If you have to argue, you argue with one person for the benefit of a third person listening in. But for the one whom you wish to win to Christ, usually it is better if you do not argue. Do not argue with him nor argue for him to hear. Why? Because argument may drive people away instead of drawing them in. You need to show a gentle spirit; otherwise people will flee from you.

Many think that argument may move a person's heart. But this is not true. Argument at most only brings people's minds into subjection. Therefore, it is better to speak less words which come from the mind and instead witness more. Tell people of how you have experienced joy and peace and rest after you believed in the Lord Jesus. These are facts that no one can argue with.

2. HOLD ON TO FACTS

Another method in leading people to the Lord is to use fact, not doctrine, while talking. It is not because of the reasonableness of the doctrine that people come into faith. Many see the logic of the doctrine but still do not believe.

Often it is the simple who can save souls. Those who preach well on doctrine may correct people's minds but fail to save souls. The one aim is to save people, not to correct their minds. What is the use in having their minds corrected but leaving them unsaved?

3. MAINTAIN A SINCERE AND EARNEST ATTITUDE

In witnessing, our attitude must be sincere and earnest, not given to frivolity. We must not argue, but only tell the facts of what we have experienced before God. If we stand in this position, we will be able to lead many to the Lord. Do not try to have a big brain; just stress facts. We may joke about other matters but in this one thing we must be sincere.

4. ASK GOD FOR OPPORTUNITIES

We should pray that God will give us opportunities to speak with people. If we pray, we will be given opportunities. Some seem to be difficult to talk with. But if you pray for them, you will be given opportunities to speak to them and they will be changed.

Therefore, we must learn to pray and also to speak. Many dare not open their mouths to speak of the Lord Jesus to their friends and relatives. Perhaps opportunities are waiting for you but you have let these opportunities slip by because you are afraid.

5. SEEK OUT PEOPLE OF THE SAME CATEGORY

According to our past experience, it is better for people to seek and save those in the same category. This is a common rule. Nurses can work among nurses, doctors among doctors, patients among patients, civil servants among civil servants, students among students. Work on those who are nearest to you. You do not need to start with open-air meetings, but with your family and acquaintances. It is natural for doctors to work on their patients, teachers on their students, employers on their employees, masters on their servants.

I do not say there are no exceptions, for there are some. Our Lord Jesus himself gave us some exceptional examples. Nonetheless, this rule regarding people of the same category is generally preferable. For a miner to preach in a college is exceptional. Yet, though the Lord does sometimes do exceptional things, yet He nevertheless cannot be expected to do such things every day. For example, for a very learned person to talk to the laborers at the pier is not quite suitable. But if a few longshoremen are saved and they go out to save the rest, it seems to me to be a more appropriate and easier contact.

6. BRING PEOPLE TO GOD DAILY THROUGH PRAYERS

There will never be a time when there is no one to pray for. You can pray for your fellow students, your colleagues, your fellow nurses or doctors, and your fellow employees. Ask God to put especially one or two of them upon your heart. When He puts a person in your heart, write his name in your book and pray daily for him.

After you have begun to pray for a soul, you should also talk to him. Tell him of the grace of the Lord towards you. This is something he cannot resist or forget.

7. IN SEASON AND OUT OF SEASON

Finally, I wish to mention that you are not forbidden to speak to those for whom you have not prayed before. There will be some to whom you will speak when you meet them for the first time. Seize every opportunity; speak both in season and out of season, for you do not know who will slip away. You must open your mouth regularly even as you should pray always. Pray for those with names and pray for many without names. Pray that the Lord will save sinners. Whenever you meet a sinner by chance, if the Spirit of God moves you, speak to him.

Household Salvation

Scripture to Memorize:
Believe on the Lord Jesus, and thou shalt be saved, thou and thy house.

Acts 16.31

Most things have their basic unit and the unit for salvation is the household. We find in the Bible that God gives many promises in regard to His dealings with men. If we know these promises, we will be greatly benefited; otherwise, we will suffer loss. The promise which God gives concerning salvation takes a household, not an individual, as the basic unit. New believers should be reminded of this, for it will solve many problems and give them great benefit.

The Unit of Salvation

When the Bible speaks of eternal life, it always takes an individual as the unit; never does it take a household as the unit. But when it deals with salvation, it actually takes the household instead of the individual. We must see that the unit of salvation is the household while that of eternal life is the individual.

The basic principle of the Bible is that God's salvation is for the household. Let us now examine the proofs in both the Old and New Testaments.

Old Testament Examples

1. THE WHOLE HOUSE ENTERED THE ARK

"And Jehovah said unto Noah, Come thou and all thy house into the ark" (Gen. 7.1).

"While the ark was a preparing, wherein few, that is, eight souls, were saved through water" (1 Pet. 3.20b).

The ark was not for one person; it was for the whole house. The Bible affirms that the man Noah was righteous before God, but nowhere does it record that Noah's sons and daughters-in-law were righteous. Noah alone was referred to as a righteous man. Yet when God prepared His salvation for Noah, He commanded all his house to enter into the ark. The ark used the household instead of an individual as its unit.

A new believer should bring all his house to the ark. You may pray: "Lord, I have trusted in You. Now I ask You to bring my whole house in because You have said that all my house may come in." God will respect your faith and bring in your whole house.

2. A PASCHAL (PASSOVER) LAMB FOR EACH HOUSE

"Speak ye unto all the congregation of Israel, saying, In the tenth day of this month they shall take to them every man a lamb, according to their fathers' houses, a lamb for a household: . . . And they shall take of the blood, and put it on the two side-posts and on the lintel, upon the houses wherein they shall eat it" (Ex. 12.3, 7).

The paschal lamb was definitely for the household, not for an individual. Thus we are shown how important is the household in the sight of God. The lamb was slain not for one person but for the whole house, and its blood was put on the door that the household might be preserved. The angel, the destroyer, would pass over the house which had the blood on the door.

How marvelous that the salvation which the Lord Jesus Christ has prepared is like the paschal lamb for the whole house. It is for the household to eat the lamb and to apply the blood. The whole family together receives the salvation of the Lord.

3. A HOUSEHOLD SAVED UNDER A SCARLET CORD

"And it shall be, that whosoever shall go out of the doors of thy house into the street, his blood shall be upon his head, and we shall be guiltless: and whosoever shall be with thee in the house, his blood shall be on our head, if any hand be upon him" (Josh. 2.19).

"And the city shall be devoted, even it and all that is therein, to Jehovah: only Rahab the harlot shall live, she and all that are with her in the house, because she hid the messengers that we sent" (Josh. 6.17).

In the case of Rahab the harlot, the whole house was also saved. Why? Because she hid the messengers. God gave her a sign—she must bind the scarlet cord on her window; all who were in the house would then be spared from slaughter. The rest of the inhabitants of Jericho were all killed. Salvation was in the scarlet cord, but this salvation saved not only Rahab but also her house.

So the scope of salvation is pretty clear—it is the household. In chapter two of Joshua, we see the promise; in chapter six, the practice. As the promise was, so was the practice. The whole house of Rahab was therefore saved.

New Testament Examples

1. THE HOUSE OF ZACCHAEUS

What about Zacchaeus? "And Jesus said unto him, Today is salvation come to this house, forasmuch as he also is a son of Abraham" (Lk. 19.9). How wonderful it is that the New Testament proclaims the same principle. We usually think of salvation as coming to the individual. Perhaps many have preached that way. But the Lord declares that "salvation has come to this house."

When you go out to preach the gospel, you should pay attention to household salvation. Do not expect only individuals to be saved. If you really believe and truly expect more, your work will undergo a great change. We want whole houses to be converted. Much depends on your faith and expectation. Should you expect unbelievers to come to the Lord one by one, they will come one by one. But if you believe in their coming house by house, you will get them house after house. The scope of God's salvation is the house; let us not reduce that scope.

2. THE HOUSE OF CORNELIUS

"A devout man, and one that feared God with all his house, who gave much alms to the people, and prayed to God always" (Acts 10.2).

"Who shall speak unto thee words, whereby thou shalt be saved, thou and all thy house" (Acts 11.14).

Cornelius invited his relatives and friends to hear Peter. As Peter spoke, the Holy Spirit fell upon them, and all who were gathered in his house were saved. This is a tremendous demonstration that God deals with households rather than just with individuals.

3. THE HOUSE OF LYDIA

"And when she was baptized, and her household, she besought us, saying, If ye have judged me to be faithful to the Lord, come into my house, and abide there. And she constrained us" (Acts 16.15). The apostles preached the gospel to the household of Lydia and they believed and were baptized.

4. THE HOUSE OF THE PHILIPPIAN JAILOR

"And they said, Believe on the Lord Jesus, and thou shalt be saved, thou and thy house" (Acts 16.31). This is one of the most famous Bible verses in Christianity.

Believe on the Lord Jesus and you shall be saved, even you and your house. I do not think we can dispute this statement. God's word does not say, Believe on the Lord Jesus and you shall have eternal life, you and your house. It says, Believe on the Lord Jesus and you shall be saved, you and your house.

5. THE PROMISE IS TO YOU AND TO YOUR CHILDREN

We have already seen how the door of the gospel was opened to the Gentiles in the salvation of the house of Cornelius. Now let us turn back to look again at the situation at Pentecost.

"For to you is the promise, and to your children, and to all that are afar off, even as many as the Lord our God shall call unto him" (Acts 2.39).

The promise given at Pentecost is that man's sin may be forgiven and he may receive the Holy Spirit. This promise is to your children as well as to you. It is therefore especially important for heads of families to lay hold of this promise, saying, "To us and to our children is this promise given. It is not for us exclusively, for our children may possess it together with us."

81

If we truly believe, the Lord will work. The way is clear: God will bless us by the household. Household salvation is a tremendous principle—one believes and the whole house shall be saved. So stand firm before God that your household may all be transformed.

BOOK THREE:
Assembling Together

Joining the Church

Scripture to Memorize:

Wherefore receive ye one another, even as Christ also received you, to the glory of God.

Romans 15.7

After one believes in the Lord, he is immediately faced with the problem of joining the church. We mentioned before that we must be separated from the world. However, that is not the end; there is yet the positive side of joining the church. (We do not like the phrase "joining the church," but use it temporarily to make the issue clear.) It is our desire now to mention four points concerning this matter.

We Must Join the Church

Many believers think they can be Christians all by themselves; they think they have no need to join any church. They say: We want Christ, but we do not want the church. We have our personal relationship with Christ but have no need for a relationship with the church. Can we not pray by ourselves? Surely we can. Can we not read the Bible alone? Doubtless we can. Then why should we go to all the trouble of trying to communicate with others? Why not just fellowship alone with the Lord? Because of the need to counteract such thoughts, young believers ought to be shown that they must join the church irrespective of their personal opinions. They should see that there are two sides to salvation.

First, there is the personal side. On the personal side, one may receive life himself and he may also pray to the

Lord. He may shut himself in a room and believe in the Lord. But if all that he knows is this personal salvation, he will not develop normally, neither will he persevere, nor will his progress be very great. We have yet to see a hermit-type Christian make much progress. There are those, though, who think that a believer can be like a hermit, hidden in a mountain, disregarding everything except communion with the Lord. We should notice, however, that the spiritual upbuilding of such persons is generally rather superficial; when it comes to a real test or trial, they are unable to stand. When the environment seems favorable, they perhaps keep on, but when the environment turns against them, they are unable to persevere.

There is another side to the Christian life—the corporate side. The word of God teaches us that from the corporate standpoint, no one can be an independent Christian. As soon as one is saved he becomes a member of the family of God; he is one of God's children. This is one of the first revelations in the Bible. One who is born again into God's house thus becomes one child amongst many children. The next revelation is that all the saved ones together become God's habitation, the house of God. This house is different from the first house in that it is a dwelling place, whereas the first one is a household. This revelation is further followed by the revelation that all Christians are united as the body of Christ, and they are members one of another. Let us look at these three aspects more closely.

1. WE ARE GOD'S CHILDREN TOGETHER WITH MANY OTHERS

The life which one receives upon believing in the Lord is a life shared with many other people. If the believer looks even from just one vantage point, whether it be that of the household of God or that of the dwelling place of God or that of the body of Christ, the picture he gets shows that he is but a part of the whole. How, then, can he desire to live in isolation? To do so surely means to miss the fullness in God. He may seek to maintain fellowship with God, yet he will miss out on much if he is not properly joined together with others. He will not be able to fully emit the light of the highest and most abundant life, for it is only in the church that fullness is found.

It is not a Christian concept for a person to be only concerned with his own welfare. Being in the family, one has to be a brother to the brothers, a sister to the sisters. Such a relationship comes from the life of God and is filled with love. Who does not long for his brothers and sisters, who does not desire to see them and have fellowship with them? This is a wonderful thing!

Please remember: though you receive the life of God personally, yet the life you receive belongs to tens of thousands of the children of God; yours is but a part of the whole. The very nature of your new life is not independence—it requires you to fellowship with the rest of the brethren.

2. THE CHURCH IS GOD'S HABITATION

Let us now turn to the second point. The Bible reveals to us a most wonderful thing when it shows us that the church is the habitation of God. This is found in Ephesians 2.22. All the revelations in Ephesians are of tremendous dimensions and this one in chapter 2 is one of them. We must know that God has a dwelling place, a habitation on earth. The thought in the Bible of a habitation for God starts with the tabernacle and continues right on up to the present. In the past God dwelt in a magnificent house, the temple of Solomon. Now He dwells in the church, for today the church is God's habitation. We, the many, are joined together to be God's habitation. As individuals, though, we are not so. It takes many of God's children to be the house of God in the Spirit. This agrees with what 1 Peter 2.5 says, "Ye also, as living stones, are built up a spiritual house . . ."

As soon as one believes in the Lord he becomes one of the stones in God's habitation. He is a stone, but until he is related to other stones, he is useless. It is like the parts of an automobile. The car can run only when the many parts are put together. What use does one have if he remains alone? He will lose out on the riches of God. We dare not say that living stones standing alone become dead stones, but it is certainly true that a stone, though living, will lose its usefulness and miss out on spiritual riches if it is not joined to other stones to become God's habitation. We can contain God's richness only when we are joined together with other living stones; then God can dwell in our midst. That is why there should be a conviction in our hearts that we must be in the church.

3. TOGETHER WE BECOME THE BODY OF CHRIST

We are one in the body of Christ; we have become one body—the body of Christ. "There is one body . . ." (Eph. 4.4). "For as the body is one, and hath many members, and all the members of the body, being many, are one body; so also is Christ" (1 Cor. 12.12). These words show us how absolutely impossible it is for one to be independent.

The Lord has not given to any one person the whole fullness of life. The life we receive does not allow us to be independent, for our life is dependent on the life of others. It is a dependent life: I depend on you and you depend on me. Do remember that no member can afford to be independent, for independence means certain death. Isolation takes away life as well as fullness.

Therefore, we expect young believers to realize that they must be joined to other Christians. They should not be Christians for several years and still remain alone.

A Christian must therefore join the church. Now this term, "joining the church," is not a scriptural one. It is borrowed from the world. What we really mean is that no one can be a private Christian. He must be joined to all the children of God. For this reason, he needs to join the church. He cannot claim to be a believer all by himself. He is a Christian only by being subordinate to the others.

How We Join the Church

Finally, let us ask the question—how do we join the church? Never once in the Bible do we find the phrase "join the church." It cannot be found in Acts nor is it seen in the Epistles. Why? Because no one can join the church. To join means that one is still outside. Can an ear decide to join my body? No, if it is in my body, it is already joined. If it is not already in my body, then there is no way for it to join. We do not join the church. Rather, we are already in the church and are therefore joined to one another.

When, by the mercy of God, a man is convicted of his sin and through the precious blood is redeemed and forgiven and receives new life, he is not only regenerated through resurrection life but is also put into the church by the power of God. It is God who has put him in; thus, he already is in the church. He *is* an insider, so he has no need of joining. Many think of joining the church. Let it be known, however, that whatever can be joined is not the real thing. One cannot join the true church of God even if he would like to. If he is of the Lord, born of the Holy Spirit, then he is already in the church and has no need to join it.

Therefore, it is neither necessary nor possible to join the church. No one can enter into the church by joining it; those who are already in do not need to join. The very desire to join reveals the fact that one is still on the outside. The church is so special that it cannot be joined. The determining factor is whether one is born of God. If one is born of God, he is already in; if he is not born of God, there is no way to join. Is not this corporate body wonderful? It cannot be joined by signing a decision card or by taking a test. All who are born of God are already in the church; therefore, they have no need to join it.

Then why do we persuade you to join the church? We are only borrowing this term for the sake of discussion. You who have believed in the Lord are already in the church, but your brothers and sisters in the church may not know you. You have believed, but the brethren may not know it. You are redeemed, yet the church may not be aware of it. Since belief is something in the heart, it may not be known to others. For this reason we must seek fellowship, just as Paul sought to receive the right hand of fellowship from those in the church at Jerusalem (Gal. 2.9). We must go to the church, telling the brethren that we too are Christians and asking them therefore to receive us as such. Since men are limited in knowledge, they need to be told that we are brothers and sisters in order that they may receive us. This is not, however, the same thing as the popular notion of joining the church.

Laying on of Hands

Scripture to Memorize:

> *Wherefore leaving the doctrine of the first principles of Christ, let us press on unto perfection; not laying again a foundation of repentance from dead works, and of faith toward God, of the teaching of baptisms, and of laying on of hands, and of resurrection of the dead, and of eternal judgment.*

Hebrews 6.1-2

"Wherefore leaving the doctrine of the first principles of Christ, let us press on unto perfection," exhorts the writer of Hebrews. In Christian life, there are a few truths which are foundational. A foundation needs to be laid only once, but it must be firmly laid. What is it that is included in the doctrine of the first principles of Christ? Not only are repentance, faith, resurrection, and judgment listed, but also baptism and the laying on of hands. These two, then, are also foundational truths in Christianity. Our foundation will not be complete if the laying on of hands is missing.

The Meaning of the Laying on of Hands

We have already seen what baptism has done for us. It calls us out of the world and thus delivers us from the world. It identifies us with Christ so that we may share in His resurrection. What, then, can the laying on of hands do for us? What is its meaning?

In the Old Testament we find that the laying on of hands has a double significance. It is mentioned most frequently in Leviticus, chapters 1, 3 and 4, so we will look there to find its first meaning.

1. IDENTIFICATION

The laying on of my hand on the head of the sacrifice in Leviticus 1 signifies that I am identified with the sacrifice and the sacrifice with me. Why do I not offer myself to God, but offer a bullock instead? "For every beast of the forest is mine, and the cattle upon a thousand hills" (Ps. 50.10), says the Lord. What is the use of bringing cattle or sheep to Him? God does not lack a bullock or a lamb. It is men that He wants to offer themselves.

But what would happen if I actually came to the altar and offered myself? I would be doing the same thing as the Gentiles did, as those who worshiped Moloch. In the Old Testament, there were people who served Moloch. Instead of offering cattle and sheep, they sacrificed their own sons and daughters on the altar to their god. Does our God desire only cattle or sheep? If we offer ourselves to God, how is our God different from Moloch? He is different in that Moloch demanded the blood of our sons and daughters, but our God requires us to offer ourselves. His charge is even more severe than that of Moloch.

It is true that God's demand is more strict, but He shows us a way whereby we may sacrifice and yet not be burned. How? I bring a bullock or a lamb to the Lord. I lay my hand upon the head of the sacrifice. Whether I pray audibly or silently, my prayer is: This is I. I myself should be on the altar and be consumed by fire. I myself ought to be sacrificed, and I would indeed gladly offer myself to You. I should offer myself to be a burnt-offering, a sweet savor unto You. Lord, I now bring this bullock with me, and upon its head I lay my hand. By doing this, Lord, it signifies that this bullock is I, and I am this bullock. When I ask the priest to slay it, it is as if I am slain. When the blood of the bullock flows, my blood flows. When the priest sets the sacrifice on the altar, he has put me on the altar. I have laid my hand on it, so it is I.

Hence, the first meaning of the laying on of hands is identification. This is its prime significance in the Old Testament. I am identified with the sacrifice and it is I. Today both the sacrifice and I stand in the same position. When it is brought to God, I am brought to God.

2. IMPARTATION

There is a second significance to the laying on of hands in the Old Testament. In Genesis we see how Isaac laid his hands on his two sons, and how Jacob laid hands on his two grandsons, Ephraim and Manasseh (see chapter 27:27-40 and chapter 48.8-20). Jacob laid one hand on each of his grandsons and blessed them. So the laying on of hands becomes the impartation of blessing. With whatever blessing one is blessed, it shall come to pass.

In short, the significance of the laying on of hands is twofold: identification and impartation. These two may again be summed up by another word, communion. Through communion, we become identified; through communion, what one person has flows to another person.

How to Receive the Laying on of Hands

We find that the meaning of the laying on of hands has two aspects: identification and impartation. The laying on of hands in the first aspect joins a person to the body of Christ and in the second aspect communicates what the Head has for the member. It requires being a member in the body as well as being subject to the authority of the Head. No one can say he is sufficient alone. The new life which he receives is corporate in nature; it does not allow independence. In the body, he lives; out of the body, he dies. On the basis of this identification is the impartation of blessing.

If a brother lays hands on me, it is not a meaningless or indiscreet act. My eyes must be opened to see that hereafter I am but a child among many children, a cell among many cells, one member among many members. I live by the life of the body of Christ just as in this physical body every member lives by the whole body. If I act independently, I come to an end and thus will be useless. If I cease to fellowship with other children of God, something is drastically wrong with me. No matter how strong I am, I cannot exist all by myself. If I am cut off from the body of Christ, I will surely die spiritually. I cannot boast of my own strength. I am strong because I am in the body. If I am disconnected from the body, I am altogether finished; by the laying on of hands, though, I am connected to the body.

At the time of the laying on of hands, I should realize, "Oh, Lord, I cannot live by myself; I have to confess this day that I am but one member in the body. Only in the body can I live, only in the body can I have the oil." (see Psalm 133.2). Is this clear? One receives the oil because the Head has been anointed. If one is subject to the Head and is also joined to all the children of God, his submission as a member within the body draws the oil upon him.

Assembling Together

Scripture to Memorize:

Not forsaking our own assembling together, as the custom of some is, but exhorting one another; and so much the more, as ye see the day drawing nigh.

Hebrews 10.25

Let us further remember that Christianity is unique in that it is not individual but collective in nature. It stresses the assembling together of the saints. Most religions advocate individual piety; Christianity calls people to assemble. God's special grace falls on the gathering of believers.

Because of this, the word of God commands us not to forsake assembling together. Even in the Old Testament, God ordained that the Jews should assemble; then He called them the congregation of the Lord. To be a congregation they had to assemble together. Thus in the Old Testament God already emphasized the gathering of His people. In the New Testament it becomes much clearer that men ought to assemble in order that they may receive His grace. The command of the Bible is, "not forsaking our own assembling together." No one can forsake such assembling without forfeiting grace. It is foolish to cease gathering with the saints.

The Bible records many occasions of assembling together. While our Lord was on earth, He often met with His disciples. Though sometimes He conversed with them individually, yet He was more interested in gathering together with them. He gathered with them in boats, in homes, on top of mountains, and even inside a borrowed upper room on the night of His betrayal. After His resurrection, He met with them behind a closed door. Before the day of Pentecost the disciples gathered with one accord and continued steadfastly in prayer. On the day of Pentecost they were also all together in one place. Again, in Acts 2, we find that all who received the word and were baptized "continued stedfastly in the apostles' teaching and fellowship, in the breaking of bread and the prayers" (Acts 2.42). Later on, under persecution, they went to their own company where there was a gathering for prayer. When Peter was miraculously released from prison, he too went to a home where the people had assembled in prayer. The epistles also command believers to not forsake assembling together. In Corinthians, special mention is made of the whole church coming together. No one who belongs to the church ought to keep himself away from such gatherings.

What is the meaning of the word "church" (more accurately, "assembly") in Greek? Ek means "out of," and klesis means "a calling." Ecclesia means "the called-out ones assembled." Today God has not only called out a people but He also wants them to assemble together. If each one who is called were to maintain his independence, there would be no church. Thus we are shown the importance of assembling together.

The Lord's Presence Is in the Gathering

Furthermore, the Lord twice promises us His special presence: once in Matthew 18 and once in Matthew 28. The latter, "Lo, I am with you always, even unto the end of the world," pertains to witnessing for Christ; the former, "for where two or three are gathered together in my name, there am I in the midst of them," pertains to meeting in His name. These two promises of His presence are different from the presence of the Lord with us personally.

Many only know His presence in a personal way, but such knowledge is insufficient. His most powerful and overwhelming presence is known only in the meeting. Although there is His presence with you personally, it is bound to be of a lesser degree. Only in assembling together with brothers and sisters do you experience His presence in a way that you never did before. Learn, therefore, to know this presence in the meetings. It is a tremendous grace which cannot be otherwise obtained.

How wonderful the assembling of God's children is! We do not know how the body of Christ operates, but we do know that it does function. As one brother rises, you see light. When another brother stands up, you sense the presence of the Lord. Still another brother opens his mouth to pray, and you touch God. Yet another says a few words, and you receive the supply of life. Let me tell you, this is something beyond explanation—how the body of Christ works together. We will not understand until we stand before the Lord at His return. Today we can only follow that which the Lord has ordained.

How We Should Assemble

How should we gather? The Bible lays down a basic principle: all gatherings must be in the name of the Lord. The meaning of this is simply that we gather under the authority of the Lord and also are centered upon Him. Our purpose in coming together is to meet with the Lord, for our attraction is to Him. Let it be clear that we do not go to the meetings to see certain brothers or sisters, for our attraction to the meeting is not them. The Lord is the center. We go, along with many other brothers and sisters, to appear before Him.

Why is it that we gather in the name of the Lord? Because, physically speaking, the Lord is not here. Were He physically present, His name would not be so prominent. But since He is absent, His name becomes more noticeable. Today our Lord is physically in heaven, yet He has left a name on earth. So today we gather in His name that we may draw near to Him. He promises us that if we do so gather, He will be in our midst: that is, His Spirit will be in the midst of our gathering.

When we assemble, we do not go to hear a preacher but rather to meet the Lord. This is a concept that must be firmly established within us. Should we meet in order to hear a certain man, are we not gathering in this man's name and not in the name of our Lord? Many advertise the names of speakers in the newspaper; unknowingly they are asking people to gather around these men.

Although our Lord is in heaven, He is yet among us because His name is in our midst and so is His Spirit. The Holy Spirit is the custodian of the Lord's name. He is sent to protect and look after the Lord's name. He is here to exalt that name which is above all names. We must therefore gather unto the name of the Lord.

Another principle which governs a gathering is the edifying or building up of God's people. According to 1 Corinthians 14, this is a purpose found in all the gatherings—that others, not just ourselves, may be edified. Paul explains how speaking in a tongue edifies oneself but that it needs interpretation so that others may receive help. If there is no interpretation, the one with the tongue should keep silent in the church. In other words, the principle of speaking in a tongue is for self-edification and not for the edifying of others, whereas that of interpretation is to impart what one has to others for their edification. That which only edifies self and not others should not be expressed in the meeting.

Therefore, when we come to the meeting, we need to consider whether or not others will be edified. Even asking questions is not merely for our personal benefit. In whatever I do, do I help the meeting or do I damage it? The place where individualism is manifested most is in the meetings. Some people can only think of themselves. If they have a hymn they want to sing, they try their best to get it in. Indeed, they themselves may be edified, but is the meeting helped?

Finally, we wish to repeat that all who gather should have one aim: the edification of one another, not of oneself alone. I should refrain from doing anything that may hinder others. If my not speaking may inhibit others, then I will speak. In all things I must learn to edify others.

Various Meetings

Scripture to Memorize:

And they continued stedfastly in the apostles' teaching and fellowship, in the breaking of bread and the prayers.

Acts 2.42

In the previous exercise we stated the principle of meeting together; now we will turn to its practice. From what I personally can see, there are five different types of meetings in the Bible. They are gospel meetings, breaking of bread meetings, prayer meetings, exercise of gifts or fellowship meetings, and ministry or preaching meetings. We can find examples of all these in the Bible. Thus we know that at the time of the apostles in the New Testament days, there were at least these five different types of meetings. The church today also needs to have all these various meetings if it is to be strong before God. We must learn how to meet in order to help brothers and sisters grow in the Lord.

Gospel Meetings

This is the first type of meeting in the book of Acts as well as in the Gospels. Judging from the history of the early church, gospel meetings were the most basic of all the church meetings.

It was not till after the church began to degenerate during the third and fourth centuries that gospel meetings gradually lost their prominence and ministry meetings took on the leading role. The popularity of listening to sermons is a reflection on the weakened condition of the church. In the early church, preaching the gospel rather than listening to sermons occupied the foremost place. Today's reverse situation is a proof of the failure of the church. To have a strong church, the preaching of the gospel should be restored to its original position of being the most basic of all the meetings.

As soon as people come to believe in the Lord, they should immediately start to help in the preaching of the gospel. Do not allow them to develop the habit of listening to sermons; instead, help them to cultivate the habit of serving by preaching the gospel.

COME AS THE BODY

Encourage all the brothers and sisters to attend the gospel meetings. Never let any brothers and sisters think they do not need to attend because they are already saved. True, you are saved, but in the gospel meetings you have work to do. Do not come passively, but rather come in order to work. Let no one be careless about the gospel meetings. The question does not lie in whether or not you know the gospel. Indeed, you should know the substance of every meeting. But you come to the gospel meetings so that you can help, thus having a part in it yourself.

Breaking of Bread Meetings

The next important meeting is that of the breaking of bread.

THE TABLE AND THE SUPPER

According to the word of God, the meeting for the breaking of bread has two different aspects: one is the Lord's table and the other is the Lord's supper. 1 Corinthians 10 refers to the Lord's table while 1 Corinthians 11 points to the Lord's supper. However, we would like to consider them in reverse order, starting with 1 Corinthians 11. In the Lord's supper, the bread is the Lord's body, alluding to the physical body of the Lord. By partaking of this body which is given for the remission of our sins, we may thus receive life. So the basic thought of the Lord's supper is to remember the Lord. The meaning of the Lord's supper lies in remembering how the Lord shed His blood in order that our sins might be forgiven.

But 1 Corinthians 10 takes up another aspect. The breaking of bread is called the Lord's table. "Seeing that we, who are many, are one bread" (v. 17). The bread in 1 Corinthians 11 is the physical body of the Lord but in 1 Corinthians 10 it is us. We who are many are one bread. In other words, the Lord's table emphasizes the communion or fellowship of God's children. Chapter 11 stresses remembering the Lord, while chapter 10 stresses the fellowship of the children of God.

Hence, we have two meanings: one is direct, our focus turned heavenward, remembering the Lord; the other focuses on having fellowship with one another, the one bread on the table. We all have part in this bread; we are all people of this one bread. You belong to this bread; so do I. You have accepted the Savior; so have I. Therefore we ought to have fellowship in the Lord. At the breaking of bread, we come before the Lord both to have fellowship with Him and with all His children.

Prayer Meetings

The prayer meeting is also an important meeting. Each kind of meeting has its own particular characteristic. The testimony which God intends us to maintain on earth is to be fulfilled jointly by preaching the gospel, breaking bread, and praying together. Prayer meetings can be both difficult and easy. New believers need to learn about this kind of meeting.

WITH ONE ACCORD

A fundamental requirement for brothers and sisters praying together is to be of one accord. The Lord tells us in Matthew 18 that we must agree on earth. Before and on the day of Pentecost, the one hundred and twenty believers prayed with one accord (Acts 1.14-15). Therefore, the first condition of a prayer meeting is to be of one heart and one mind. How can people gather for prayer if each one has his own mind? The word "agree" in Matthew is most weighty. The Lord promises that "if two of you shall agree on earth as touching anything that they shall ask, it shall be done for them . . ." (v. 19). This particular word in Greek is used in music to denote harmony. If a person is playing alone, there is no problem. But if three play together—one the piano, one the violin, and one the flute—and should one of them play out of tune, the result is discord. Likewise, our prayers should not be out of harmony. If we are able to agree with one another, God will hear whatever we ask. What we bind on earth shall be bound in heaven, and what we loose on earth shall be loosed in heaven. (see Matthew 18.18). The basic condition is harmony. Therefore let us learn to be harmonious and not to pray each according to his own wish.

Exercise of Gifts Meetings

The gifts found in each local church are different. To some local churches, God may give words of revelation as well as gifts of prophecy and of teaching; to others, He may add the gift of tongues and the gift of interpreting tongues. In some places, He may give only the gift of teaching without giving any miraculous gifts; or it could be just the opposite, there being miraculous gifts without the gift of the word. We cannot dictate what God will do in His church. But what we do know is the principle of such meetings: God wishes His children to exercise their gifts. It is evident that we cannot exercise the gifts which we do not have but that we can use the gifts we do possess. Hence, no local church can imitate other local churches in this matter of exercising gifts. Each church must exercise before God whatever gifts the local brothers and sisters have. What we are describing here are meetings according to the principle of 1 Corinthians 14.

One thing new believers ought to know: not everyone may speak in the meetings for the exercising of gifts. Only those who have gifts may speak. We do not approve of a one-man ministry, neither do we sponsor an every-man ministry. God judges both the one-man ministry and the every-man ministry as wrong. Only the gifted should supply the word; not everyone can speak. Where does the difficulty lie today? The problem is that brothers with ministry adopt an attitude that the meeting is open to every brother, whereas in actuality it is open only to those brothers gifted in ministry, not to every brother and sister. They who are mouths refuse to speak while expecting the hands, the feet, and the ears to speak! What can you expect in such a meeting but confusion? Therefore, all the brothers who are gifted should open their mouths in the meeting. As to the rest, let them speak only when they have something of value to say.

Ministry Meetings

This is the least important of all meetings; still, it is a part of God's established order and thus should not be neglected. Through such meetings, we may receive the supply of God's word. We may have the opportunity to hear the word when an apostle comes our way or when some teachers and prophets reside with us. I do not suggest this is not an important meeting; I merely say it is the simplest. Nevertheless, there are also matters to be learned in this meeting. When people come, they should learn to be punctual, lest they compel others to wait. They should follow the directions of the ushers and not insist on choosing their own seats. They should also bring their own Bibles.

LET HEARTS BE OPEN

In attending such meetings, on the spiritual side the first preparation is that the heart must be open. He who listens with prejudice will never get anything. He whose heart is closed will not receive any blessing from God. Let no one sit there to criticize. It is the hearer, not the critic, whom God will bless. I often say that whether a message is well delivered or not depends half on the preacher and half on the audience. No preacher can carry a meeting if he is met with closed hearts, tightly shut minds, or critical attitudes.

The Lord's Day

Scripture to Memorize:

This is the day which Jehovah hath made; we will rejoice and be glad in it.

Psalm 118.24

God's Creation and Rest

God measured each day by the evening and the morning. He repaired the earth in six days, and on the seventh day He rested. About two thousand five hundred years later, He gave the ten commandments in which He charged men to remember the Sabbath. All the other commandments are "shall" and "shall not"; only the fourth commandment calls us to remember God's work. In other words, this remembrance points back to the creation of the world. It is to recall how God restored the world in six days and how He then rested on the seventh day. Therefore, the seventh day is God's Sabbath. After more than two thousand years from the creation, God gave His Sabbath to men with the charge that they should rest on that day.

When God first gave the seventh day, the Sabbath, to men, He desired them to rest physically. Since God himself rested on the seventh day and ceased from all His labor, He also desired men to work for six days and rest on the seventh day. The Sabbath was originally God's day of rest but He gave it to men, especially to the people of Israel in order that they too might cease from all works and thus might rest. The thought of rest on the Sabbath is quite clear in the Old Testament.

The Sabbath in the New Testament

When it came to New Testament days, conditions were somewhat changed. It seems as if the Sabbath day became more positive in the New Testament. Whereas in the Old Testament there was the emphasis on not doing any work, in the New Testament the Lord Jesus read the law and the prophets in the synagogue on the Sabbath. That which was originally intended for physical rest had by then become a day for spiritual pursuit. This element is not found in the Old Testament. So there is progression in the New Testament: to physical rest has been added the hearing of the law and the prophets. The principle of setting apart one day out of seven for God is implied.

It is indeed marvelous to see the Sabbath in the New Testament turned into something more positive. On the Sabbath, people attended the synagogue to listen to the law and to the prophets. The Lord Jesus preached in the synagogue on the Sabbath; the apostles, including Paul himself, also preached and reasoned in the synagogue on the Sabbath. The Sabbath became not only a day of rest but also a day of positive use. Special emphasis was now laid on the spiritual side.

The Lord's Day in the New Testament

The New Covenant, however, does have its own day, based not on the Sabbath, but on one day out of every seven days. The Sabbath day has not been changed to become the Lord's day; another day entirely has been chosen. Under the Old Covenant God chose the seventh day, but in the New Covenant He chose the first day of the week.

Scriptural Basis for the Lord's Day

We think the following passages are of great importance: "The stone which the builders rejected is become the head of the corner. This is Jehovah's doing; it is marvellous in our eyes. This is the day which Jehovah hath made; we will rejoice and be glad in it" (Ps. 118.22-24).

"Be it known unto you all, and to all the people of Israel, that in the name of Jesus Christ of Nazareth, whom ye crucified, whom God raised from the dead, even in him doth this man stand here before you whole. He is the stone which was set at nought of you the builders, which was made the head of the corner" (Acts 4.10-11).

Here is found the phrase, "the stone rejected by the builders." Who decides whether a stone is usable or not? It is the builders. If the mason says that a certain stone is unfit to build the house, you do not need to ask anybody else. Whatever the builder decides is final. But a strange thing happened. The stone which the builders rejected became the head of the corner. God put upon it the most important responsibility. What the builders considered useless, God made the chief cornerstone. This is the Lord's doing. It is marvelous in our eyes. It is indeed marvelous. Verse 24, however, gives us an added marvel related to the Lord's day. "This is the day which Jehovah hath made; we will rejoice and be glad in it." The day which the Lord has appointed is the day when the stone rejected by the builders became the chief cornerstone.

It is a day when we will rejoice and be glad. All should fear God and rejoice in His presence. Let us, then, find out what day it was when the stone rejected by the builders became the head of the corner. This we discover in Acts 4.10-11. Verse 10 says, "Whom ye crucified, whom God raised from the dead." Verse 11 continues, "He is the stone which was set at nought of you the builders, which was made the head of the corner." In other words, this is the day of the resurrection of the Lord Jesus. God, not man, determined the day when He who was rejected by men was to be raised from the dead. Let there be no confusion. The Bible puts it very clearly that this is the day the Lord has made. What day is it? It is the day of resurrection. So let all the children of God gather in the name of God's Son on that day and be glad.

Do you see the difference between the Lord's day in the New Testament and the Sabbath day in the Old Testament? The latter is negative, full of "shalt not's" and the threat of the punishment of death; the former, though, is a day of great rejoicing.

Things to Be Done on the Lord's Day

In regard to the first day of the week, three things receive special attention in the Bible:

1. REJOICE—THE PROPER ATTITUDE

The first thing concerns our attitude. As we have just read, all the children of God should rejoice and be glad on the first day of the week, for this is the day our Lord was raised from the dead. There was no need to tell Peter and the other apostles to rejoice. During the days when their Lord was laid in the tomb they experienced great disappointment and sadness. Then they found that the tomb was empty! They could not but rejoice and be glad.

2. ASSEMBLE TO BREAK BREAD

"And upon the first day of the week, when we were gathered together to break bread" (Acts 20.7a). Notice the grammatical structure here. The second clause is in apposition to the preceding phrase, meaning that the first day of the week is the time when they gathered to break bread. It does not point to any specific first day of the week, but simply refers to every first day of the week. So naturally this has become the day when all the churches gather to break bread in remembrance of the Lord. What day is more excellent than this, the first day of the week?

3. GIVE

"Now concerning the collection for the saints, as I gave order to the churches of Galatia, so also do ye. Upon the first day of the week let each one of you lay by him in store, as he may prosper, that no collections be made when I come" (1 Cor. 16.1-2). Here we find the second thing which should be done on the first day of the week. Paul repeated an order to the churches in Achaia which he formerly had given to the churches in Galatia. On each Lord's day there was something to be done. It is quite evident that during the apostolic time, the first day of the week was a special day.

If Paul wanted to find the Jews, he looked for them on the Sabbath; but if he wanted to find the Christians, he had to do it on the first day of the week. This was not only true of the churches in Achaia and in Galatia but also true of the churches everywhere, for the first day of the week is a very special day to Christians. On that day we break bread to remember the Lord. On that day we give as the Lord has prospered us. Is it not surprising to find that giving is to be done once a week, not once a month? Many wait until the end of the month and some even wait until the end of the year; but Paul tells us, we must balance our accounts before God on the first day of each week. We should lay aside our contribution to the Lord as He has prospered us each week.

Hymn Singing

Scripture to Memorize:

Let the word of Christ dwell in you richly; in all wisdom teaching and admonishing one another with psalms and hymns and spiritual songs, singing with grace in your hearts unto God.

Colossians 3.16

Understanding Hymn Singing

We would like now to consider the matter of hymn singing. We need to instruct new believers how to sing hymns. Even as prayer is often neglected, perhaps even more so is singing.

1. KNOW THE HYMNS

We wish to point out that our intention is not to make musicians out of the brothers and sisters. That would be purely worldly. What we do desire, though, is that they may know the hymns they sing. This we consider to be of great importance. In a meeting, those who sing the loudest all too frequently are those whose hearts are least touched. Our aim is not to produce fine voices or good music. What we want to appreciate before God is the hymn itself.

2. CULTIVATE A DELICATE FEELING

In the Bible we find that as well as prophecies, history, doctrines, and commandments, there are also hymns. One basic reason for the presence of these hymns in Scripture, I believe, is to train God's people to have finer, more delicate feelings.

Poems or hymns show man's tenderest feelings. The sentiment we exhibit in prayer cannot exceed in its delicateness that expressed in singing hymns. God purposes that we should have delicate feelings. For this reason, He gives us all kinds of poems in abundance in the Bible. We not only have the Psalms, the Song of Songs, and Lamentations but also other poems mingled in the historical sections and the commandments. Even in Paul's letters, so full of doctrine, he has unconsciously interspersed some poems.

One thing marvelous to observe is that the longer a person is a Christian and the more he has learned before God, the more tender his feelings become. On the contrary, if he has had few dealings with God and has learned but little, he seems to be rough and unpoetic.

4. INCENSE TO GOD

I have used this metaphor before. Incense in Scripture sometimes represents prayer and sometimes a poem of praise to God. Incense comes from trees. It is the sap or juice of the tree—an extraction of the very life of the tree. Made into incense and burned before God, it gives forth a most delicate fragrance. It is not the burning of wood or bark or leaves, but the consuming of the exuded juice and sap. It is something which flows from within and thus becomes a poem of praise to God.

Three Basic Requirements of Hymns

What is a hymn or a poem? According to what we read in the Bible, a proper hymn or poem must fulfill at least three basic requirements. The lack of any of these three requirements renders the hymn unusable.

1. SOUNDNESS OF TRUTH

The first criterion for a hymn to be usable is soundness in truth. Many hymns are well qualified in other areas, but if there are errors in truth they lead God's children into a wrong sentiment. It is extremely difficult for people to approach God while they are filled with human errors. In singing, we must let our delicate feeling ascend to God. If there is error in truth, we deceive ourselves and thus fail to touch reality. God never allows us to deal with Him according to the hymns we sing. He permits us to deal with Him only in accordance with the truth we hold. In other words, we can approach God only in truth. Things that are not of the truth are not acceptable.

2. POETIC FORM AND STRUCTURE

All good hymns must possess a poetic form and structure. A hymn is supposed to be poetical. If the truth is accurate but the form not poetic, it cannot be considered a good hymn. Soundness in truth alone does not make a hymn. There needs to be poetic form and structure.

Not any of the Psalms in the Bible are crude; all are exquisitely delicate. Each one is written in poetic form and structure. God's thought is expressed in poetic words.

In writing a hymn, it is not the meter alone that counts. The whole song must be poetically constructed.

3. TOUCHES REALITY

A hymn requires sound truth, poetic form and structure, and also a spiritual touch.

To illustrate, let us use Psalm 51 which tells of David's repentance. The truth is right and the psalm is poetically constructed. Its words are intricately designed; they are not sudden, brief utterances. In reading this psalm, you are aware of David's repentance; yet you would never just treat it as doctrine, for it touches spiritual reality. Hence, it draws from you a spiritual feeling. This we call the burden of the psalm. David repents, and this deep sense of repentance pervades the whole psalm.

In other words, a hymn must be able to touch your emotions deeply. It can either make you cry or rejoice as the content dictates. It should not be just poetically constructed and yet void of the power to move people to cry or to rejoice. A poetic sentiment is necessary to a hymn, a feeling which one cannot fail to sense. How can you sing a hymn on repentance and feel like laughing or sing a hymn of praise and not feel uplifted?

Three Different Types of Hymns

There are three different types of hymns in the Bible.

1. HYMNS TOWARD GOD

The principle objective of a hymn is for it to be sung to God. Hence, most of the Psalms in the Old Testament are of this nature. In fact, most hymns should be Godward.

2. HYMNS TOWARD MEN

Proverbs is also poetic writing, but it is of a different type, for it is directed to men. Among Christians, however, such hymns should be limited in number. The vast majority of the Psalms are Godward, though there are some which are manward. Generally speaking, hymns should be Godward; hymns that are manward are permissible only in a small number. Too many of the latter are contrary to the significance of hymns. Hymns of praise, of thanksgiving, and of prayer are all directed toward God. Gospel hymns and hymns for exhortation are of the second type and these are directed toward men.

3. Hymns Toward Self

In the Bible, especially in the book of the Psalms, we find a third type of hymn—those sung neither to God nor to men but to self. In many places there are expressions such as, "O my soul!" It is the communion of myself with my soul before God, the fellowship of myself with my heart, the consultation or communication between my heart and myself. All who know God and who have communed with God will understand this matter of communion with their own heart. So in this third type of hymn, I commune with myself and I consult with my heart. I sing to myself, calling myself and awakening myself; I make decisions, I remind myself. Usually at the end of these hymns one is led to God, for a spiritual person cannot be in communion with himself long without being drawn to God. His fellowship with his heart invariably changes into communion with God.

Let me tell you: the whole Bible is a poem. Those who are insensitive in their feeling are not able to touch its spirit. We thank God for we know that in the eternity to come our feelings will be much more delicate than those we have today. We know there will be more praises in heaven than prayers on earth. Prayer shall pass away and praise shall fill eternity. How excellent that day will be when all our feelings become exquisite and tender.

Finally, we are not attempting to make brothers and sisters musicians. We are not musicians but we are songsters(singers)! Christian hymns help us to develop delicate spiritual feelings. May we so learn that we are able to come to God with a more tender spirit and be brought closer to Him. May the Lord be gracious to us.

Praise

Scripture to Memorize:

Through him then let us offer up a sacrifice of praise to God continually, that is, the fruit of lips which make confession to his name.

Hebrews 13.15

Praise is the greatest work God's children can ever do. It is the loftiest expression the saints can ever show. The highest manifestation of spiritual life is seen in men praising God.

Though the throne of God is the heart of the universe, it is nonetheless established on the praise of the children of God. God's name is exalted through praise. There is nothing a Christian can offer which surpasses praise.

Sacrifice is very important to God, yet "The sacrifice of the wicked is an abomination" (Prov. 21.27a). Never, though, do we hear of praise as being abominable. There is abominable sacrifice but never abominable praise.

Prayer also occupies a very big place in the Bible, but we are told that, "He that turneth away his ear from hearing the law, even his prayer is an abomination" (Prov. 28.9). We have never read, however, of any praise being abominable. Is this not quite wonderful? David in his psalms says: "Evening, and morning, and at noon, will I pray and moan aloud; and he will hear my voice" (Ps. 55.17 Darby); also "Seven times a day do I praise thee, because of thy righteous ordinances" (Ps. 119.164). He prays three times a day, but praises seven times a day. As moved by the Holy Spirit, he acknowledges the significance of praise.

Praise Is Added to Priestly Functions

One thing we know: all matters related to worship, the tabernacle, the sacrifices, and the priesthood are given in detail in the book of Exodus. The pattern shown to Moses in the mount was not open to any addition or subtraction. All who know God know that Moses did not dare add any of his own ideas in building the tabernacle in the wilderness. Since the whole project was divine, no one was allowed to tamper with the pattern. Everything was done exactly according to God's command. Yet years later, David and Solomon seemed to make changes in the priesthood when they added something to the functions of the priests. They appointed a great number of people to the work of praising God. This change, though, was not rejected, but accepted, by God.

The Nature of Praise

Praise in its nature is a sacrifice. If suffering were incidental, then it would not be a part of the nature of praise. But we know suffering is not accidental but planned by God. This means that praise derives its character from suffering and from darkness. Hence the writer of Hebrews says: "Through him then let us offer up a sacrifice of praise to God continually, that is, the fruit of lips which make confession to his name" (Heb. 13.15).

Brethren, what is a sacrifice? It involves death and loss. He who sacrifices incurs loss. The bullock or the lamb used to be yours, used to be your possession and property. Today you bring it before God as a sacrifice; you suffer its loss. God wants men today to offer praise as if offering a sacrifice. In other words, He enables you to offer praises to Him by wounding you, grinding you, and cutting you deeply. God's throne is established on praises. How will He obtain these praises?—by His children's coming to Him, each bringing the sacrifice of praise. New believers must learn to praise. We mentioned in an earlier chapter the need to pray to God. Now we shall consider how to praise Him. David received grace to praise God seven times a day. Shall we do so less than that? No, let us praise God incessantly. Let us learn to say, "Lord, I praise You."

The Way to Victory

First we need to see that praise is a sacrifice. Then we shall see that it is also a way to victory. It is a very common strategy of Satan to attack God's children in the area of prayer. Many brothers and sisters complain to me that they are so frequently under attack that they cannot pray very well. We often read in spiritual books that what Satan fears most is God's children in prayer, that he will flee when God's children are on their knees. This is quite familiar to us. But what I would like to say today is, that what Satan attacks most furiously is not prayer, but praise.

I do not say Satan does not attack prayer. When a Christian starts to pray, Satan begins to attack. It is therefore relatively easy to talk with people, but quite difficult to pray. Indeed, Satan does attack prayer. However, he also assaults the praise of God's children. If he could prevent all words of praise from rising up to God, he would gladly use all his strength to do so.

Do remember: whenever God's children are praising, Satan must flee. Prayer frequently is a battle, but praise is victory. Prayer is spiritual warfare; praise is the shout of triumph. For this reason, praise is what Satan hates most. He will exert all his strength to quench our praise whenever possible. The children of God act foolishly when they look at their environment or consider their feelings and then stop praising the Lord. If they really know God, they will see that even in the jail at Philippi there was a place for song. As Paul and Silas were praying and singing hymns unto God, all the doors of the prison opened (Acts 16.25-26). Prayer may not always open prison doors, but praise does!

Why is praise also triumph? Because when you pray, you are yet in the environment; but when you praise, you have risen above the environment. Whenever you are praying and pleading, you are involved in the thing you ask for. The more you plead, the more you are surrounded by that thing, for it is before you all the time. But if you are brought by God beyond the prison, beyond the stocks, beyond the shame and suffering, then you are able to raise your voice and sing praise to the name of God.

What prayer may fail to accomplish, praise can. This is a basic principle to be remembered. If you cannot pray, why not praise? The Lord has not only given us prayer but also praise that through it we may claim the victory. "But thanks be unto God, who always leadeth us in triumph in Christ" (2 Cor. 2.14). Whenever your spirit is pressed beyond measure so that you can hardly breathe, let alone pray, why do you not try to praise God? Pray when you are able to pray; but praise when you cannot pray.

The Basic Substance of Praise

In Psalm 106 which depicts the situation of the Israelites in the wilderness, there is one word which is most precious: "Then believed they his words; they sang his praise" (v. 12). They believed, therefore they sang; they believed, so they praised. Within praise there is the basic content of faith. No one should lightly praise or casually say, "I thank the Lord; I praise the Lord!" No, such words cannot be reckoned as praise, for praise must be substantiated by faith. In a time of distress you pray; when in sorrow you pray. You pray and pray until you are able to believe in your heart. Then you open your mouth to praise.

Praise, therefore, is living. It is not something carelessly uttered. Whenever one is troubled, he ought to pray. But once there rises within you a little faith enabling you to believe in God, in His power, greatness, mercy and glory, then you should start to praise. Remember, if one has faith within him and fails to praise, that faith will sooner or later fade away. I make this statement on the basis of experience. Let me say it most emphatically: if you find faith in you, you must praise, or else you will soon lose the faith.

Glorifies God

Finally, I wish to read with you one passage found in Psalm 50. "Whoso offereth the sacrifice of thanksgiving glorifieth me" (v. 23). The Lord is seeking our praises. Nothing glorifies God more than praise. We know that one day all prayer shall become a thing of the past, all works shall have passed away. Prophecy shall be gone, labors shall cease. But in that day, praise shall be increased far above that of today. It shall continue without end. Praise will never cease. In heaven, in our heavenly home, we shall praise more and learn more how to praise God. I believe it is best that we start to learn this most excellent lesson right here on earth.

The Breaking of Bread

Scripture to Memorize:

*Wherefore whosoever shall eat the bread or drink
the cup of the Lord in an unworthy manner, shall
be guilty of the body and the blood of the Lord.*

1 Corinthians 11.27

Dual Meaning of the Lord's Supper

1. REMEMBER THE LORD

The basic thought of the Lord's supper is to remember
the Lord. The Lord himself says, "This do in remembrance
of me" (1 Cor. 11.24b). He knows how very forgetful we
are. Do not think that because we have received such an
abundance of grace and experienced such a wonderful
redemption that we will never be able to forget. Let me
warn you that men such as we, are most forgetful. For this
reason, the Lord especially desires us both to remember
Him and to remember what He has done for us. The Lord
wants us to remember Him not only because we are so
forgetful, but also because He needs our memory. In other
words, He does not want us to forget Him. The Lord is so
great and so transcendent that He could let us forget Him
and not be bothered by it. Yet He says, "This do in
remembrance of me," thus revealing how condescending
He is in desiring our remembrance.

That the Lord wants us to remember Him fully is an
expression of His love. It is the demand of love, not of
greatness. So far as His greatness is concerned, He can
afford to be forgotten by us. But His love insists that we
remember Him. If we do not remember Him, we will suffer

125

great loss. If we do not remember Him often and keep the redemption of the Lord always before us, we will easily be conformed to the world and become contentious toward the children of God. Thus, we not only need to remember Him, but we are profited by so doing. It is a means by which we may receive the grace of the Lord.

DISASSOCIATES YOU FROM THE WORLD

One cardinal value in remembering the Lord lies in the fact that the world will not be able to exert its influence continuously upon you. If every few days you remember how the Lord died for you and received you, let me tell you, the world will have no place in you. Since my Lord suffered death here in the world, what have I to say? If they had not killed my Lord, there might still be some ground for them to talk with me. But now that they have already killed my Lord and His death is exhibited before me, I have nothing more to say and no way to communicate with the world. I cannot have any fellowship with it. This is one of the prime benefits of the breaking of bread.

ENLARGES YOUR HEART

Another advantage in remembering the Lord is that each one who remembers Him will quite naturally have his heart enlarged to embrace all children of God. It is but natural to see that all who are redeemed by the Lord's blood are the beloved of the Lord; therefore, they are also the delight of my heart. If we are all in the Lord, can there be jealousy, reviling and unforgivingness? How can you continue in strife with the brother or sister who sits next to you at the Lord's supper? What right do you have to demand anything of your brother when you recall how many of your sins have been forgiven? If you insist on strife, jealousy and an unforgiving spirit, you will not be able to remember the Lord.

Every time we gather to remember the Lord, we are bidden to review His love once more. We should reexamine the corruption of the world and the judgment upon it. We should renew the conviction that all the redeemed are beloved of the Lord. Every time we remember the Lord, we review His love, how He loved us and gave Himself for us. In love, He descended to hades for us. The world has already been judged, for it crucified our Lord. But all of God's children are our delight, because they have all been bought by the Lord's blood. How can we hate them? How can we harbor any thought of hate?

2. PROCLAIM THE LORD'S DEATH

The Lord's supper has a second meaning. This is found in 1 Corinthians 11.26: "For as often as ye eat this bread, and drink the cup, ye proclaim the Lord's death till he come." We need to proclaim or exhibit the Lord's death that all may see.

From a human standpoint, God has left nothing on the earth other than the cross. The work of the cross is finished but the fact of the cross remains. Indeed, many today have forgotten the cross, but not the believers. To them, the cross is something forever remembered. Every Lord's day we see in the Lord's supper the cross of the Son of God exhibited in the church. This suggests that though we may forget everything else, we must remember the fact of our Lord's death for us.

Meaning of the Lord's Table

1 Corinthians 11 speaks of the Lord's supper with its dual meaning of remembering the Lord and exhibiting the Lord's death. Chapter 10 of the same book, however,

speaks of it as the Lord's table. Though the subject is the same, yet two different designations are used. Like the Lord's supper, the Lord's table also has a double meaning. "The cup of blessing which we bless, is it not a communion of the blood of Christ? The bread which we break, is it not a communion of the body of Christ? seeing that we, who are many, are one bread, one body: for we all partake of the one bread" (vv. 16-17). Here the table carries a double significance: first communion, then oneness.

1. COMMUNION

The first and primary meaning of the Lord's table is communion. "The cup of blessing which we bless, is it not a communion of the blood of Christ?" As 1 Corinthians 11 delves into the relationship of the believer with the Lord, so 1 Corinthians 10 deals with relationships among believers. The former (chapter 11) does not touch upon our mutual relationships; it merely stresses remembering the Lord and proclaiming the Lord's death till He come. One the other hand, the latter (chapter 10), emphasizes the communion of the blood of Christ.

Notice that the cup of blessing which we bless is singular in number. We all drink out of the same cup; therefore it demonstrates the sense of communion. Unless people are very intimate, they will not drink from the same cup. The fact that so many of God's children drink from the same cup fully attests to the communion aspect of the Lord's table.

In chapter 11 our eyes are focused on the Lord, but in chapter 10 we see our brethren. We see them in the cup. The cup is for drinking, and we all drink of the same cup. In so doing we have communion with all of God's children. Let us be careful to not lose sight of this aspect.

2. ONENESS

The second meaning of the Lord's table is oneness. "Seeing that we, who are many, are one bread, one body: for we all partake of the one bread" (v. 17). In this we can see at once that all the children of God are one. The bread of chapter 11 and that of chapter 10 have different emphases. Whereas in chapter 11 the Lord says, "This is my body which is for you. . ." (v. 24), thus making reference to the bread as His physical body, in chapter 10 the verse reads, "We, who are many, are one bread, one body," this time suggesting that the church is the bread.

Even as we need to learn before the Lord the various meanings of the Lord's table as remembrance, exhibition, and communion, so also we must learn its meaning as oneness. All God's children are as one as the bread is one. We have only one loaf; each believer breaks off a piece. If it were possible to gather all the broken pieces, we could restore that one loaf of bread. The bread scattered among many would still be one loaf if the pieces were reunited. Physically, after the bread is broken and eaten, it cannot be recovered. But spiritually, we are yet one in the Holy Spirit. The Holy Spirit gives Christ to us; yet Christ is still in the Holy Spirit. What has been distributed is the bread, but in the Holy Spirit we are still one and have never been divided. So in the breaking of bread, we confess that the children of God are one. This bread signifies the oneness of the church of God.

The basic question with the Lord's table lies in the bread. As God's children gather together to break bread, if the bread only represents themselves, it is too small; it should not be broken. The bread must stand for the whole church, including all the children of God on earth as well as those in your particular locality. Hence, it testifies to the oneness of all the children of God.

The Principle of Receiving

How, then, do we receive people to the table of the Lord? Remember, we are not the hosts; we are at best but ushers. This is the Lord's supper, the Lord's table, not ours. We have no authority whatsoever over the Lord's table. We are privileged to eat the bread and drink the cup, but we cannot withhold it from others. We cannot forbid any of the blood-redeemed ones from coming to the Lord's table. We have no authority to refuse it to anyone. We cannot refuse those whom the Lord has received, nor can we reject those who belong to the Lord. We can only refuse those whom the Lord refuses or those who do not belong to Him. The Lord only refuses those who do not belong to Him or those who yet remain in sin. Since their communion with the Lord is already interrupted, we, too, do not have fellowship with them. But let us take note that we are the Lord's and have no authority to exercise other than what the Lord exercises.

Every time we break the bread, we should think of all those who have received grace. We should not think only of those brothers and sisters whom we personally know. If those gathered at the table in one place refuse to have fellowship with God's children in other places, they are too exclusive.

We hope the hearts of brothers and sisters in every place will be so enlarged that they can embrace all the children of God. To stand on the ground of the church is not to discriminate against any of God's children, as if some were welcome and others not. Every time we come to the Lord's table, we are enabled to see Him once more; thus our hearts are enlarged once again to include all the children of God. The heart is a great mystery. It does not expand by itself; rather, it tends to become narrowed by the least bit of carelessness. Its natural inclination is to contract, not to expand. But at the time of remembering the Lord, our hearts should be expanded.

IN A WORTHY MANNER

"Wherefore whosoever shall eat the bread or drink the cup of the Lord in an unworthy manner, shall be guilty of the body and blood of the Lord. But let a man prove himself, and so let him eat of the bread, and drink of the cup. For he that eateth and drinketh, eateth and drinketh judgment unto himself, if he discern not the body" (1 Cor. 11.27-29). It is extremely important that we eat and drink worthily. This does not refer to the person's own worthiness but to the way in which he partakes. A person's worthiness is already taken care of in his being redeemed by the precious blood. If he is not the Lord's, he cannot have any part in the Lord's table. But some who are the Lord's may eat in an unworthy manner; that is, they may receive the bread casually without discerning the Lord's body.

Therefore, we exhort young believers to receive the bread respectfully. You are qualified before God to come, but you are asked by the Lord to examine yourself. You must discern that this is the Lord's body. Hence, you cannot take it lightly. You must receive it in a manner worthy of the Lord's body. Since the Lord gives His blood and His flesh to you, you need to receive them respectfully. No one but a fool would despise what God has given to him.

BOOK FOUR:
Not I But Christ

If Any Man Sin

Scripture to Memorize:

If we walk in the light, as he is in the light, we have fellowship one with another, and the blood of Jesus his Son cleanseth us from all sin.

1 John 1.7

If a redeemed person should inadvertently sin, how can he be restored to God? This is a very pressing problem. Unless he knows the way of restoration, he will not be able to come back to God.

By His death on the cross the Lord Jesus cleansed and redeemed us from all our sins. At the time we came to Him, the Holy Spirit enlightened us and showed us our sins. But what the Holy Spirit showed us was not as comprehensive as what the Lord did on the cross. The difference is worth noticing. Even as the sin-offering in Leviticus 16 included every sin, so also the Lord Jesus on the cross bore all of our sins. His redemption covered every sin that you could possibly commit in your lifetime. Indeed, when He died on the cross, He bore all the sins of your life.

How to Return to God after Sinning

We have no intention to encourage young brothers and sisters to live a loose life. In another exercise we will point out to them the way of victory (Exercise 26, "Deliverance"). Our purpose for this exercise is to show how one who has sinned can be restored to God

1. WALK IN THE LIGHT

"If we walk in the light, as he is in the light, we have fellowship one with another, and the blood of Jesus his Son cleanseth us from all sin" (1 John 1.7). What does the "light" here refer to? It has two possible meanings: one possibility is the light of holiness; the other possibility is the light of the gospel, that is, God revealed and manifested in the gospel.

Many would like the "light" here to refer to the light of holiness. Thus the first section of this verse might be paraphrased as: "if we walk in holiness as God is in holiness." Such a rendering, however, would make what follows meaningless. It is quite evident that we have no need of the blood of Jesus, God's Son, to cleanse us from our sins if we are holy.

God has distinctly declared that He comes to save us and give us grace. If we are in this light as God is in the light of grace, the light of the gospel, then we can have fellowship one with another. By grace we come to God, as He also comes to us in grace. Thus we have fellowship with God, and the blood of Jesus His Son cleanses us from all our sins. This truly is grace.

2. CONFESSION AND THE GRACE OF FORGIVENESS

"If we say that we have no sin, we deceive ourselves, and the truth is not in us" (1 John 1.8). We deceive ourselves if we say we have no sin. It is evident that the truth is not in us. This is certain.

"If we confess our sins, he is faithful and righteous to forgive us our sins, and to cleanse us from all unrighteousness" (v. 9). If we know we have sinned and also confess it, God will forgive our sins and cleanse us from all unrighteousness. He is faithful to His own word and righteous toward His own work, faithful to His own promise and righteous toward the redemptive work of His

Son on the cross. He cannot but forgive for He has said it; He must forgive because of the work of redemption. Due to His faithfulness and righteousness, He will forgive us our sins and cleanse us from all unrighteousness.

"If we say that we have not sinned, we make him a liar, and his word is not in us" (v. 10). How can we say we have never sinned? That would make God a liar and would refute the necessity for redemption. God provides us with redemption because we have sinned.

"My little children, these things write I unto you that ye may not sin. And if any man sin, we have an Advocate with the Father, Jesus Christ the righteous" (1 John 2.1). "These things" refers back to the words in chapter 1.7-10; there God depicts in principle our various conditions before Him due to our sins. Because of the blood of Jesus His Son, God forgives us our sins. Owing to His faithfulness and righteousness, He forgives and cleanses all our unrighteousness. No matter what kinds of sins we have committed, they all are forgiven.

What the Lord has done is to wholly forgive and totally cleanse us from all our sins and all our unrighteousness. When He says "all," no doubt He *means* "all." Do not change His word. He forgives not only our sins of the past but all of our sins—sins that we are conscious of as well as those of which we are unaware. We go away with a perfect and complete forgiveness. "These things," therefore, alludes to how our sins are forgiven through the promise and work of God. God has spoken to us that we may not sin. When we see the Lord's great forgiveness to us, far from becoming careless, we rather are constrained not to sin.

What follows is something quite specific. The sins already mentioned are more general in nature and the forgiveness experienced is also general in principle. But what about the sins committed after we have believed in the Lord? What specific forgiveness is there? "And if any man sin"—this refers to a child of God—"we have an Advocate with the Father, Jesus Christ the righteous." "With the Father" shows that it is a family affair. We are counted among the children of God; we belong to the family. We have an advocate with the Father, even Jesus Christ the righteous, who is the propitiation for our sins. Because He became the propitiation for our sins in His death, He is now our advocate with the Father.

If a Christian should sin, he has an advocate with the Father. There is a Father-son relationship if the one who sins is a believer. The word *advocate* in the Greek is *parakletos* which means "called to one's side." It has two different usages: in civil use it means one who stands by and is ever ready to help; in legal use it means a counselor or attorney, one who takes full responsibility for the case. Our Lord took us in when we first came to His cross. How did He assume our case? By being "the propitiation for our sins; and not for ours only, but also for the whole world" (1 John 2.2).

New believers should clearly be exhorted not to sin. They ought not to sin and it is actually possible for them not to sin. But if they should unfortunately sin, let them remember that the blood of the Lord Jesus can still cleanse them from all their sins. He is their champion; He is the righteous One. The very fact that He is now with the Father guarantees the forgiveness of their sins.

Since this is so, do not linger in the shame of sin as if such suffering will bring in holiness. Do not think that to prolong the consciousness of sin is in any way an indication of holiness. If any man sin, the first thing to do is to go to God and confess, "I have sinned." This is judging oneself, calling sin by its right name. "If we confess our sins, He is faithful and righteous to forgive us our sins, and to cleanse us from all unrighteousness." If you do this, you will then see that God forgives you and that your fellowship with Him is immediately restored.

3. THE WAY TO RESTORATION

If a child of God should sin and continue in that sin without confession, he yet remains God's child and God is still his Father. Nevertheless, his fellowship with God will be lost. There is now a weakness in his conscience; he is unable to rise up before God. He may try to fellowship with God, but he will find it most painful and quite limited. It is just like a child who has done something wrong. Even though his mother may not know and may not scold him, he is still very uneasy at home. He finds it impossible to have sweet fellowship, for within him there is a sense of distance.

There is only one way to be restored. I must go to God and confess my sin. I believe that the Lord Jesus is my advocate and has taken care of all my sins. So here I am before God, humbly acknowledging my failure. I look to the Lord that hereafter I may not be so arrogant and careless. I have learned how prone I am to fall. I am no better than others. So I pray that God may be merciful to me, that I may continue on with the Lord step by step. Praise God, we do have an advocate with Him, One who does come alongside.

Apology and Restitution

Scripture to Memorize:

Herein I also exercise myself to have a conscience void of offence toward God and men always.

Acts 24.16

The Needed Habit of Apology and Restitution

After we believe in the Lord, we need to cultivate the habit of apologizing and making restitution. (We are not here referring to the things of the past. We have already dealt with that subject in Exercise 2.) If we offend or hurt anyone, we ought to learn to make amends for our fault either by an apology or by restitution. If we confess to God and apologize to men, our conscience will be kept sensitive and keen. Otherwise our conscience will become hard, and a hardened conscience is unable to receive God's light. Light does not shine easily upon a person with a hardened conscience.

The famous Welsh revivalist, Evan Roberts, always liked to ask people, "When was the last time you apologized?" If the last apology was a very long time ago, something must be wrong. It is inconceivable that one could live for years without offending someone. More likely, we have offended others without being conscious of our sins. If so, it proves that something is wrong with our conscience; it is in darkness, void of light and sensitivity.

"When was the last time you apologized?" By noticing the length of the time lapse, we can know if there is anything between the person and his God. If the time lapse has been great, we know that his spirit lacks light. But if he

141

has recently apologized to someone, then we know that his conscience is sensitive. New believers should see the importance of a sensitive conscience, for this alone enables us to live in God's light. With a sensitive conscience, we will continue to condemn our sins as sins. Many times we will have to confess our sins to God and also apologize to men.

Sins Requiring Apology

For what kind of sins do we need to apologize? Not all sins require an apology, but we should apologize for those which damage or hurt others. If I sin and what I do causes loss to my brother or to an unbeliever, I ought to express my regret to that person. I should not only confess to God but also apologize to the person involved.

We can ask God himself to forgive us our sins, but how can we ask Him to forgive us on behalf of other people? Surely, we must confess to God and ask Him to forgive us, but also we should make it right with those whom we have hurt. It is very important that we never get the idea that to ask God alone for forgiveness is sufficient to cover up our offenses against others.

On the other hand, it is absolutely unnecessary to apologize for sins which are unrelated to men. May young believers be kept from overdoing, from going too far. Whatever sin is committed against God but is totally unassociated with man needs only to be confessed to God, but that which is a sin against man needs an apology to man.

Do not easily offend people, especially do not offend a brother. But if you do, you will fall under a judgment from which it is hard to be extricated. The Lord puts it emphatically, "Agree with thine adversary quickly while thou art with him in the way," (Matt. 5.25). How? "While thou art with him in the way." Today we all are yet in the way. Neither he nor you has died. Both of you are living and therefore yet in the way. So make up with him quickly.

The Practice of Matthew 5:23-26

DEAL WITH ALL INDEBTEDNESS

The last farthing in Matthew 5.26 does not refer to an actual amount of money; rather, it suggests that if any indebtedness is not cleared the person is still not free.

FIRST BE RECONCILED TO YOUR BROTHER

Let us look more closely at this passage. "If therefore thou art offering thy gift at the altar, and there rememberest that thy brother hath aught [something] against thee" (v.23)—here it refers especially to matters among God's children, matters between brother and brother. It is when you are offering your gift at the altar, not when you are praying. At that very time you remember that your brother has something against you. This, indeed, is God's guidance. Frequently, in matters of this nature, the Holy Spirit recalls a certain incident or puts an appropriate thought into your mind. When it comes, do not push the thought aside as if it were merely something fleeting. Rather, deal faithfully with it.

When you remember how your brother feels it must be because you have offended him. Such indebtedness may or may not be material in character; nonetheless it is an indebtedness. You may have offended him by an unrighteous act pertaining either to material or nonmaterial things; if so, then he has something against you. Should a brother or a person whom you have offended moan and grieve before God because of you, then you are seriously hampered in God's sight.

If, when about to offer your gift at the altar, you remember that a brother has something against you, it is better that you do not proceed. Leave your gift, for it is right to leave it with God with a view to offering it later. "First be reconciled to thy brother, and then come and offer thy gift" (v.24). Though the gift is for God, there must first be reconciliation with man. Whoever fails to be reconciled to man cannot come to God and offer. "Be reconciled to thy brother"—what does it mean? It means to appease his wrath, whether by apology or by making restitution. You must apologize or repay until he is reasonably satisfied.

How to Apologize and Make Restitution

Now, let us see how we should apologize and how we should make restitution.

1. THE SCOPE

In this matter of making apology or restitution, the sin itself determines the scope of the apology or of the restitution. We do not want people to go to extremes. We desire that brothers and sisters act in accordance with God's word and not be excessive. It is in excessiveness that Satan has ground to launch his attack. The scope of the apology should be as wide as the scope of the sin. If the sin is against all, then confess to all. If the sin is against one person, confess only to that person. To confess to one person when the sin is against all is not sufficient; to confess to all when the sin is against only one person is overdoing it. The scope of the sin determines the scope of the confession. Of course, giving testimony is another matter. I have sinned in a personal way frequently, but sometimes I want to testify about it to brothers and sisters. This is something else again, to be treated separately. But as for apology and restitution, these two are definite in their scope. This point must be carefully observed.

2. UNRIGHTEOUS TO INCRIMINATE OTHERS

If two people sin together, say for example, stealing or using falsehood to obtain something, then the one who apologizes or makes restitution should not incriminate the other. Whatever knowledge we have is a trust. He who violates a trust is unrighteous. If anyone informs me of a certain matter, it is like entrusting me with a sum of money. I cannot sell my trust because it would be unrighteous. Remember, it is unrighteous for you to reveal any trust that people confide to you. So, in making apology or restitution, do not incriminate the other person lest you be unrighteous.

3. SINS NOT TO BE CONFESSED

There are certain sins which should not be confessed. You should not confess for the sake of appeasing your own conscience if the one who hears your confession will lose his peace as a result. To make yourself peaceful but to take away another's peace should not be done. For example: Suppose a girl did something terribly wrong, sinning against her mother, but her mother was unaware of it. Her mother, though a church member, is uncertain of her salvation, and, besides, has a fierce temper. The daughter, having been enlightened by God, is convicted of her sin. She feels terribly bad about it and is constantly troubled by it. So she tells her mother about the sinful thing she did against her. After the confession, the daughter has peace in her heart. But the mother, since that day, becomes so disturbed that she loses her temper and rants day and night. The mother loses her peace while the daughter regains hers. The principle is: never gain your peace at the price of another's peace.

4. CONSULT THE RESPONSIBLE BROTHERS

In making apology, new believers should learn to frequently consult the responsible brothers of the church. Thus, the new believers, under the protection of the church can carry out their task properly and without excess. Confer with the responsible brothers so that they may instruct you as to what things should be confessed and what things need not be.

5. LETTERS OF RESTITUTION

Concerning restitution, it is possible that you may not have the ability to repay. To make restitution is one thing, to be able to repay is another thing. If you do not have the ability to reimburse, you still must write a letter of restitution. You can honestly write: "I will repay but am unable to do it just now. Please forgive me. As soon as I am able, I will immediately pay back." This, too, ought to be done.

6. CONSCIENCE CLEANSED

Finally, it is important that one not fall under excessive accusation because of making apologies. This is something quite possible. Each person needs to see how the blood of the Lord cleanses his conscience. Through His death, one can have a conscience void of offense before God. The Lord's death enables him to draw nigh to God. Such is the reality. On the other side, he must also see that in order to be a clean person in the sight of the world, he has to deal with his many sins. Whether he sins against people in material things or in other matters, he should be ready to deal with it. Never, however, allow Satan to attack with excessive accusation.

Restore Your Brother

Scripture to Memorize:

Brethren, even if a man be overtaken in any trespass, ye who are spiritual, restore such a one in a spirit of gentleness; looking to thyself, lest thou also be tempted.

Galatians 6.1

One problem that must be solved is, what should we do if someone sins against us? The question under consideration now is not what should we do if we sin against others, but what should we do if people sin against us. Let us read Matthew 18.15-35, for this passage gives special instruction on the subject.

In analyzing this passage, we find it can be divided into two parts: forgiveness (vv. 21-35), and persuasion (vv.15-20). The Lord tells us that if our brother should sin against us, our first responsibility is to forgive him before God, and our second responsibility is to persuade him before God. We often mention the first matter of forgiveness, but we should equally emphasize the second matter of persuasion.

The First Responsibility—Forgiveness

"Then came Peter and said to Him, Lord, how oft shall my brother sin against me, and I forgive him? until seven times?" (v. 21). We find this not only in Matthew but also in Luke. And Luke records it a little differently.

1. FORGIVE BOUNDLESSLY

"Take heed to yourselves: if thy brother sin, rebuke him; and if he repent, forgive him. And if he sin against thee seven times in the day, and seven times turn again to thee, saying, I repent; thou shalt forgive him" (Luke 17.3-4). This is similar to Matthew's record but not entirely the same. The words in Matthew seem to be weightier. Forgiveness there is not to be given seven times, but seventy times seven. "Seventy times seven" means that the forgiveness the children of God extend toward their brethren is to be unlimited. There is no counting the number of times, for it is not seven times but seventy times seven.

The point which Luke stresses is that if the brother who sins against us repents and asks for forgiveness, we must forgive even if it is seven times in one day. The question is not whether his repentance is true or false. We are to disregard that. If he says he repents, we forgive and leave the matter of repentance with him.

2. FORGIVE GENEROUSLY

The Lord then uses a parable in verses 23-27.

There are a few special points that require our attention. What we owe forever exceeds what we can repay. We owe God ten thousand talents, far beyond our ability to pay back for we have nothing with which to repay. All of us need to have a right estimate of our own indebtedness to God so that we may generously forgive our brother's debt. If we forget how great the grace we have received from God, we then become the most ungracious of men. In order to see how little that people owe us, we need to see how much we owe God.

The Lord expects you to treat others as He has treated you. Since He does not demand of you according to righteousness, He expects you not to demand righteousness of others. The Lord forgives your debt according to mercy. With what measure He has meted out to you, He wants you to mete out to others. He gives you in good measure, pressed down, shaken together and running over; He wishes you to do likewise. (see Lk. 6.38). As He treats you, so should you treat your brother.

It is exceedingly ugly in the sight of God for the forgiven person to be unforgiving. Nothing can be uglier than for the one who was forgiven to be unforgiving, the one who received mercy to be merciless, and the one who was given grace to be graceless. We must learn before God to treat others as He has treated us. Let us be so humbled by what we have received that we treat others according to the same principle.

The Second Responsibility—Persuasion

I believe many of God's children have learned the lesson of forgiveness. Many, though, have forgotten what we should do after someone has sinned against us. According to Matthew 18.15-20, we must persuade or exhort our brother. We must not only forgive but we must persuade as well.

1. TELL HIM

"And if thy brother sin against thee" (v. 15). It is quite common for God's children to sin against one another. Although such things may not happen too often, neither are they too scarce. The Lord shows us what we should do if anyone sins against us. "Go, show him his fault between thee and him alone." Should anyone sin against you, the first thing to do is to tell him, not to tell others. This is a word we should rightly understand. Show his fault to him when you and he are alone.

The Lord says, "Show him his fault." But how? The Lord does not suggest you write a letter but that you go to him. Talk to him when you and he are alone. This is the Lord's command. In dealing with personal sin, the two of you are sufficient; a third party is absolutely unnecessary.

Let us learn this lesson before God. We must control ourselves and never speak behind the back of the brother who has offended us. Nor should we speak in public against him. It is only when you and he are alone that you show him his fault. This requires the grace of God. When you speak, you are to show him his fault, not to talk about other things. To point out his fault is not an easy thing to do, but you have to do it. This is one of the lessons which the children of God must learn. Go to him and say, "Brother, you hurt me by doing such a thing. It was wrong for you to do it. You have sinned."

PURPOSE: TO GAIN YOUR BROTHER

God's children should learn to overlook offenses. But if an offense must be dealt with, deal with the offender directly. In such dealing, we need to remember this fundamental principle: "If he hear thee, thou hast gained thy brother" (v. 15). This is the purpose of telling. The motive is not to lessen your difficulty nor to demand reparation from the offender. The purpose is to gain your brother.

2. TAKE ONE OR TWO MORE

If you discover that your brother will not accept your word, the Lord says, "Take with thee one or two more." (v.16). These may be the elders of the church or they may be other brothers. Even at this juncture, you do not tell it to just anybody. You tell it to one or two brothers in the Lord who are well experienced and have spiritual weight. You lay the matter before them and ask their advice. Is it true that this brother is wrong? What do you brothers think about it? After these two brothers have considered the matter prayerfully before God and judged according to their spiritual discernment, they may agree that this brother has indeed done wrong. Now the question is no longer your hurt feelings. You may take these two or three witnesses to the brother and say, "You have done wrong in this matter. It will obstruct your spiritual future. You must repent and acknowledge that you are wrong."

"That at the mouth of two witnesses or three every word may be established" (v.16). These two or three witnesses cannot be persons who are talkative or who talk carelessly. If they are, they will not be respected and honored. They must be dependable persons with honesty, weight, and experience in the Lord. Every word is then established in the mouths of two or three witnesses.

3. TELL THE CHURCH

The rule of the church is: it is best if you personally can resolve the problem; otherwise you have to seek for a way to purity. If the difficulty is minor, you may simply forgive and forget. But if it affects fellowship, you must learn to deal with it. If you fail in your dealing with it personally, then you can bring in two or three witnesses. "And if he refuse to hear them, tell it unto the church" (v. 17). I think the church here refers to the responsible brothers of the church privately, not at a time when the whole church assembles. You tell the responsible brothers of the difficulty between you and your brother and ask them for advice.

If the church is one about it and if the conscience of the church condemns a brother, he must be wrong. If he is a brother who lives before God, he will set aside his own opinion and accept the testimony of the two or three

151

witnesses. If he refuses to accept their witness, he should at least accept the decision of the church. "Since all the brothers and sisters judge that I am wrong, I must be wrong no matter how right or wrong I think I am." The consensus of the church is the mind of the Lord. The Lord is here in the church; this is His judgment. How we need to learn to be soft and tender when we hear what the church has to say to us. We should not trust our own feeling, nor be confident of ourselves. We ought to accept the feeling of the church.

The Believer's Reaction

Scripture to Memorize:
Ye therefore shall be perfect, as your heavenly Father is perfect.

Matthew 5.48

At least half, if not more, of our lives are lived in reactions. People talk and we feel happy; this is reaction. They talk and we become angry; this also is reaction. Somebody does a certain thing and we consider it wrong; this is reaction. Someone does something against us, so we lose our temper; this too is reaction. We become irritated when provoked, we defend ourselves when misunderstood, we endure when ill-treated; these all are reactions. In analyzing our lives, it seems that more than half of them are lived in reactions.

Difference in Reaction of Believer and Unbeliever

We Christians also live in reactions, but ours are different from those of the unbelievers. By observing how a person reacts, we can judge who he is. A Christian should not have unchristian reactions, nor can a non-Christian have true Christian reactions. If you want to know what sort of person someone is, just notice the kind of reactions he has.

Believers' reactions should differ from those of other people. The Lord both charges us as to how we should react and gives us the power to do it. He does not want us to react carelessly. Christian life is a chain of reactions. If we react properly, we are good Christians; otherwise, we are poor Christians.

After we believe in the Lord and are saved, we are Christians. The Lord has given to us definite commands as to how we must react whenever we are faced with trials and persecutions. We are not given the liberty to react as we please. Christians' reactions, as well as their lives, should be under the control of God. If God controls our reactions, we will not react freely. As He commands us, so will we react. It is His life within us, the life He has given us, that does the reacting.

Teaching of the Lord on the Mount

How did people in the Old Testament under the dispensation of the law react? "Ye have heard that it was said, An eye for an eye, and a tooth for a tooth" (Matt. 5.38). This passage is rather simple; it speaks of reactions. If anyone hurts my eye, I will hurt his eye; if anyone breaks my tooth, I will do the same to him. I do something because you have done something—this is reaction. The Old Testament under the law produces this kind of reaction.

New Testament believers, however, have a different kind of reaction. The Lord says, "But I say unto you, Resist not him that is evil" (v. 39). Your reaction should be different; you should not resist evil people.

Before we became Christians, we had our reactions. But now we should not react as in former days. We must react as Christians.

"Give to him that asketh thee, and from him that would borrow of thee turn not thou away" (v. 42). These are all reactions. If anyone asks of you, give it to him. If anyone desires to borrow from you, do not turn him away unless you have nothing you can give.

"Ye have heard that it was said, Thou shalt love thy neighbor, and hate thy enemy" (v. 43). These are the reactions of those under the law. If you are my neighbor, my reaction is love; but if you are my enemy, my reaction is hate.

"But I say unto you, Love your enemies" (v. 44). The Christian reaction is different. He is your enemy, but you love him. "And pray for them that persecute you." He is intent on persecuting me, but my reaction is to pray for him.

"That ye may be sons of your Father who is in heaven: for he maketh his sun to rise on the evil and the good, and sendeth rain on the just and the unjust" (v. 45). These are God's reactions. God makes His sun shine on the evil as well as on the good; He sends rain on the unjust as well as on the just. His reactions remain constant. He has no evil reaction against men.

"For if ye love them that love you, what reward have ye? do not even the publicans the same?" (v. 46). What reward will you have if you react in love to those who love you? The publicans [tax collectors] do the same thing. You are no different from the publicans. Such reaction is too easy, too cheap, too low.

"And if ye salute your brethren only, what do ye more than others? do not even the Gentiles the same?" (v. 47). He and I are brothers, so I salute him; but if we have something between us, I will not even speak to him. Then am I different from the Gentiles? Such reaction is too low, as low as that of the Gentiles.

"Ye therefore shall be perfect, as your heavenly Father is perfect" (v. 48). This is to say that in the matter of reaction, we must be like God.

Basic Principle of Reaction

Having briefly gone through this passage in Matthew, we can now discover what the basic principle of the Christian reaction is. Man's reactions to ordinary matters may be divided into three levels: first, the level of reason; second, the level of good conduct; and third, the level of God's life. He who lives on the level of reason will react temperamentally and angrily; he who lives on the level of good conduct will react patiently; but he who lives in God's holy life will react transcendently.

If someone strikes your right cheek, you will say, "Why did you hit me?" Your heart is full of reasoning. Your cheek has been hit, you are angry and thus you reason with the one who did it. You are standing on the level of reason, and your reaction is anger and loss of temper. Or perhaps you are aware of the fact that Christians ought to behave well and that it is wrong for you to get angry. So you react as one whose coat has been taken from him by someone; you bear it with patience; you let them take it without uttering a word. You feel that as a Christian you cannot say anything but should be patient. Such reaction seems to be better than losing your temper. But the Lord tells us there is still another kind of reaction—a reaction which He expects of us.

The reaction which the Lord has ordained for us is not that we get angry when people strike our cheek, nor that we try to be patient when others take our coat. The Lord has not said if people force you to walk one mile, walk that mile patiently. He says, instead, turn your left cheek to him. If he wants your coat, give him also your cloak; or, in modern terms, if he wants your shirt, give him also your coat. If he compels you to walk one mile, go the second mile with him. Such reaction is not called patience but transcendence. It rises above the demands of man. Man only demands so much, but, because we are before God, we give much more than his demand. It is not just being patient but transcending man's demand.

Brothers and sisters, I desire that from the first day of your faith in Christ, you may know what a believer's life is. The Lord has shown us that Christians should have only one reaction. That reaction is neither reasoning nor enduring, but transcending. Remember, if it is not transcendent, it is not Christian. To be patient is insufficient for a Christian. The Lord no longer says, an eye for an eye: if someone hurts my eye, I will hurt his. He says instead, add another eye. If someone hurts my eye, I give him another. Do you see that the Christian reaction is neither revenge in striking back nor patience in enduring? It is to give another eye.

What, then, is the Christian reaction? The Christian reaction is not to do the right thing nor the good thing but the transcendent thing. The more a child of God is persecuted and pressed and frustrated, the higher he climbs. How pitiful if you fall the moment you are squeezed. It is really regretful to lose your temper, to argue, or even to endure. The time when you are severely pressed against the wall is the time for you to rise up. Let me tell you, this is what a Christian is.

Two Things Concerning the Reaction of Life

Finally, concerning this reactive life there are two things worth special notice.

1. PRAY DAILY TO NOT BE BROUGHT INTO TEMPTATION

First of all, we need to pray daily that the Lord not bring us into temptation but deliver us from the evil one. Having a life principle such as this, we are unable, according to the world's estimate, to live at all. The reaction which the Lord has given us is something impossible on earth. After a few attempts on our own, all the resources we have will be gone. For this reason, the Lord inserts such a prayer in the teaching on the mount. "And bring us not into temptation, but deliver us from the evil one" (Matt. 6.13). Only by the Lord's protection are we able to live in this world. Without His protection, we cannot live a day. Hence, this prayer is a must. It would not matter if we did not live such a life nor have such a reaction. But if we do live by the life of God, then we have to pray this prayer daily.

2. KEEP THE PROPER CHRISTIAN REACTION

We do not seek for trouble. However, if under God's permission or arrangement or control of the Holy Spirit, we are faced with such a situation, whether it comes from unbelievers or from believers, we must not draw back. We must maintain a proper reaction.

I believe the words we have said are sufficient. A Christian life is surprising. The more you are persecuted, troubled, and unreasonably treated, the happier you are before God. This alone is the way of happiness. Will you try it out? If you smite a person, will you feel comfortable or uncomfortable? It is better if you are smitten. If I were to smite a brother and he immediately turned the other cheek to me, I would be uncomfortable for a whole month.

As a Christian, do not live on earth taking advantage of people. If you take people's advantage, you will at least lose sometime before God, for you will not be able to rise up spiritually. Taking advantage on earth is not worth it. It is better to be beaten; then you will sleep well, eat well, sing well. Do not even think that taking advantage is really advantageous. I trust that if we react aright, we will walk aright. This is a basic life principle which must not be overlooked.

Deliverance

Scripture to Memorize:

*The law of the Spirit of life in Christ Jesus made
me free from the law of sin and of death.*

Romans 8.2

A person who believes in the Lord may immediately be
delivered from sin. This experience, however, is not
necessarily shared by all new believers. Many are not
delivered from sin after they first trust in the Lord. Instead,
they often find themselves falling into sin. There is no
question at all that they have been saved, that they belong
to the Lord and have eternal life. Yet the great difficulty
remains that they are frequently disturbed by sin. Because
of this, they are unable to serve the Lord as they would like.

It is most painful for a saved person to be disturbed by
his continuing sins. Since he is enlightened by God, his
conscience is sensitive. In him is the life which condemns
sins; so he has the consciousness of sin. He deeply feels his
corruption and he abhors himself. This is really an
exceedingly painful experience.

The word of God does not tell us that we should
overcome sin; it tells us, instead, that we must be delivered
from sin, freed from sin. These are the words of the Bible.
Sin is a power which holds people. We are to be delivered
from its grip, not to destroy its power. We cannot put it to
death, but the Lord has removed us from it.

The Law of Sin

That which I do I know not: for not what I would,
that do I practise; but what I hate, that I do . . . for
to will is present with me, but to do that which is
good is not. For the good which I would I do not:
but the evil which I would not, that I practise. But
if what I would not, that I do, it is no more I that
do it . . . I find then the law, that, to me who would
do good, evil is present. For I delight in the law of
God after the inward man: but I see a different
law in my members, warring against the law of my
mind, and bringing me into captivity under the law
of sin which is in my members. . . So then I of
myself with the mind, indeed, serve the law of
God; but with the flesh the law of sin.

Rom. 7.15-25

You need to find the key to Romans 7. In verses 15 through 20, such words as these are used: "I would," "I would not," "I hate," "to will is present with me," "the good which I would," "the evil which I would not," and so forth. The thoughts constantly repeated are "would," "would not," or "will." But verses 21 through 25 show us another point. The emphasis is no longer "would" or "would not," but is repeatedly seen in words like "the law," "a different law in my members," "into captivity under the law of sin which is in my members," "I of myself with the mind serve the law of God; but with the flesh the law of sin." If you keep these two points of emphasis before you, you will be able to solve the problem.

In verses 15 through 20, though Paul wills to overcome, yet he suffers total defeat. This shows that the way of victory does not lie in "would" or "would not." Victory is not to be found through man's will. Paul wills and wills, but he ends up in defeat. Therefore, do not think that everything will be all right if only you have the will to do good. To will is with you, but to do is not. All you can do is to will; there is not much use in it.

However, after verse 21 Paul himself finds out why his will to do good is unsuccessful. The reason is that sin is a law. Since sin is a law, it is futile to will. Paul shows us the reason for his defeat. He explains that though he would do good, evil is present with him. He delights in the law of God after the inward man, but with the flesh he serves the law of sin. Whenever he decides to delight in God's law, a different law in his members—the law of sin—brings him into captivity. Any time he wills to do good, evil is present. This is a law.

Many who have been Christians for years still do not see that sin is a power which seems to be quite authoritative. They do not see sin as a law. I hope newly saved brothers and sisters will see this: sin in human experience, as well as in the Bible, is a law. It is not only an influence, a power, but it is also a law. Paul discovered how useless it was for his will to battle against a law.

The Inability of the Will to Overcome the Law

Will is the inner power of man, while law is a natural power. Both are powers. I like to use an illustration to help people understand this matter of law. We know that the earth exerts a gravitational force. This force of gravity is a law. Why do we call it a law? Because it is always so. That which is not incidental is a law. That which is occasional is an historical accident, not a law.

Every law has its natural power—something not manufactured by human effort. We may use the earth's gravitation as an example. Wherever I drop something, that thing gravitates downward. I do not need to press it down for there is a natural force which causes it to go down. Behind the law is the natural power.

What, then, is the will? Will is man's determination, man's decision. It speaks of what man decides or desires or wills. The exercise of the will is not without its power. If I decide to do a certain thing, I start out to do it. If I decide to walk, I walk; if I decide to eat, I eat. As a person I have a will, and my will produces a power.

However, the power of the will and the power of a law are different. While the power of the law is natural power, the power of the will is human.

In Romans 7 the subject is the contrast between law and will. Its theme is very simple, for it deals only with the conflict between will and law. At an earlier time, Paul was not conscious that sin is a law. Paul is the first one in the Bible to discover this truth. He is also first to use the term "law." People know that gravitation is a law, that heat expansion is also a law, but they do not know that sin is a law. At first even Paul did not know this; only after repeatedly sinning did he discover that there was a power in his body which gravitated him to sin. He did not sin purposely, but the power in his body pulled him to sin.

It is a great discovery when the Lord has mercy on you and opens your eyes to see that sin is, indeed, a law. If you see this, victory is not far away. Should you consider sin merely a matter of conduct, you will no doubt try to pray more and to resist more in order to overcome the next time. But it is futile. As the power of sin is strong and constant, so our strength is weak and untrustworthy. As the power of sin is always triumphant, so our power is always yielding. Sin's power is victorious and our power is defeated. The victory of sin is a law, even as our defeat is a law. When I would do good, evil is present. Paul says he has found this to be a law, an unconquerable law.

The Way of Victory

We know man is not delivered by exercising his will. When he is using his willpower, he is unable to trust God's way of deliverance. He has to wait for the day when he submits himself to God and confesses that he is utterly undone. Then he will pray, "Lord, I am not going to try again." Whenever one has no way but still thinks of finding a way, he will draw upon his will to help. It is only when he acknowledges he has no way and is not going to find a way that he forsakes calling upon his will for help. Then he will begin to see how to get real deliverance. Then he will read Romans 8.

Paul said in Romans 7 that it is useless to battle, for who can overcome a law? Thus, at the start of Romans 8 he says, "There is therefore now no condemnation to them that are in Christ Jesus. For the law of the Spirit of life in Christ Jesus made me free from the law of sin and of death" (vv. 1-2). You have seen that sin is a law. You have also seen that it is not possible for man's will to overcome that law. Where, then, is the way of victory, the way of deliverance?

The way of victory is here: "There is therefore now *no condemnation* to them that are in Christ Jesus." The word "condemnation" in the original Greek has two different usages, one legal and the other civil. If the word is used legally, it means "condemnation" as found in the English translation. But in its civil usage, the word means "disabling" or "handicap." According to the context of this passage of Scripture, probably the civil usage is clearer.

We are no longer disabled. Why? Because the Lord Jesus Christ has given us deliverance. It is something the Lord has done. But how does He do it? It is very simple, for it is explained by the second verse: "For the law of the Spirit of life in Christ Jesus made me free from the law of sin and of death." This is the way of victory.

May new believers see that the Holy Spirit in them is a spontaneous law. If anyone is to be delivered from sin, he has to come to that deliverance naturally. Should he try to get deliverance by exercising his willpower, he will again be defeated. But now those who are in Christ Jesus are no longer handicapped, for the law of the Spirit of life in Christ Jesus has made them free from the law of sin and of death. It is all so simple and so natural. We have been given another law which naturally delivers us from the law of sin and of death.

The law of the Spirit of life is in Christ Jesus and I am also now in Christ Jesus; therefore by this law I am made free from the law of sin and of death. "There is therefore now no disabling to them that are in Christ Jesus." The man in Romans 7 is labeled, "disabled." But this disabled person who is so weak and always sins is now, Paul says, no more disabled in Christ Jesus. How? By the law of the Spirit of life in Christ Jesus which has set him free from the law of sin and of death. Therefore, there is no more disabling. Do you see now how this problem of deliverance is completely solved?

Our Life

Scripture to Memorize:

I have been crucified with Christ; and it is no longer I that live, but Christ liveth in me: and that life which I now live in the flesh I live in faith, the faith which is in the Son of God, who loved me, and gave himself up for me.

Galatians 2.20

Many people greatly misunderstand Colossians 3.4, Philippians 1.21, and Galatians 2.20, especially the latter two. In Philippians 1, Paul tells us that "to me to live is Christ." To him, this is a fact. But among God's children today, there is a big misunderstanding. They think that, "to me to live is Christ" is a goal to reach. They must try to so live that they may arrive at the goal. It is a standard to reach; it is their expectation. Let us remember, however, that Paul is not telling us here that his goal is "to me to live is Christ." He is not saying that he must go through many years, trials, and dealings of God before he can reach the goal. What he says is that the reason why he lives is Christ. Without Christ, he cannot live at all. This describes his present condition, not his goal. This is the secret of his life, not his hope. His life is Christ; he lives because Christ lives in him.

Galatians 2.20 is another familiar verse among Christians. The misunderstanding many have with this verse is even graver than with Philippians 1. Again, they take this verse as their goal, as their standard. How they pray and wait and long to arrive at a point where "it is no longer I that live, but Christ liveth in me."

But is Galatians 2.20 a hope? Is it a goal? Is it a standard to arrive at? Many make it so. They hope that one day they will arrive at the place where they no longer live, but Christ lives in them. This is their goal. What they fail to see is that this is God's *way* of victory, not a goal or a standard. It does not say what I should do that I may live; neither does it say what I can do to make me live. It simply says that Christ lives in me.

Galatians 2.20 is not a standard or a goal. It is not something which is set high above man for him to exert his utmost strength to reach. Rather, it is the secret of life.

1. VICTORY THROUGH A SUBSTITUTIONARY LIFE

What is the secret of life? It means that the way of victory is not a goal but a process. Do not confuse the process with the goal. This is a marvelous grace God has given us. It is a way by which the defeated may overcome, the unclean may be clean, the common may become holy, the earthly may be heavenly, and the carnal may become spiritual. It is a way, not a goal. The way lies via a substitutionary life. As Christ is our substitute in death, so is He our substitute in life.

At the beginning of our Christian life, we saw how the Lord Jesus bore our sins on the cross so that by His death we were delivered from death, our sins were forgiven, and we were condemned no more. Today Paul tells me that because Christ lives in me, I am delivered from living. The meaning here is simple: since He lives in me, I no longer need to live. As He died on the cross for me, so now He lives in me in my place. This is the secret of victory. This is Paul's secret. He does not say, "I hope I will not need to live," or, "I hope I can let Him live." He just says, "No longer live I, for I have let Him live. Now it is no longer I who live, but Christ who lives in me."

Let us pray much that God will enlighten us to see that man has no need to live for himself because Christ can live in him. The day that you heard you did not need to die, you felt this was a great gospel. Now, in another day, you are hearing that you do not need to live. This is also a great gospel.

Death is painful, but for us to try to live before God is also painful. How can people such as we, who know nothing about God's holiness, love, the Holy Spirit, or the cross, live in the presence of God? Such a heavy burden is unbearable. The longer we live, the more we sigh. The longer we live, the more frustrated we are. The gospel delivered to you today is that you do not need to live. God has exempted you from living. This, indeed, is a great gospel.

2. NOT I, BUT CHRIST

As it is good news that we need not die, so it is good news that we need not live. For a person to strive to live as a Christian is really an exhausting, impossible task. To ask an impatient, ill-tempered, proud person to live humbly will soon wear him out; he will be worn out by trying to be humble. No wonder the man in Romans 7 was tired! "For to will is present with me, but to do that which is good is not" (v.18). To daily will to do good, yet daily be unable to do it—how very tiring this is. Then one day the gospel is preached to him, telling him that the Lord does not expect him to do good. Oh, this is a great gospel. The Lord does not require you to do good, neither does He want you to will to do good. He wants to come and live in you. The issue is not whether there is any good, but who does the good.

It is painful for you to try to live before God, for you can never satisfy His demands. You have to confess: "Lord, I knew thee that thou art a hard man, reaping where thou didst not sow, and gathering where thou didst not scatter" (Matt. 25.24). You are totally unable to answer God's requirement.

Therefore, God's way and His secret for me is not in asking me to imitate the Lord Jesus, nor parceling out power to me in response to my begging that I may be like Christ. God's way for me is what Paul expresses, "No longer I that live, but Christ liveth in me." Do you notice the difference? It is neither a life of imitating Christ nor a life of having power given; rather, it is a substitutionary life. It is no longer you, for God will not allow you to live before Him. It is Christ who lives in you and stands before the presence of God. So, it is not my imitating Christ, not my receiving the power of Christ, but letting Christ live in me.

You have to come to this point of not I, but Christ. This is the believer's life. Formerly I lived but Christ did not; now I do not live but Christ does. If a person cannot say, "Not I, but Christ," he has no knowledge of what Christianity or the Christian life is. It is evident that he is merely hoping to so live that it may be Christ and not him. But Paul tells us it is not this way. He tells us that the way is to let Christ live.

Crucified with Christ

At this point, you will most likely ask, How can I get out of the way so Christ can live? This is indeed a big problem. How can it be, "no longer I"? The answer is found in the first part of Galatians 2.20: "I have been crucified with Christ." Unless I am crucified, I cannot be removed. Unless I am crucified, it will still be I. It can be no longer I only if I am crucified with Christ.

Please remember: your sin problem was solved on the cross, and on the same cross you yourself were also finished. We must recall what Romans 6 states, "Knowing this, that our old man was crucified with him" (v. 6). It is not that my old man wishes to be crucified with Him, but that my old man *was* crucified with Him. It is not wishing or hoping. The word in Greek is quite emphatic. It is *"was,"* distinctly indicating that I have once and for all, absolutely and unchangingly, been crucified with Him. Since God put me in Christ, I died when He died on the cross.

This is something you must believe. As your eyes were once opened to see your sins laid on Christ, so must your eyes be opened to see your person hid in Christ. Your sins were borne, your person was crucified. This is not your problem, but Christ's, for He has done it for you. Do not look within yourself. Your sins are no longer in you but on the cross. So is your person no longer here but there on the cross. Those who are defeated always look within themselves; those who believe look at the cross. Our sins are there, on the cross, not here; the sinner is also there, not here. We must see that the man is on the cross, not here in us. This is what the Lord has done. It is finished. God has put us in Christ and made us die with Him. Christ has died, we too have died.

The Victorious Life

Now I declare that I am a crucified person. If I am to live today, it is no longer I who live but Christ lives in me. I am undone, but Christ has come. This is the way of victory. This is what Paul has shown us. This is how he lives the Christian life. What is the Christian life? Only this—that it is no longer I who live but I let Christ live for me.

I have been wrong all these years: sinful, weak, undone, proud, ill-tempered. But now I come into the presence of the Lord, saying, "Lord, I am undone. Starting from today I wash my hands of my own efforts. Please take over." This is what is meant by "no longer I that live but Christ liveth in me." "I have lived long enough; I am sick of living; now, Lord, will you please try?" Let me tell you, it is as simple as that. The victorious life is none other than this: you need not live. You do not need to exhaust yourself in living; you need only look up and say, "Hereafter I will manage no more; You live and manifest Yourself!" So shall it be done.

Hereafter, you take a positive course. As you deal with the Lord, you tell Him, "Lord, I accept You to be my life. Hereafter, I acknowledge Christ as my life. I confess that to me to live is Christ." This will become your daily life before God, trusting in the Lord. "Lord, this is Your business, not mine." Your temptation is not to sin; rather, your temptation is to act on your own.

"And that life which I now live in the flesh I live in faith, the faith which is in the Son of God." What does Christ living in me mean? It simply means that hereafter I live in the faith of the Son of God. I daily believe that the Son of God lives in me. "Lord, I believe You live for me. Lord, I believe You are my life, and I believe that You live in me."

The Will of God

Scripture to Memorize:

I delight to do thy will, O my God; Yea, thy law is within my heart.

Psalm 40.8

What we will now consider is how a new believer can know the will of God. This is of great importance, for the lack of such knowledge causes great damage to His service.

From the day he is saved a child of God undergoes a drastic change in his life. Formerly he felt frustrated if he could not do as he wanted but happy if he could do according to his desire. Such happiness was derived from his own will. But now, his center is changed, for he has a Lord. If he still lives according to his own will, as before, he will not be satisfied; on the contrary, he will feel most uncomfortable.

After you are saved, you discover that the cause of your discomfort lies in following your own will. The more you do things according to your desire, the less happy you are. But if instead of following your own thought you learn to follow God by the new life in you, you will have peace and joy. This, indeed, is a wonderful change. To do God's will is joyful. Never for a moment think that following your own will make you happy. The way to happiness is not in following your will but in following the will of God.

The life we have received has a primary demand: we should walk according to God's will. The more we do God's will, the happier we are. The less we walk in our own way, the straighter our path before God is. If we do not live according to our own mind, we will have a more ascendant life in God's presence. But if we follow our own will, the going will get harder. Happiness is found in obedience, not in self-will.

Brethren, as soon as you become a Christian, you should start to accept God's thought. His will alone should govern everything. No one should live according to his own idea. You will be saved many unnecessary wanderings if you are soft and tender before God and learn from the start to submit to His will. The reason many fail in their Christian lives is because they follow their own wills. Remember, to walk according to your own will will give you nothing but sorrow and spiritual poverty. Eventually God will still bring you around to following His will, but He will have to get your submission through special circumstances or unusual dealings. If you were not His child, He could let you go. But since you are His child, He will in His own way steer you onto the road of obedience. All your disobedience will merely cause you to wander unnecessarily. In the end, you will yet obey.

How to Know the Will of God

How can we know God's will? So often we make mistakes. It is not easy for us earth people to understand God's will. However, we have one comfort before God: it is not only that we desire to do God's will, but also God himself wants us to do it.

We seek to understand His will, and He calls us to know it. Since He wants us to do His will, surely He will enable us to understand. Therefore, it is God's business to reveal His will to us. No child of God need worry about how he can do God's will when he has no knowledge of it. Although it is quite difficult to know God's will, to worry about it is unnecessary. Somehow, God *will* make His will known to us.

172

By what means can you know the will of God? There are three things to which you must pay attention. When these three factors fit together, you can be rather sure of what the will of God is. But if these three do not line up, if one of them does not harmonize with the others, then you know you have to wait further before God.

1. ENVIRONMENTAL ARRANGEMENT

Let us look at the factor of environment first. The Bible tells us, "Are not two sparrows sold for a penny?" (Matt. 10.29). In another place, it says, "Are not five sparrows sold for two pence?" (Lk. 12.6). Mathematically, if one penny buys two sparrows, then two pence would buy four sparrows. But the Lord says, two pence will buy five sparrows. This shows how cheap sparrows were. One penny for two, two pence for five, the extra one being added without cost. Yet not even this fifth sparrow could fall to the ground apart from the will of God.

I do not wish to speak of the first or second sparrow, but of the fifth one. Unless it is God's will, this fifth sparrow will not fall to the ground—though it was bought without price, simply being added to the purchase. Thus, the Bible indicates to us that all environmental arrangements, all things which happen in the environment, are expressions of the will of God. No one shall fall to the ground outside of the will of the heavenly Father. Hence, if you see a sparrow on the ground you have met with the will of God.

New believers ought to learn to know God's will through their environment. There is nothing in our lives that is accidental. Every day's happenings are measured by the Lord. We need to see that everything in our lives— events, families, husbands, wives, children, schoolmates, relatives —everything is arranged for us by the Lord. Things which befall us daily are all within the Father's ordering. We must learn to know God's will in the environment. This is the first factor.

Many new believers have not yet learned how to be led of the Holy Spirit; they may know very little of the teaching of the Bible. God, though, is still able to guide them, for they can at least see the hand of God in their environment. This is the very first step.

2. GUIDANCE OF THE HOLY SPIRIT

We have seen how the hand of God is manifested in our environment. God does not want us to be like the horse or the mule which has no understanding. He will give us guidance from within. "For as many as are led by the Spirit of God, these are sons of God" (Rom. 8.14). Who can be led by the Spirit of God? The sons of God can, for the Holy Spirit leads us from within. God will not only guide us through environment but also lead us by His life in our spirit. Remember, we are indwelt by the Holy Spirit; we do have Him in us. Because of this, God can make His will known to us in the deepest part of our beings.

New believers, you have a new spirit, and the Spirit of God also dwells in you. That indwelling Spirit of God will tell you what God's will is. The witness is within you. This is a characteristic of today's believer: he not only knows through environment but also from within. Not only can he see the Lord's arrangement in his environment but also the Lord himself reveals within what His will is. Learn, then, to trust in the guidance of the Holy Spirit within you as well as in God's arrangement of your environment. At the most appropriate moment, the time of need, the Spirit of God within you will not be silent but will enlighten you and show you whether or not the matter is of God.

As soon as one believes in the Lord, he is able to be led by the Holy Spirit. He need not wait for some future time.

In order to know God's will, you need to know something of this inner feeling. However, you should not overemphasize it lest you fall into analysis. What you should see is simply that God's Spirit dwells in the innermost recess of man, that is, in his spirit. That is why the consciousness of the Holy Spirit cannot be shallow or external; it comes from the depth of your being. It does not sound like a voice, and yet it is like a voice. It is not exactly like a feeling, and yet it is like a feeling. The Spirit of the Lord within you will tell you what is His will and what is not His will. If you are the Lord's, when you follow the movement of this life, you have the sense of being right. But if you rebel a little or resist, you feel upset and uncomfortable within you.

3. SCRIPTURAL TEACHING

The will of God is not only manifested in environment and by His indwelling Holy Spirit, it is also made known to us through the Bible. His will has been revealed many times in the past, and this is recorded in the Holy Scriptures. God's will is one will, not two or ten or a hundred or even a thousand wills. God's will is one. He does not change today from yesterday. His will remains the same forever. For this reason, God's children must know the Bible. In it they will find the revelation of God's will.

The way which God views a thing today is the same as He viewed it in the past. What He condemned before, He condemns now. That which He delighted in before is still His delight today. The Bible is the place where God reveals His mind. God manifested His own will concerning many people and many things in the former days. All these are recorded in the Bible. Since God's will is uniform, there are already a number of examples written in the Bible to show us what it is. It is absolutely impossible for God to condemn something today which He has approved in the

175

Bible. Likewise, the Holy Spirit today will never lead us to do what God has already denounced in the Bible. The will of God is one.

GOD'S WILL KNOWN IN THE AGREEMENT OF THESE THREE FACTORS

These three factors together manifest the will of God— environment, man's spirit, and the Bible. By the agreement of these three we learn to know the will of God. What should we do if we desire to seek God's will in a particular matter? For us to be sure, these three factors must agree. It cannot be just one factor but, rather, the agreement of all three. Then we can be clear of His will.

4. THE PRINCIPLE OF THE CHURCH

God has shown us that His will is manifested in His word, in man's spirit, and in environment. Now we will add one more factor: God's will is manifested through the church. There is no guidance which can stand independently. God's children today are quite different from His people in the Old Testament. During that time, they became the people of God individually; but today we are God's people corporately. They became God's people as a nation, while we are the people of God as a body.

No hand can move without getting other parts of the body involved. How can the hand move without the body being moved? How can the eyes see and the body not see? Can the ears hear and the body not hear? The hearing of the ears is the hearing of the body; the seeing of the eyes is the seeing of the body. Although the feet do the walking, the body has walked. Likewise, all of God's guidance is corporate, non-personal, involving the whole body. The light of God is in the holy sanctuary; the glory of God is also there. Whenever the church of God is like a sanctuary,

God's glory is manifested there, for the glory of God is in the sanctuary. It is not only that we are individually led of God, but also that the whole body of brothers and sisters receives the Lord's guidance. It is not one person who makes a decision; rather, it is the body which decides. We must learn to know God's will by the principle of fellowship.

When these four factors stand in a straight line, all is well. God's will is manifested in environment, in the guidance of the Holy Spirit, in the Bible, and through the church. After one has examined the first three factors, he still needs to consult the church. God tells His will not just to one person but to a body, that is, to all the brothers and sisters. So it is important to be clear in one's inward feeling, in the word of God, in the environment, and finally in the consent of the church.

The Problem of Man

Finally, though all the preceding four factors seem to give a positive indication, it still does not necessarily guarantee that one has found the will of God, for he who trusts in methods may not be right. He needs to cry from the bottom of his heart, "Lord, I am Your servant; I will do Your will."

I am often troubled that many seek to know how to know God's will without really having the heart to do it. They want to know the proper method. They seem to look upon God's will as a kind of knowledge to be stored away unused. They consult with God to know His will, but then they confer with their own thoughts. Do not forget the word of the Lord Jesus, "If any man willeth to do his will, he shall know" (John 7.17). Let us really desire to know God's will. Let us take God's will as our food and our life. Let us learn to obey His will.

BOOK FIVE:
Do All to the Glory of God

Managing Your Finances

Scripture to Memorize:

Give, and it shall be given unto you; good measure, pressed down, shaken together, running over, shall they give into your bosom. For with what measure you mete [give] it shall be measured to you again.

Luke 6.38

The way Christians manage their finances is totally different from the way of unbelievers. The Christian way is to give, the unbelievers' way is to hoard. Our concern now is to know how a Christian should live on earth so that he may never be in want. Has not God promised us this? As the birds of the air have no lack of food or the lilies of the field of beautiful garments, so God's children should not lack anything. If they are in need, there must be a loophole somewhere. Those brothers who have a problem with income are usually those who have not managed their finances according to God's principle.

The Christian Principle of Financial Management

How should a Christian manage his finances? Read Luke 6.38. "Give, and it shall be given unto you; good measure, pressed down, shaken together, running over, shall they give into your bosom. For with what measure ye mete it shall be measured to you again."

As believers, we look to God for all our supplies. We live only through His mercy. The wealthy cannot depend on their wealth for food and clothing. During wartime, we have seen many rich people short in both of these. Paul exhorts us not to have our hope set on the uncertainty of riches nor be desirous of getting rich, for to do so will only pierce us with many sorrows (see 1 Tim. 6.7-10, 17-19). Only those who put their trust in the Lord, though they have no savings, shall not be in want. The Lord is well able to supply all their needs. But they do need to know that God's supply does have a condition attached to it.

If God is able to feed so many birds of the sky, He certainly can support us. No one but God could feed all the birds of the sky and nourish all the lilies of the field. He alone has the superabundance of riches to take care of the birds and the lilies as well as His own children. He would not have us be in such straitened circumstances that we can hardly live. Whoever has fallen into privation has not managed his finances according to God's principle. God has appointed a way for us to use our money. If we do not follow this law of spending, we will naturally fall into poverty. Only by following this law of God shall we be kept from want.

God is willing to supply our needs, superabundantly if need be. Never for a moment think that He is poor. The cattle upon a thousand hills are His; all things belong to Him. Why should God's children be poor? Why should they be in want? God is not one who cannot supply. He most assuredly can. But there is one thing we must do, that is, we must fulfill His condition before we are supplied. What, then, is His requirement?—give and it will be given to you.

New believers ought to learn this basic lesson from the outset of their Christian lives. Otherwise they will not be able to go very far. Christians have a special way of managing their finances: give as you would like to be given. In other words, measure your income by giving. The world measures giving by its income, but we Christians measure income by giving. The measure we give will be that which we receive. Consequently, all who love money and bargain in giving are not able to receive God's money; they will not get God's supply.

We like to tell the brothers and sisters that everyone must look to God for the management of his or her needs. But, actually, God is pledged to supply only to one kind of person—those who are willing to give. The wording in Luke is indeed marvelous. It says, "good measure." When giving, God never calculates. He always gives bountifully. Our God is most generous; His cup always overflows. He is never stingy. He declares that He will give with good measure: "Pressed down, shaken together, running over." Have you ever bought rice or wheat? Many sellers will pour the grain out of the measure without allowing you to shake it down. Not so with God. He will give with good measure, not only pressed down and shaken together but also running over. Truly our God is most liberal in giving. Listen, however, to what He says: "With what measure you mete [give] it shall be measured to you." If your giving is calculating and exacting, then, when God moves people to supply your need, it will also be strictly measured or calculated.

The Christian Way of Managing Finances

The Christian way of financing is to not hold money tightly in hand. The tighter one holds on, the deadlier it becomes. Such money will be useless; it will melt away like ice. Only in giving is money increased. If God's children learn how to give, God will perform miracles everywhere. Holding on to money will reduce the children of God to poverty. Young believers must learn this lesson. They should not be content just to be saved; they must learn to experience the blessedness of giving. God cannot trust anyone who holds money tightly and does not give it out, for such a one is untrustworthy. The more one gives, the more God will give to him.

1. SOWING FOR GOD

"But this I say, He that soweth sparingly shall reap also sparingly; and he that soweth bountifully shall reap also bountifully" (2 Cor. 9.6). This Scripture also relates to the principle of Christian finances. Christians give money but they do not throw it away. It is not he who throws away that shall receive more; nor is it that he who throws away less shall receive less. What God says is that he who sows bountifully shall reap bountifully and also he who sows sparingly shall reap sparingly. Do you expect your money to grow? If you do, go and sow it. If you sow, the money will grow. Otherwise it will remain the same.

2. BRINGING TO GOD

God's word concerning needs is very clear in the Old Testament: "Bring ye the whole tithe into the store-house, that there may be food in my house, and prove me now herewith, saith Jehovah of hosts, if I will not open you the windows of heaven, and pour you out a blessing, that there shall not be room enough to receive it" (Mal. 3.10), said God to the people of Israel. This gives the same principle we have just explained.

3. SCATTERING FOR GOD

"There is that scattereth, and increaseth yet more; and there is that withholdeth more than is meet, but it tendeth only to want" (Prov. 11.24). Many do not scatter, so they have nothing left. But they who scatter become rich before God. This too is shown us by God's word.

4. SPENDING FOR GOD

There is another wonderful event of which we may take note. (see 1 Kings18). When Elijah prayed for rain, the nation was suffering under a great drought. Both the king and his chief chamberlain were out searching for water. Such a scarcity of water can easily be understood. But when Elijah offered a sacrifice and prayed for rain, he ordered them to pour water on the burnt-offering. How very precious water was at that time, yet Elijah made them pour water three times on the sacrifice till the water ran round about the altar and filled the trench. Considering the fact that rain from heaven had not yet descended, was it not a pity to pour away so much water? What if the rain did not come? But Elijah commanded them to pour out the water. He knelt down and prayed that God would send fire to consume the offering on the altar. God heard that prayer and also his prayer for rain; He sent down a great rain. Let me tell you, if you want heaven to send down a great rain, you must first pour on your water. If you spare the water, you will not get the water from heaven.

5. Supplied from God

"My God shall supply every need of yours according to his riches in glory in Christ Jesus" (Phil. 4.19). This indeed is a marvelous verse. The Corinthian believers were tight in giving, but the Philippian believers were generous. Time and again, the Philippians had sent supply to the apostle Paul. Paul, in turn, answered them that his God would supply all their needs according to His riches in glory in Christ Jesus. Do you see the wonder of the verse? Paul especially mentioned "my God," that is, the God of the one who received the supply, for had not the Philippians sent money to Paul? "My God shall supply"—He would supply those who had supplied Paul. It was the God of the recipient of the gift supplying the needs of the givers of the gift.

Many today try to lay hold of Philippians 4.19. Do we, though, see in this verse that God shall supply the givers, not the askers? Only the givers have the right to use this verse; those who do not give are not entitled to the privilege. After giving to others, you may say, "O God, supply today all my needs according to the riches in Christ." God supplied all the needs of only the Philippians. God supplies on the principle of giving.

The Christian Way Is in Giving

Both the Old and New Testaments lay down the same teaching. God does not want us to be poor or in distress. If there is poverty and distress among us, it may be that we have held our money too tightly. The more we love ourselves, the more we will be hungry. If the money question is not solved, nothing is solved. To whomever money looms big, the threat of poverty is near. I may not be able to testify to other things, but to this I can testify; the tighter one holds on to money, the poorer he becomes. May we release our money and allow it to be in circulation doing miracles for God.

The cattle on a thousand hills and the sheep on ten thousand hills all belong to God. Who but a fool would think he must earn them? All we need to do is to bring our all to God. We should send money out as soon as it comes in. We should take care of brothers and sisters in need. To hoard for ourselves is foolishness. The way of a Christian lies in giving. Let all the money in the church be living money. Then when you are in need, God will perform miracles, even sending the birds of the air to supply you.

Put yourselves into the word of God, or else God has no way to perform His word in you. First give yourselves to God, and then release your money that God may give to you.

Occupation

Scripture to Memorize:

If any will not work, neither let him eat.

2 Thessalonians 3.10b

The occupation of a Christian is a major consideration in life. If he or she chooses the wrong occupation, that person will be hampered in his or her progress in the Lord. Hence a Christian must be careful in the choice of occupation.

At the time of creation, God not only created man but also planned for his occupation. He appointed Adam and Eve to dress and to keep the garden of Eden. Hence their job before the fall was that of a gardener.

After the fall, they had to toil with sweat in order to have bread, for the ground was cursed because of them. This indicates that after the fall the appointed occupation for man is that of a farmer. God knows better than anybody else that farming is the best pursuit for a fallen mankind.

From Genesis chapter 4 we find Cain was tilling the ground while Abel his brother was tending the sheep. Thus shepherding is added as another occupation besides that of being a farmer, and this is also acceptable to God.

As the earth's population began to increase, all sorts of craftsmen were raised up: the ironsmiths, the coppersmiths, the makers of musical instruments, and the manufacturers of sharp tools. And by the time of the building of the tower of Babel (see Gen. 11), there were masons and carpenters as well. Although the tower of Babel ought not to have been built, men nevertheless learned to build during that period.

From Genesis chapter 12 we learn that God chose Abraham. And Abraham was a shepherd: he had many cattle and sheep. His grandson Jacob followed the same occupation—that of pasturing.

Later on we find the people of Israel making bricks in Egypt for Pharaoh. They were masons. But when they came out of Egypt, God gave them two blessings: one was to shepherd the flocks, and the other was to till the land of Canaan that was flowing with milk and honey. That a branch with a cluster of grapes took two men to carry clearly indicated the work of husbandry (gardener). That God warned that if they rebelled against Him and worshiped idols He would cause the heaven to be like brass and the earth as iron so that the ground would yield no produce, was further evidence that their main employments in the promised land of Canaan were to be farming and pasturing. The above are the various God-approved occupations shown in the Old Testament.

What about the basic occupations mentioned in the New Testament? From the parables spoken by the Lord Jesus we find that farming and pasturing are again the main occupations—Matthew 13, the parable of the sower; Matthew 20, the parable of the vineyard; Luke 17, the servant who serves the master at table after coming in from having ploughed or kept the sheep; and John 10, the Lord as the good shepherd who lays down His life for the sheep.

When the Lord called His twelve apostles, most of them were fishermen. Were any of them a tax-collector, the Lord would demand that he leave his post. To the fishermen among them, however, He said this: "I will make you fishers of men" (Matt. 4.19b). Consequently, fishing was also a God-approved vocation.

Luke was a physician (Col. 4.14a), and Paul was a tentmaker (Acts 18.3). Tentmaking is different from fishing, in that it is manufacturing work. Whereas farming is a direct work, the labor of spinning, weaving, cutting or tentmaking involves an additional step in the laboring process, and is therefore manufacturing work.

We may say that from the Old Testament to the New, God has made His arrangement for occupations. The disciples of the Lord were either farmers or shepherds or craftsmen or fishermen or manufacturers. We can add one more occupation, that of a laborer. For the New Testament does have this word: "the laborer is worthy of his [wages]" (1 Tim. 5.18b). A laborer is one who works with his hands in unskilled or manual labor. Such employment is also sanctioned in the Bible.

The Principle Governing Occupations

In searching the Scriptures, we find that God has ordained for men various kinds of jobs. Underlying these occupations, there is a basic principle—which is, that men ought to be profited from nature through earning their hire by putting in either their time or their strength. Apart from this principle operating in any given occupation, the Bible does not seem to approve of any other kind of employment. Let us discuss several facets of this principle, as follows:

1. DRAW RESOURCES FROM NATURE FOR THE INCREASE OF WEALTH

How are we to explain this statement? Perhaps we can best explain in this way: a sower sows his seed, and later he gets thirty or sixty or a hundredfold yield. Such multiplication comes from the supply of nature which is abundant and open to all. For God causes the sun to shine on the unrighteous as well as on the righteous. He also causes rain to fall on them both. This is the advantage of farming. Since it is God who gives the increase, this shows that God's purpose is for men to take grace from nature. The same rule applies to pasturing. As one tends the flock, he is profited with many lambs as well as with wool and milk. This is production increase obtained from nature.

In the New Testament, we observe fishing as an occupation. To fish in the sea is still drawing resources from nature. No one will become poorer because I fish in the sea. I may get richer through fishing, but no one will become poorer for my sake. My sheep may give birth to six lambs and my cattle may beget two calves, yet no one will become poorer because of me. Or I may be farming and obtain an hundredfold increase. I certainly will not cause anyone or any family to suffer hunger or loss because of the good yield from my land. Thus the basic principle for human occupations is: I gain but nobody will lose. The noblest occupations as appointed by God come under this rule.

2. MANUFACTURING—THE INCREASE OF VALUE

Paul's tentmaking comes under the same principle, though not without some variation. He does not make his profit by going directly to nature as in fishing, pasturing or farming; rather, he puts his effort and time into a kind of manufacturing work. We may view such work as that which increases the value. For example: A piece of cloth may be worth one dollar. If I cut it, sew it, and make it into a tent, it can be sold for, say, two dollars. But this means I increase its value and earn my wages. Nobody will become poorer as a result of my earning a fair share. I simply increase the worth of this piece of cloth by adding my labor to it. It is therefore proper for me to earn my wages in this way. Such employment may be called a value-increasing occupation.

3. A LABORER'S WAGES

In the case of an employee who works for another, or in the case of a mason or a physician, such a one is simply earning the wages derived from his own labor. Though he does not make his profit out of nature nor does he increase any value by means of manufacturing, he has nevertheless expended so much of his time and exerted so much of his strength that he is entitled to receive precisely that much in wages which is commensurate with his effort and time. God permits a laborer to have his share of wages.

From the standpoint of God's word, trading is the lowest form of all employments. If opportunity is given us to choose our occupation, may we choose that which will increase wealth or value rather than that which only increases our money. It is very selfish if we choose the latter.

Today we are poor; beware lest we become rich. For I must acknowledge that it is actually not hard for us to get rich because we as believers are honest and diligent, and because we do not waste our money in smoking and drinking and luxurious living. Do remember that before John Wesley died he said that he was deeply concerned with the Wesleyans for they would soon become the wealthiest people in the world since they were honest, diligent, and thrifty. And his prediction has indeed come true: the Wesleyans are wealthy, but are they rich in God?

In conclusion, let me say that we expect young believers to earn their money with honest labor. Do not aim at making a great deal by means of buying and selling. Our principle must always be to increase wealth but not money. And thus the money we earn will be clean, and it will be blessed as it is offered to God. The rule, then, is to labor or to produce. Although we dare not forbid trading, we nevertheless maintain that we should try our best to avoid pure commerce. It is a base employment which can easily drown a Christian in destruction and pierce him through with many sorrows (1 Tim. 6.9,10).*

---

*This is in no way overlooking the law of availability in trading as supplied by transporting goods from one place to another. It simply illustrates the absence of the basic principles of increasing wealth or increasing value.—*Translator*

Marriage

Scripture to Memorize:
*Two are better than one, because they have a good
reward for their labor.*

Ecclesiastes 4.9

To be a good Christian, one needs to deal faithfully
with all one's basic problems. If there is a moral issue in
any of these basic areas, whether it be family or profession
or whatever, other problems will later on crop up. One
undealt difficulty is strong enough to hinder growth and
deter one from walking uprightly.

In this exercise we will consider the matter of marriage.
New believers especially need to know what the word of
the Lord says about this matter. Let us, then, look at the
problem from various directions.

Sex Consciousness Not Sinful

People are conscious of sex just as they are conscious
of hunger. If hunger is a natural, physical demand, then sex
is also a natural requirement of the body. For a person to
feel hungry is natural and it is not a sin. But if he steals
food, then it is sinful. It is something unnatural. Likewise,
the consciousness of sex is natural and is not reckoned as
sin. Only if one uses an improper way to satisfy his desire
does he fall into sin.

Sex consciousness is God-given. Marriage was
ordained and created by God. It was instituted before, not
after, the fall of man. It happened before Genesis 3. As a
matter of fact, God introduced it in Genesis 2. Hence, sex
consciousness existed before, not after, sin entered into the

193

world. It is important to know that there is no sin in being sex conscious. Sin is not primarily involved, for the very presence of this consciousness was created by God.

The Lord tells us through His apostle, "Let marriage be had in honor among all" (Heb. 13.4). It is not only something to be honored but is holy as well. God considers sex both holy and natural.

Three Basic Reasons for Marriage

1. FOR MUTUAL HELP

Marriage is ordained by God: "It is not good that the man should be alone" (Gen. 2.18), says God. All things created by God are good. On the first day of creation, God saw the light and said it was good. On every day except the second, God proclaimed it was good. (The second day was an exception because then the firmament, Satan's dwelling place, was created.) But on the sixth day, after God created man, He said, "It is not good that the man should be alone." This was not to suggest that the man had not been well created; it only meant that it was not good because only half of man was created.

So, God made "a help meet" for man. Eve was also made on the sixth day and was brought by God to Adam. She was made for the express purpose of marriage.

The words "help meet" means "meet [suitable] to help"; that is, she must first answer or correspond to Adam before she can be of help to him.

When God created man, He created them male and female. It seems as if He first created half of man and then made the other half so that there would be one whole man. Only after the two halves were joined together was man completed. Then God pronounced that "it was very good" (Gen. 1.31). First of all, it needs to be pointed out that marriage was initiated by God, not by man. Further, it did not originate after the fall of man, but before man ever sinned. Man did not sin on the first day of his creation, but he was married that very first day. After God created Eve, on the same day He gave her to Adam. So marriage is indeed instituted by God.

2. FOR PREVENTION OF FORNICATION

In the Old Testament, before sin came into the world, God had already instituted marriage. But now, in these New Testament days, sin has already come in. So Paul shows us in 1 Corinthians 7 that, because of the entrance of sin, marriage not only is not prohibited but, rather, has become a necessity.

In order to prevent fornication, Paul tells us that each man should have his own wife and each woman her own husband. He does not condemn sex consciousness as sin; instead he suggests that marriage can prevent the sin of fornication.

"It is better to marry than to burn" (1 Cor. 7.9b). Paul writes strongly here. Those who have a compelling desire for marriage and who burn with passion should be married. He does not reprimand them for their strong sensation, as if it were sinful, nor does he make provision for the flesh. He only states that if people have a strong feeling toward marriage it is better for them to marry than to be consumed with desire. The word of God is clear on the matter. Sex consciousness is not sin. Even a strong sexual urge is not sin. But God does prescribe marriage for such people. They should not refrain from marriage because to do so might cause them to fall into sin.

3. FOR RECEIVING GRACE TOGETHER

In speaking to husbands and wives, Peter says, "as being also joint-heirs of the grace of life" (1 Pet. 3.7). In other words, God delights in having the husband and the wife serve Him together. He looks for Aquila and Priscilla to serve Him, for Peter and his wife as well as Jude and his wife to serve Him.

New believers should know that there are three basic reasons for Christian marriage: first, for mutual help; second, for prevention of sin; and third, for receiving grace together before God. Marriage does not involve just one Christian, but two Christians together in the presence of God. Not merely one person receives grace, but two are joint-heirs of the grace of life.

The Other Party in the Marriage

The Lord has laid down definite conditions as to whom one can or cannot marry. The Bible indicates clearly that the marriage of God's people should be limited among themselves. In other words, if there is to be a marriage, the opposite party must be sought among God's own people. One may not marry someone outside the scope of God's people.

BE NOT UNEQUALLY YOKED

Paul tells us whom we may marry in this famous passage, "Be not unequally yoked with unbelievers" (2 Cor. 6.14). Though this word is not directed exclusively to marriage, it does include marriage. For a believer and an unbeliever to work together in order to arrive at one goal is like putting opposite types of animals together under one yoke to till the ground. This is something God forbids. God does not allow the believer to bear the same yoke with the unbeliever. In the Old Testament it is specifically charged, "Thou shalt not plow with an ox and an ass together" (Deut. 22.10). The ox is slow, while the ass is fast. One wants to go one way; the other wants to go another way. One goes heavenward; the other goes to the world. One seeks for spiritual blessing; the other for earthly abundance. One pulls in one direction while the other pulls in another direction. This is an impossible situation. Such a yoke cannot endure.

The most serious yoke of all is marriage. Of three examples—partnership in business, an enterprise jointly undertaken, or marriage—the last constitutes the heaviest yoke. It is really difficult to bear the responsibility of the family together. The ideal second person in the marriage must be a brother or a sister. Do not carelessly choose an unbeliever. If you do, you will immediately get into great trouble. The believer pulls one way, while the other migrates toward the world. One seeks for heavenly gifts, but the other looks for earthly wealth. The difference between the two is tremendous. Because of this, the Bible commands us to marry those in the Lord.

Choosing a Mate

Scripture to Memorize:

Be not unequally yoked with unbelievers: for what fellowship have righteousness and iniquity? or what communion hath light with darkness?

2 Corinthians 6.14

Concerning the matter of choosing one's mate, we hope young brothers and sisters will be open and unprejudiced before God about this. Deal with the matter objectively, not subjectively. To be too subjective easily makes one's heart and head too hot to be able to see clearly or to see everything. Learn to remain calm and objective. Deliberate everything carefully before God. Do not leap into anything on the impulse of over-heated emotion. A Christian can jump into marriage but he cannot jump out of it. We Christians cannot behave like people in the world who easily marry and easily divorce. We cannot jump out. Therefore, before you jump in, consider carefully. I will mention some basic conditions for choosing a mate, going from the outward to the inward. I do so with the hope that young brothers and sisters will calmly consider them one by one before God.

Natural Attraction

The marriage between Jacob and Rachel was more easily concluded than that of Jacob and Leah, for the former was based on natural affection. We must not despise natural attraction. In choosing a mate, not just any brother or sister will do. To be brothers and sisters involves no question of attraction, but to be joined in matrimony involves consideration of many factors. Attraction is one of these factors.

When you are choosing a mate, you must love to be with the other person and enjoy his or her company. You should not merely endure the presence of the opposite one but should find delight in being together. If you do not enjoy each other's company, you should not be married, for a basic condition is lacking. Furthermore, such delight in, or enjoyment of, the company of the other party must not be of a temporary nature; rather, it should be of long duration. You should sense that even after thirty or fifty years you will still love to be together.

Health

I believe for a marriage to be successful both the man and the woman should be comparatively healthy. Neither of them should be seriously ill, or else in a time of special trial the burden may become unbearable.

Heredity

Marriage must be coolly considered from a long-term point of view. Therefore, the matter of heredity needs to be taken into account. One should take into consideration the health of the ancestors as well as that of the potential spouse.

Family Background

There is a Western proverb which says, "I marry her, not her family." This is not strictly true, for when a girl marries, her family usually comes along.

A person is more or less influenced by his or her family. In considering marriage, one should pay attention to the moral standard of the other person's family. Are they of noble ideals? How strict a standard do they maintain? What is the attitude of the men toward women and vice versa? By looking into questions such as these, one may safely deduce what one's future home will be like.

A boy or a girl who has been under his or her family's education for twenty years or so will unconsciously carry the old family way into the new home. This will happen even if he or she is dissatisfied with the old family. Sooner or later the old ways will crop up. I dare not say this will happen ten out of ten times, but I dare say it will occur seven or eight out of ten times. Although the old family ways may not appear all at once, they gradually will seep in. So young people need to know that to safeguard the success of their marriage they should notice these things and carefully weigh them one by one.

Age

1. PHYSICAL

Generally speaking, women mature faster than men, but women also age faster. Women usually mature about five years ahead of men but age around ten years earlier. So in marriage, so far as the physical body is concerned, it is permissible for the man to be five, six, or even seven or eight years older than the woman.

2. MENTAL

On the other hand, there is the mental age. It is quite possible for a person to be physically matured yet mentally a child, old in body but young in mind. One may be over thirty in physical age but have a mental age of only twenty. For this reason, it is permissible for a brother whose mind matures earlier to marry a somewhat older sister whose mind is still young.

201

The decision rests on whether you pay more attention to physical age or to mental age. As far as physical age goes, it is better for the brother to be older than the sister. But as far as mental age is concerned, it is all right for a sister to be older than the brother. This is something each one has to decide for himself or herself.

Temperament, Interest, and Goal

The above five considerations are those matters that have more to do with the physical side. Beginning with the item now before us, we shall consider those things that are more concerned with nature or character.

For a marriage to be successful, there must not only be physical attraction but also proximity of temperament, interests, and goals. If natures and interests are too far apart, the family will eventually lose its peace and both the husband and the wife will suffer. Young people should know that natural or physical attraction is only temporary, but natures are more permanent.

Love among unbelievers is mostly natural attraction. It is not the love which the Bible mentions. There is natural attraction in love, but natural or physical attraction by itself is not love. Love includes natural attraction, but it also includes proximity of temperament. Hence, love possesses two fundamental elements: natural attraction and proximity of temperament and interests.

ACCEPTANCE OF THE OTHER

Many have the wrong concept of thinking they can change someone else's temperament. This never happens. For the Holy Spirit to change a person's character takes lots of time; how could you, then, succeed in this impossible task? Even marriage has not the power to change one's nature. Many brothers and sisters, aware of the disparity of their temperaments, hopefully wait for a change. But the expected change does not come. If there is one hope in the world which is doomed to despair, this one certainly is. I have yet to see a husband who has changed his wife, or a wife who has changed her husband. As I once said, in marriage you can only get ready-made goods, not made-to-order goods. Whatever the brother or the sister is, that is what you get. Before marriage you should first observe whether the brother or sister's present condition is commendable or not, for you cannot afterward expect to change the temperament of your marriage partner to suit yours.

Weaknesses

The above matters refer only to differences of nature without any involvement of a moral problem; now, though, we shall see that human beings do have weaknesses.

What should one do about the weaknesses of the opposite party? This is rather hard for an outsider to decide. Before young brothers and sisters marry, they need to find out the weaknesses of their proposed partner. These must be found before they are engaged, not afterward. It is wrong to look for the weaknesses of the opposite party after marriage. It is more than wrong: it is foolish. After marriage is too late to do such a thing. Once married, the husband and the wife should be as blind and deaf as possible. Even without looking, you will see plenty; what, then, if you should search carefully? Marriage should not be used as an opportunity for finding fault. You should not use your eyes after you are married. But before you are engaged, at the time you are choosing your mate, do not be so blinded by natural attraction that you fail to notice the weaknesses of the other person. Do not be so eager for marriage that you cannot see any weakness in the other party.

Character

For a marriage to be successful, it is necessary for the two to have mutual respect. If either one of them looks down on the other, the family is doomed. The husband must respect his wife's character; the wife must appreciate the quality of her husband's character. This is not a matter of temperament or of weakness, but of character.

Consecration

The first set of items in this exercise on choosing a mate touched on the physical side; the second set dealt with matters of personality or character—the soulical side; now in the third set we shall consider the spiritual side.

1. SAME PURPOSE

A Christian must not marry an unbeliever. We must see that to attain to the highest meaning of marriage, there must be oneness of spiritual purpose in addition to physical attraction and complementary natures. This means that both must have the desire to serve God. Both must be fully committed to the Lord. Both must live for God. This is more important than having an admirable character. Though the latter cannot be omitted, the former is absolutely indispensable. In big things and small things, both must live for the Lord.

Such a marriage has a solid foundation, for the two parties have a strong bond of unity before God.

2. CHRIST AS LORD

In a family having oneness of purpose, there is no striving as to who stands in the position of head and who obeys. Christ is the head who is to be obeyed. Christ is the Lord of the house. The question of saving face is altogether eliminated. Many husbands and wives quarrel, not because they care for right and wrong, but because they want to save their faces. Were they both consecrated Christians, this problem would be non-existent. Both would be willing to lose face before the Lord. Both would be able to confess their fault. Since both desire most of all to do the will of God, everything can be settled on that basis.

Young brothers and sisters should know that they must be fully consecrated. If both parties to a proposed marriage serve the Lord with all their hearts, the probability of success in their marriage is exceedingly high. Even though there may be some natural differences and even though physical attraction may somewhat fade, the family will prosper without hindrance.

May young brothers and sisters see that there are conditions for marriage. Simply speaking, these conditions may be divided along three lines: the physical or external, the psychological, and the spiritual. These three need to be placed in their proper respective positions.

Husband and Wife

Scripture to Memorize:

Wives, be in subjection to your husbands, as is fitting in the Lord. Husbands, love your wives, and be not bitter against them.

Colossians 3.18-19

First of all, the married person—husband or wife—must see that to be a husband or a wife is a most serious matter.

Before a person can enter into a profession, he must be properly prepared. To be a physician requires college plus several more years of training; a teacher needs to spend four or five years in a teachers college; an engineer must at least finish a four-year course in college; a nurse must study four years in a nursing school. Is it not strange, then, that one can be a husband or a wife without even one day of training? No wonder there are so many poor husbands and poor wives. They have never learned how! If I am sick, would I trust myself to the care of a medically untrained doctor or nurse? If I need someone to teach a child, would I ask the help of an unschooled person? If I am going to build a house, would I dare engage an unqualified architect? How, then, can I think it well for a man to be a husband or a woman to be a wife who has never learned how?

Therefore, all married brothers and sisters should learn to take up their responsibility before God. Since marriage is more difficult than any other profession, no one should delay to diligently learn how.

Close Your Eyes

The first thing to learn after marriage is to close your eyes that you may not see.

When two people live together as husband and wife, day after day, year after year, without vacation or sick leave, each one has plenty of time to find out the weaknesses of the opposite party. So, as soon as you are married, you must close your eyes. The aim of marriage is not to discover the weaknesses of your life partner. Remember, she is your wife, not your student; he is your husband, not your apprentice. You are not required to find the difficulties and weaknesses of your mate in order to help and correct them. A family should be built on a solid foundation. Hence, before you are married, you have to open your eyes wide so as to understand everything, even the possible difficulties. But after you are married, you must not seek to understand anymore. If you want to split hairs, you have plenty of opportunity to do so. Since God has put you together, you both have plenty of time, perhaps fifty years, to discover the weaknesses of the other one. For this reason, the first thing the married brothers and sisters should do is close their eyes to the difficulties and weaknesses of their counterparts. You will see enough without looking! How many more difficulties there will be if you seek them on purpose.

In joining two people together as husband and wife, God has arranged that there be subjection and love in the family. He has not asked the husband and wife to find and correct each other's faults. He has not set up husbands to be instructors to their wives or wives to be teachers to their husbands. A husband need not change his wife or a wife her husband. Whatever the manner of person you marry, you must expect to live with that for life. Do not purposely look for difficulties and weaknesses with a view to helping.

Such a concept of helping is basically wrong. Married people should learn to close their eyes. They should learn to love and not to help or correct.

Learn to Accommodate

To accommodate is a lesson which needs to be learned immediately after marriage. No matter how much alike the dispositions of the couple are, sooner or later they will discover lots of differences. They still will have different viewpoints, likes and dislikes, opinions and inclinations. Hence they must learn soon after they are married to accommodate themselves to each other.

1. GO HALFWAY

What is meant by accommodation? It means that I will meet the other party halfway. It is best if this is mutual. But in case it is not reciprocal, you yourself can at least go half of the way. However, many problems will be solved if you can leave your position and go over all the way. When this is not possible, it is still good to meet your partner halfway. In other words, after the brother and the sister have become husband and wife, they both should learn to make adjustments in all things. If you can adjust all the way, fine; if not, adapt yourself at least half of the way. Learn to go out and meet the other. Do not insist on your opinions, but be willing to change your views. Although you have your ideas, learn to accommodate yourself to the thoughts of your life partner.

2. LEARN TO DENY YOURSELF

As Christians, we must learn to deny ourselves. To deny oneself means to accommodate oneself to others. Both the husband and the wife should learn to be more accommodating. Then there will at least be peace in the family. Where there is self-denial, there will be accommodation. Where self-denial is absent, accommodation will also be absent.

Be Appreciative and Sensitive

Once you are married you should learn at once to appreciate the strengths of your partner.

1. NOTICE THE OTHER'S STRENGTHS

We must not only be accommodating and close our eyes to weaknesses, we must also learn to appreciate the strengths of the opposite party. We should be sensitive to things that are well done. Family relationships will greatly suffer if the husband does not know how to appreciate his wife, or if the wife does not value her husband. Remember, we need neither flatter our wives nor seek to satisfy our husbands' vanity. What is needed is to appreciate each other. Learn to see the strengths, the virtues, the beauty of the other.

2. MAKE YOUR APPRECIATION KNOWN

A husband's appreciation of his wife must not be less than anyone else's. His appreciation may not be higher, but at least it should not be less than other people's. Why did you marry her if you appreciate her value so little? Either your perception was wrong then or it is wrong now. The same applies to the wife. Why did you marry that man if you feel he is the wrong person? You yourself must be wrong. To have a happy family, mutual appreciation is essential. Let it not be that others praise your life partner while you criticize. Notice your partner's strengths and be aware of his or her virtues. Whenever opportunity offers itself, confess publicly what you have observed and felt. This is not being pretentious, for you are telling the truth.

When the husband and the wife appreciate each other in this way, the family tie is strengthened.

Be Courteous

A family must be courteous to each other. It is abominable not to be courteous.

We all should be courteous to everyone. However familiar you are with a person, you will lose him as a friend if you are lacking in politeness. Paul tells us that love "doth not behave itself unseemly" (1 Cor. 13.5). Oftentimes family troubles are caused by small things. The time a person is least gracious is when he is at home. You think since your wife or your husband is the person most intimate to you, you may be less thoughtful. But you should remember that courtesy beautifies human contact. Once it is removed, all the ugly parts of life will be revealed. However familiar people are, courtesy must be maintained. One brother explained this well by saying that courtesy is like the lubricating oil put in machinery. Without courtesy there will be friction and unpleasant feelings.

Let Love Grow

For a family to be successful, love must grow continuously and not be allowed to die.

Love needs to be fed by accommodation, sacrifice, self-denial, understanding, sympathy, and forgiveness. All of these must be repeated over and over. If it is nourished, love can grow beautifully. But if people do not seek the pleasure of others but think only of their own welfare, their love will soon be starved and die.

Be Unselfish

Another important condition of family life is to not be selfish.

1. SEEK TO PLEASE THE OTHER

If you are married, live like a married person. You should not live like an unmarried person. The word of God says: "he that is married is careful for the things of the world, how he may please his wife. . . [and] she that is married is careful for the things of the world, how she may please her husband" (1 Cor. 7.33-34). The greatest difficulty a family faces is probably selfishness.

Permit Freedom, Privacy, and Private Possessions

In the family, one must allow the other party certain freedom, privacy, and private possessions.

In the family, both the husband and the wife should learn to give freedom to the other. Each of them should have his or her own time, money, and things. Just because there is a husband-and-wife relationship, these things should not be usurped. You need to learn to keep your place. Otherwise, a small thing like this can cause a big problem.

Every husband and every wife should be allowed to have his or her own privacy. This is perfectly legitimate. It is permissible for the left hand to do something without notifying the right hand (see Matt. 6.3). Learn, therefore, to respect each individual's privilege of some privacy. This will help the family avoid many troubles.

Learn to Solve Problems

The matter now before us is how to solve family problems. Husbands and wives cannot avoid having some differences and difficulties. Since both are grown-ups and both are children of God, they need to understand first where their differences and difficulties are. Before any difficulty can be solved, one needs to know where the problem is. After identifying where the problem is, they need to find the solution to it.

It is best for the husband and the wife to talk things over with each other. Outsiders should not interfere at the beginning, though there may be occasion to help later on. First let the two people exchange their views freely. The news should not be known to others and travel far and wide while it has not yet been discussed at home. Sometimes things concerning the husband are known twenty miles away and yet the husband is ignorant of them. Things between a husband and wife ought to be told to each other. Provide opportunity for such a family council. Let your partner finish speaking before you speak. Guard against the talkative one monopolizing the conversation. The husband should listen to the wife and the wife to the husband.

When you are sitting down to talk, discuss your conflicts objectively. If they are brought out subjectively, the conference will not be successful. The purpose of your talking is to find out what is right. Neither one of you knows who is right, so both of you must be intent on finding the truth. You should both talk and afterward both pray. Through prayer seek a solution. Ask the Lord to make you both understand where the trouble lies. Usually by the time you pray the second time, most matters will be solved. The problem of many is that they have not sat down and listened objectively. When they do, their difficulty is half solved; they will soon be able to discover the real trouble spot.

In family life, husband and wife often need to confess to each other and forgive each other. They should not just casually pass over their faults but should confess them. One should confess one's own fault and forgive the other's fault.

When you are at fault, confess. But what should you do when the fault is your partner's? Remember, your family relationship is like all other Christian relationships. When your counterpart is wrong, learn to forgive instead of probing. For love "taketh not account of evil" (1 Cor. 13.5). Love does not record every wrong; rather, love learns to forgive. As soon as a sin is forgiven, it is forgotten. Love will not behave as Peter in Matthew 18 did, counting every sin and limiting the measure of forgiveness. True forgiveness takes no account of time; as soon as a sin is forgiven it is forgotten. For a family to be successful, there must be forgiveness.

Live Together before God

To solve family problems and to live happily together, it is necessary for the couple to have a positive life together before God. Especially parents with children need to have a time to pray together. Every couple needs such a time to wait on God and to deliberate spiritual things. Whether it is the husband or the wife, both must gladly accept the judgment of God's light. The husband must not try to save his face, nor the wife her's. There must be fellowship together. Spend time in praying and deliberating together. In order to have a good family, both must live before God.

Parenthood

Scripture to Memorize:

Fathers, provoke not your children to wrath: but nurture them in the chastening and admonition of the Lord.

Eph. 6.4

New believers, especially parents and future parents, should know that even as it is not easy to be a husband or a wife, it is even harder to be a father or a mother. To be a husband or a wife is mostly one's own concern; to be a parent affects others. A husband or a wife only touches his or her mate's personal happiness, but a parent influences the happiness of the next generation. The future of the children depends upon the parents. Therefore, the responsibility of parents is great. God has delivered our children's bodies, souls, thoughts, lives, and futures into our hands. No person can influence another's destiny more than parents can their children's. They can almost direct their children to heaven or to hell. How tremendously important their responsibility is. They must learn how to be good parents as well as how to be good husbands and wives. Their responsibility as parents probably is more serious than their responsibility as husbands and wives.

Let us fellowship a little on how to be a Christian parent.

Sanctify Yourself

1. YOU SHOULD SANCTIFY YOURSELF

All parents should sanctify themselves for their children's sake. This means that though they are free to do many things, for the sake of their children they will not. There are many words they no longer feel free to utter because of their children. From the day a child comes into the family, the parents need to sanctify themselves.

If you cannot control yourself, how can you control your children? If you cannot govern yourself, how can you govern your children? A person without children only hurts himself by his lack of control, but one who has children destroys his children as well as himself. Therefore, as soon as a Christian is entrusted with children, he must sanctify himself. For the rest of his life there are two or four or more pairs of eyes watching and watching. Even after he has left this world, those eyes will continue to remember what they have seen.

2. DEVELOP A SENSE OF STEWARDSHIP OVER YOUR CHILDREN

Neither failure in work nor failure in marriage can be compared with failure in parenthood. Why? Because when one is already grown up, he is well able to protect himself. But the child who is committed to you cannot protect himself. Could you go to the Lord and say, "You entrusted me with five children, and I lost three of them," or, "You trusted me with ten and I lost eight of them"? The church cannot be strong if this sense of stewardship is missing. How can the gospel be spread over the earth if you lose those born to you and then have to try to recover them from the world? You should at least bring your own children to the Lord. For you to not nurture them in the chastening and admonition of the Lord is wrong. Remember, it is the responsibility of the parents to bring up their children in the Lord.

3. Do Not Have a Double Standard

To lead your children to God, you must yourself walk with God. Do not fancy that by pointing your finger towards heaven you may lead them to heaven. You yourself must walk ahead and let them follow. The reason for the failure of many Christian families is that the parents expect their children to be better than they are. They expect their children not to love the world and to go on with the Lord while they themselves stay behind. Such an expectation is futile. It is important that the parents have the same standard as the children. You cannot set up a standard for them and not live by it yourself. The standard which you follow in spiritual things will eventually be the standard of your children.

Parents Must Be of One Mind

For a family to be solid, the Christian father and mother must be of one mind. For the sake of God, they must agree to sacrifice their own freedom and establish a strict moral standard. Neither the father nor the mother can have his or her special opinion.

Oftentimes the father and mother provide an opening for their children to sin because they themselves do not stand together. It is difficult for the children to follow a definite standard if the parents do not agree. If the father says yes and the mother says no (or vice versa), the children can choose to ask whoever is more lenient. This will further enlarge the gap between the father and the mother.

Do Not Provoke Your Children to Wrath

Paul shows us that it is of utmost importance that parents not provoke their children to wrath.

1. USE AUTHORITY WITH RESTRAINT

What is meant by provoking the children to wrath? It means the excessive use of your authority, overpowering your children with your strength, financial or physical or whatever. In every way you are stronger than your child. You may overwhelm him with your monetary strength if you threaten: "If you don't listen to me, I won't give you any money," or, "If you don't listen, I won't give you food or clothing." Since you support him, you can oppress him by withdrawing financial support. Or you may simply subdue him by your physical strength or perhaps by your overbearing will. You provoke him to wrath. You press him to such an extent that he just waits for the day of liberation. When that day comes, he will throw off all restraint and claim freedom in everything.

2. SHOW APPRECIATION TO THE CHILDREN

When the children do well, parents should show proper appreciation. Some parents only seem to know to beat and to scold. This easily provokes the children and discourages even those who really have a desire to be good. Paul says, "Provoke not your children, that they be not discouraged." Children should be encouraged when they do well. They need to be rewarded as well as disciplined. Otherwise, they will be disheartened.

Nurture Your Children in the Chastening and Admonition of the Lord

What is meant by the admonition of the Lord? It means instruction on how one should behave. In so instructing your children, you must treat them as Christians, not as unbelievers. The Lord wants you to expect your children to become Christians; hence you must treat them as such. You should instruct them according to the norm of a good Christian.

1. CHANNEL CHILDREN'S AMBITION

A great problem with children is ambition. Every child has his ambition. If children could print their name cards, many of them would write such titles as "The Future President," "The Future Chairman," or, "The Future Queen." If you are worldly, your children will naturally think of being a president, a millionaire, or a great educator. Whatever your world is, that will be your children's ambition. Because of this, parents must try to correct and channel their children's ambition. You yourself must be a lover of the Lord, not a lover of the world. Instill in their young hearts the understanding that to suffer for the Lord is noble and to be a martyr is glorious. You yourself need to set an example for them. You must often tell them what your ambition is. Tell them what kind of Christian you want to be. In this way you can turn their ambition to that which is noble and glorious.

2. DO NOT ENCOURAGE CHILDREN'S PRIDE

Besides outward ambition, children also have the problem of inward pride. They like to boast of their cleverness, talent, or eloquence. Usually a child can find many things to brag about, imagining himself to be someone very special. Parents should not stifle their children, neither should they nurture their pride. Many parents educate their children in a wrong way by encouraging their vanity. When people praise your child before him, you may tell him that there are many other children like him in the world. Do not encourage his pride, but instruct him according to the chastening and admonition of the Lord. Do not let him lose his self-respect, but also do not allow him to be proud. You should not break down his self-respect, but you must show him wherein he has overestimated himself. Sometimes it takes young people ten to twenty years of social grinding before they start to do well. This is a waste of much precious time, all because they have been so proud and indulgent at home that they cannot humble themselves enough to really do any work well.

3. TEACH CHILDREN HOW TO CHOOSE

Give children the opportunity to make choices when they are still young. Do not always make decisions for them in everything until they are eighteen or twenty, and then suddenly thrust them into the world. If you do that, they will not know how to choose for themselves. So, in bringing up your children, give them ample opportunity to choose. Let them express what they like or dislike. Show them whether what they like is the right thing or not. Help them to choose rightly. Some children like to be dressed in one color while some others prefer another. Let them have their choice.

If children are not given the opportunity to choose, they will not be able, when they reach the age of marriage, to rule in their families. Give your children as much opportunity as possible to choose; also, you should instruct them about their choice.

Lead Your Children to the Lord

One way of leading children to the Lord is an effective family altar. In the Old Testament the tent and the altar were joined together. In other words, the family and consecration are connected; united family prayer and reading the Bible together are indispensable.

1. HAVE FAMILY WORSHIP ON THE CHILDREN'S LEVEL

Some so-called family worship is a failure, either because it is too long or too deep. The children sit through without knowing what it is all about. I am opposed to families inviting us to preach deeper truth to them with the children sitting there. Sometimes a family gathering continues for an hour or two and what is considered is all deeper truth. This is really a hardship on the children. And sometimes parents are not sensitive to it at all. In a family gathering, the children must be the first consideration. The gathering is not for you, because you can worship in the church. Never force your level on the family gathering. All that you do in the family must be on the level of the children and best suited to their taste.

2. LEAD THE CHILDREN TO REPENTANCE

You need to show your children what sin is. Notice if they are repentant. Bring them to the Lord. When the time is ripe, help them to accept the Lord in a definite way. Then take them to the church that they may have a part in the life of the church. In this way you will lead your children to the true knowledge of God.

Discipline Your Children Wisely

When children do wrong, they should be disciplined. It is not right not to chasten a child.

221

1. USE THE ROD WHEN NECESSARY

Children must be chastened. "He that spareth his rod hateth his son; but he that loveth him chasteneth him betimes [diligently]" (Prov. 13.24).

This is the wisdom of Solomon. Parents must learn to use the rod, for it is necessary.

2. CHASTEN JUSTLY

However, chastening must be done justly. Never spank your child because you have lost your temper or when you are out of sorts. If you spank in anger, you yourself are wrong. You are not qualified to chasten your child. You need to have your wrath calmed down before God.

3. SHOW THE CHILDREN THEIR FAULT

In some cases, spanking is necessary. But you must show your child why he deserves it. Doubtless he is in need of chastening, yet he also has the need of being shown his fault. Each time you chasten a child, tell him wherein he was wrong.

Friendship

Scripture to Memorize:

Ye adulteresses, know ye not that the friendship of the world is enmity with God? Whosoever therefore would be a friend of the world maketh himself an enemy of God.

James 4.4

Friendship Not Emphasized in the Bible

It is rather special that the Bible hardly mentions the matter of friends in relation to God's children, though the word "friend" occurs many times. It is found in Genesis and Proverbs and in Matthew and Luke. Most of these times it refers to people outside of Christ. Rarely is it used of friends in the Lord. If I remember correctly, the word "friends" is used only twice in reference to Paul, both times being in Acts. Once was when ". . . certain also of the Asiarchs, being his [Paul's] friends, sent unto him and besought him not to adventure himself into the theatre" in Ephesus (Acts 19.31). Again, on the way to Rome, ". . . Julius treated Paul kindly, and gave him leave to go unto his friends and refresh himself" (Acts 27.3). In a third New Testament reference, John wrote, "The friends salute thee. Salute the friends by name" (3 John 14b). The fact that there are so few references to Christian friends indicates that the Bible does not stress this matter.

Why is it that friendship is not emphasized in the Bible? It is because the word of God emphasizes another relationship, that of brothers and sisters. How to be brothers and sisters in the Lord is of basic and primary importance.

223

eds to be strengthened, not the matter of

ndships in the World Terminated

As ꜱ~ ı as one believes in the Lord Jesus, he is charged by God to desist from his former friendships.

1. ENMITY WITH GOD

"Friendship of the world is enmity with God" (James 4.4). The "world" here may mean "the people of the world." If we would be friends with the people of the world because we love the world, then we make ourselves enemies of God. "If any man love the world, the love of the Father is not in him" (1 John 2.15b).

2. UNEQUAL YOKING

"Be not unequally yoked with unbelievers" (2 Cor. 6.14). Many people seem to think this refers exclusively to marriage. I believe it does include marriage, but more than that too. It comprises all kinds of friendships and relationships between believers and unbelievers. Here we are shown the utter incompatibility of believers and unbelievers.

To be unequally yoked is not a blessing but a sorrow. I hope Christians will see that we must not maintain an intimate relationship with unbelievers, whether in the sphere of society, business, friendship, or marriage. Believers have one standard and unbelievers another. Believers have the teaching of faith, but unbelievers follow their doctrine of unbelief. Believers possess a believing viewpoint, and unbelievers hold on to an unbelieving viewpoint. When you try to bring these together, the result is not blessing but pain. Their viewpoints, opinions, moral standards, and judgments are so different from ours that there is a tugging in two directions. To put these two under one yoke will either break the yoke or cause the believer to follow the unbeliever.

3. THE INFLUENCE OF BAD CONVERSATIONS

"Be not deceived: Evil companionships corrupt good morals" (1 Cor.15.33). "Evil companionships" means improper communications, while "corrupt" carries the thought of wood being corrupted by worms.

BRINGS CORRUPTION

"Good morals" in a lighter vein is "good manners." Improper communications will corrupt your good appearance. At first you were pious before God, but, in the company of unbelieving friends, you begin to jest and laugh. Some of the jokes you ought not to laugh at, for they are unbecoming. But you set aside your self-control in their midst because you know they welcome looseness.

Evil communications corrupt good manners. These two are opposites. One is evil and the other is good. Evil corrupts good. It will corrupt the life of the Lord in believers. Believers ought to have good habits. They should spend time cultivating good habits before the Lord. They should learn to control themselves. They should gradually exercise themselves unto godliness.

A New Kind of Friendship in the Church

Tell new believers that soon after they are saved, they need to take care of the question of friendships. They must change their friends. They should tell their former friends what has happened to them. Although they may still keep some contact, they most definitely should not continue any deep and intimate friendships. Rather, they should learn to be brothers and sisters in the church. They should substitute the brethren in the church for their former friends.

We must not be extreme. We do not hate unbelievers nor will we neglect them. But we communicate with them now on a different ground. Now we learn to witness to them and bring them to the Lord.

CHRIST, THE SINNERS' FRIEND

The Lord Jesus is the friend of sinners. If He had stood strictly on His position, He could not have become the sinners' friend. He became a friend because He left His exalted position. Otherwise, though He could be a Savior, He could not be a friend. I hope you see what is meant by Christ being a friend. The Lord and sinners are irreconcilable. He is the Judge, and we are the judged; He is the Savior, and we are the saved. But the Lord laid all this aside to be the sinners' friend. People called Him the friend of sinners. As a friend, He is able to lead us to accept Him as our Savior.

THE APOSTLE JOHN'S FRIENDS

I believe that after a child of God has been a brother for a sufficient length of time and has come to a deeper knowledge in the Lord, he may become friends with some in the church. This naturally shows that he has transcended a formal position. This is distinctive of 3 John.

Third John was written when the apostle John was very old. Probably it was written about thirty years after Paul was martyred. When John wrote the letter, old Peter had already gone, Paul had passed away, and the rest of the twelve apostles had also departed from the world. He wrote not as an apostle but rather as an elder (v. 1). He was really advanced in age. I like his third letter. It is quite different from the other two. In 1 John he said, "Fathers," "young men," "little children," and "my little children" as if he spoke formally to them. But in the last verse of 3 John, he stood in a very special position. He would soon depart from the world. He was very old, probably in his nineties. He had known so much of the Lord and he had walked so far with God that, when writing this letter, instead of calling them brothers, sisters, little children, young men, or fathers, he said, "The friends salute thee. Salute the friends by name." Can you get the taste of it? If you can enter into the spirit of it, you will comprehend the meaning. Otherwise, you will not see. Here was a man who was so old that he outlived all his friends. Peter was dead, Paul was dead. But he could yet say, "The friends salute thee. Salute the friends by name." How very rich he was. He had arrived at the zenith of richness. For many years he had followed the Lord and had touched many things. Now he was so full of years that he could very well have patted the head of a sixty or seventy year old and called him, "My child." But he did not do this. Instead he said, "My friend." The position of formal ground was forgotten. He spoke from a position of exaltation and thus could exalt others. As the Lord became the sinners' friend, as God made Abraham His friend, so here John treats these children, young men, and fathers as friends.

As Brethren

Some day the young ones in the church may arrive at such an exalted place. But today they must learn to stand in the place of brethren. The matter of friendship in the church occupies a very high ground. Some day, when you are very mature, you may make little children your friends. By then you will have far exceeded them in spirituality. You will be able to exalt them to be your friends. Until that day comes, however, what the church stresses is not friends but brothers and sisters.

Recreation

Scripture to Memorize:

All things are lawful; but not all things are expedient [profitable]. All things are lawful; but not all things edify.

1 Corinthians 10.23

The Purpose of Recreation

The first purpose of recreation is to meet the family's needs. It is not for ourselves that we consider this matter, but for the children in the family. To us, if we are consecrated, recreation is a very minor thing. But in our family, not only are there our own children but also there are our younger brothers and sisters. These younger ones have been entrusted to our care. If it is that they too are consecrated, the problem of recreation does not exist. However, these children, and nephews and nieces too, may not be fully consecrated; thus our attitude has much bearing upon them. What we allow or what we prohibit has a great effect upon their lives. That is why recreation is primarily a consideration for family folks, that they may give proper guidance to those of the younger generation.

The second purpose of recreation is for ourselves. A believer sometimes does need a change. The only question is how much or what kind of change is good. Adults need diversions just as the children do, but what is suitable and becoming to a Christian is something basic to settle before God. This is not too difficult for us, but for the children it may be quite necessary. What recreation will we permit our children to have? Every child of God must be clear on this.

If any loopholes are left, the world will immediately invade the situation. Once in, it is not easy to drive the world away. Therefore, for the sake of keeping our family in the Lord, we must pay attention to this matter of recreation.

Principles Governing Recreation

1. NEED

Recreation according to the Lord's will grows out of a recognition of the need for it. A Christian should not go to extremes. Man does have a need for recreation. Many people are so busy that if they do not have some sort of relaxation, they may get sick and lose their health. Hence, renewal is the basic principle of recreation. This is especially important to young people. You cannot ask your children to study from morning till night. You must give them some kind of diversion, provide some change. This is a rule to be observed.

Recreation is for the sake of renewal. When one has worked five or eight hours on a project, he gets tired. When doing one thing for a long time, one's nerves get strained and one's body becomes fatigued. To refresh oneself, a change of work is needed. For example, after a child has studied for several hours at school, when he comes home he needs to play for a while. Such playing is perfectly right because it is the child's relaxation. But if the child should play eight hours in succession, his playing is more than renovation. There is a need for renewal, but to make recreation our life is unjustifiable. When a person is tired, for him to do something else for a change is right. Yet it would be wrong if he were to play from dawn to dusk. In the summer, people like to go swimming. We find no fault with it. When one is tired, it is all right to swim for half an hour or an hour. But should one immerse himself in water from morning till evening like a duck, this would no longer be recreation. We need to see the difference between recreation as renewal and recreation as our life.

2. POSSIBLE FORMS

Recreation may take many different forms. A Christian might enjoy any of the following:

REST

The best form of recreation for a Christian is rest. I am tired today, so I rest a while. The Lord Jesus and His disciples were tired working, so He told them, "Come ye yourselves apart into a desert place, and rest a while" (Mark 6.31). His rest includes the idea of recreation. He does not say, "Rest awhile," but He says, "Come . . . apart into a desert place, and rest a while." Oftentimes our fatigue is relieved after resting beside the hill or the water. The most common form of Christian recreation is rest.

CHANGE OF WORK

Sometimes you can feel yourself becoming dull and inactive. If so, take a change by working on something else. Usually you work eight hours. Take out two hours to do some other work. If you always work sitting, stand up for a change. If your work is mental work, change to a little physical exertion and immediately your weariness will be gone. Though this is not what the world calls recreation, yet, by changing your work, you may get rid of your tiredness. Furthermore, this is something you can easily arrange to do. Since the principle of recreation is renewal, a change of work fits the requirement.

HOBBIES

There are many hobbies proper for a Christian. Some people like to take pictures. Some like to keep a bird or two. Some like to plant flowers. Some like to paint. All these are legitimate and within a proper Christian domain. Some may like music, such as playing the piano or writing musical compositions. Others may like to practice calligraphy. Any of these is appropriate.

However, there is a principle governing any recreation: you must be able to lay it down as well as take it up. If you cannot lay it down, something is wrong. For example, it is innocent to take pictures and research a bit into photography. But do not let it influence you too much. If you are well along on the spiritual course, these things will not disturb you. But it would be wrong for you to feel you *must* take pictures.

GAMES

There are many games of skill such as chess, ball games, and riding which are commendable. Although there is the element of victory and defeat, they are nonetheless proper because they are entirely games of skill. It is well to let the children play table tennis or basketball or tennis or chess. There is nothing inherently sinful in these games. Parents should be more lenient with their children in such things. Older people may not have time for strenuous sports, but they should not hinder the young from engaging in such games. True, we want them to spend their time for the Lord, but they do also need some recreation. Let us be glad to let them have it.

Thus far we have mentioned four kinds of recreation—rest, a change of work, a hobby, and games. All these are permissible for Christians. But a Christian must never be under the power of any of them. To be under their control is an error.

3. To Help Us Work

Why do we need recreation? It is to help us work better. Recreation has a purpose; it is not an end it itself. I do not play ball just because I like to play ball. I play ball that I may work better. I do not sleep just because I love to sleep. I sleep so that I may work better. I do not plant flowers just for enjoyment but so that I may work efficiently. These things are permissible only because they help us work better and serve God in a stronger way. They should never be a disturbance to us. Sometimes you see people work on one thing day and night. If they continue like this for two or three weeks, their mind and their physical strength will be exhausted. It would be better for them to seek the Lord about having some diversion. After working seven or eight hours, they should change their work—play the piano or play ball. Such diversion is for the purpose of restoration. It is to increase, not decrease, their efficiency. Because of the refreshment of recreation, their work can be better done and thus they can serve God in a stronger way.

4. No Games of Chance

There is a special requirement as to what games should be allowed: all games must involve skill. None of them should be pure chance. A game is commendable only if it depends on skill, not on chance. If it requires both skill and chance, it becomes a gamble. If it is all chance and no skill, it most definitely is gambling. Games which Christians play must be games of skill, not of chance. Dice is purely a game of chance. It is gambling and Christians should not be involved in it. The young may play chess and checkers because it is a matter of skill, not of chance.

5. HEALTH FOR THE BODY

All recreation must be agreeable to the body. This is one of the first principles: the recreation must benefit the body. So, before entering into recreation, one should consider whether or not it is of physical benefit. If the recreation should damage the body, it is in violation of a first principle and is highly questionable. For example, if a brother has tuberculosis, his recreation must be of a nature not to adversely affect his sickness. Or if a sister has heart trouble, she may need some light recreation to help relieve her fatigue yet not affect her heart.

I hope we may see that our whole body belongs to the Lord. If we refresh ourselves, it is for the Lord, and if we do not, it is also for the Lord. Nothing is for ourselves. When we have recreation, let us do it for the Lord's sake. When we do not have it, let it also be for His sake. Whether we have or have not, the principle is to not hurt the body. If the presence or absence of recreation hurts our body it is a loss. Not only is it wrong for us to destroy our body with improper things; also it is wrong to destroy our body with proper tasks. The body of a child of God does not belong to him. Hence, in considering recreation, always consider whether or not it would be good for the body. If good, do it; if not, refrain from it. The question should not be decided on the basis of likes or dislikes. If a sister with heart trouble is attracted by the ball game the brothers outside are playing, and joins in with them, she may suffer the consequences of it. It is not wrong for the brothers to play, but for that sister to play is wrong. May all the children of God see that everything we do is for serving God. If we engage in some recreation, our purpose is to serve God better.

6. NOT A STUMBLING BLOCK

As Christians, we must be examples in all things. Even in the matter of recreation, we must not be a stumbling block to others. We live for our brethren as well as for the Lord; we do not live for ourselves. As Christians we are highly influential. We must therefore be concerned not only for ourselves, but also for others. God asks Christians to be as contagious as the plague. We cannot murmur and say, "Why do people look to us?" Whom else can they look to if not to us? Of course they will look at us. Who can fail to see the city that is built on the hill? Who will not see the light on the mountain? No matter how we ourselves feel, we must consider how the younger brothers and sisters will be affected by us. Will we stumble them in the things that we do? We are God's children; we have believed in the Lord. Hereafter we must cultivate a delicate sensitivity. We are responsible not only to God but also to our many brothers and sisters.

7. NOT CONSIDERED IMPROPER

Whatever recreation unbelievers judge improper, we Christians should not take up. Even certain kinds of recreation which they do approve, we still may not take up. These are the two rules about recreation in relation to unbelievers. What they disapprove, we certainly do not allow. And even what they approve we may not accept. To frequent theatres, to dance, to gamble—we do not approve.

Speech

Scripture to Memorize:
Set a watch, O Jehovah, before my mouth; keep the door of my lips.

Psalm 141.3

Speech Comes Out of the Heart

"Out of the abundance of the heart the mouth speaketh" (Matt. 12.34b), the Lord Jesus said. Man's speech represents his heart; it reveals what is there. One's actions do not always declare the person, but his word often does. Actions may be so careful as to mislead people, but speech is not so easily guarded as to be under perfect control. Thus speech reveals more clearly what is in the mind of a person. Out of the abundance of the heart, out of what is stored within, the mouth speaks. If a lie or deception is expressed by the mouth, it must be also in the heart. When a person is silent, it is difficult to know his heart. But once he opens his mouth, his heart is unveiled. Before he speaks, no one can fathom his spirit. When he speaks, though, others may touch his spirit and discern his condition before God.

Having trusted in the Lord, we must learn afresh how to live and how to speak. Old things and old ways are passed away. Today we start anew.

How to Speak

There are a few passages in the Bible which teach us how to speak. Let us look at them one by one.

237

1. WITHOUT LIES

"Ye are of your father the devil, and the lusts of your father it is your will to do. He was a murderer from the beginning, and standeth not in the truth, because there is no truth in him. When he speaketh a lie, he speaketh of his own: for he is a liar, and the father thereof" (John 8.44).

SATAN THE FATHER OF LIARS

When Satan speaks a lie, he speaks from himself, for he is a liar. But today he is more than a liar; he is the father of all liars. How prevalent lies are in this world. There are as many liars as there are subjects of Satan. They lie for him because he needs the lie to establish his kingdom and to upset God's work. Everyone who belongs to Satan knows how to lie and how to do a lying work.

As soon as one is saved, he must learn the basic lesson of dealing with his words. He must learn to resist all lies, whether spoken knowingly or unknowingly, and he must refrain from uttering inaccurate words, words that are either less or more than the truth. Lies of all kinds must be removed from the midst of God's children. If any trace remains, Satan has some ground to attack.

Therefore, learn to speak as before God. Speak accurately. Avoid all lies. Do not speak according to your own preference or opinion. Resist all lies absolutely. Speaking should be objective, not subjective, in nature. It should be according to fact or truth.

2. WITHOUT IDLE WORDS

"The good man out of his good treasure bringeth forth good things: and the evil man out of his evil treasure bringeth forth evil things. And I say unto you, that every idle word that men shall speak, they shall give account thereof in the day of judgment. For by thy words thou shalt be justified, and by thy words thou shalt be condemned" (Matt. 12.35-37).

Verses 35-37 should be connected with verse 33 which says: "Either make the tree good, and its fruit good; or make the tree corrupt, and its fruit corrupt: for the tree is known by its fruit." We can readily see that the fruit here refers to words rather than to conduct. If a man is good, his words assuredly will be good; if he is evil, then his words no doubt will be evil also. By listening to his words, you may know what sort of person he is. Should he sow seeds of contention from morning to night, criticizing people, speaking slanderously and destructively, and using dirty words, he is definitely a corrupt tree.

It will not help for a brother or a sister who continually speaks evil, critical, sinful words to try to correct his or her statements. Rather, he or she should be bluntly told that to gossip at all is profane. New believers need to know that their words are their fruits.

One whose heart is holy will speak purely. One whose heart is full of love will not utter words of hate. By its fruit the tree is known.

3. WITHOUT EVIL WORDS

"Not rendering evil for evil, or reviling for reviling; but contrariwise blessing; for hereunto were ye called, that ye should inherit a blessing. For, he that would love life, and see good days, let him refrain his tongue from evil, and his lips that they speak no guile: And let him turn away from evil, and do good; let him seek peace, and pursue it. For the eyes of the Lord are upon the righteous, and his ears unto their supplication: but the face of the Lord is upon them that do evil" (1 Pet. 3.9-12).

One kind of word which should never come from a Christian's mouth is evil words. Evil words are words of reviling, words of cursing. A child of God cannot return evil for evil, or insult for insult.

THE MARK OF SELF-CONTROL

"In many things we all stumble. If any stumbleth not in word, the same is a perfect man, able to bridle the whole body also" (James 3.2). Whether or not one can bridle himself hinges on whether he is able to bridle his words. To judge if he has the fruit of the Spirit in self-control, one only needs to observe how he controls his words. Do you know what self-control is? Oftentimes brothers and sisters have a wrong concept about the matter. They think that self-control as the fruit of the Holy Spirit means moderation, the middle way. No, self-control here means nothing but control over self, bridling oneself.

In other words, to be able to control oneself is the fruit of the Holy Spirit. What is the mark of this fruit of the Holy Spirit by which it can be recognized? James tells us that if a man is able to bridle his tongue he can bridle his whole body. Such a man has self-control. A loose tongue betrays a loose life. He who speaks thoughtlessly leads a careless life. Too much speaking dissipates a person. May young believers start to learn to bridle their words.

Do you wish that God in His mercy would deal with you? Let me tell you: if He is able to deal with your words, then He has found the way to deal with you. For many people, their words are the center of their being. Their words serve as their backbone. Discipline the words and the person is disciplined. If the matter of one's words resists breaking, the person remains unchanged. In order to determine whether one can control himself, do not look at his outward appearance (for that may be deceiving); just talk with him for half an hour or so. Then you will know. As soon as one talks, he is known. Nothing reveals a person more than his words.

How to Listen

In considering the matter of speech, we must pay attention to listening as well as to speaking.

1. RESIST AN ITCHING EAR

May I be frank with you? If brothers and sisters knew how to listen, the church would be rid of many improper words. The reason there are so many inappropriate words in the church is because so many want to hear them. Since there is such a desire, there is such a source of supply. Why should men have so much destructive criticism, wicked slandering, double-talk, unclean words, lies, and words of contention? It is because so many are willing to listen. How treacherous and crooked and defiled is the human heart that itches to hear such unedifying words.

If God's children knew what kind of words to speak and what kind not to, they would quite naturally know what to listen to and what not to listen to. What you listen to betrays you; it reveals what kind of person you are.

2. TURN A DEAF EAR

"But I, as a deaf man, hear not; and I am as a dumb man that openeth not his mouth. Yea, I am as a man that heareth not, and in whose mouth are no reproofs" (Ps. 38.13-14). When people talk improperly, be as a deaf man who does not hear. Let them say what they like, but do not listen. Or, instead of being as one deaf, you may testify to them, even reprove them, by saying, "Who do you think I am that you pour all that rubbish on me? I think a Christian should not say these things. They are not suitable for a believer." There is great blessing in learning to be deaf and dumb, for talking and listening are tremendous temptations. May young believers know how to overcome.

Clothing and Eating

Scripture to Memorize:

Whether therefore ye eat, or drink, or whatsoever ye do, do all to the glory of God.

1 Corinthians 10.31

We have before us the practical matter of a Christian's clothing and food.

Clothing

1. ITS MEANING

In order to find the meaning of clothing, we must trace it back to the beginning.

BEFORE THE FALL

Before the fall, probably Adam and Eve were clothed with light. They were innocent. Although they both were naked, they were not ashamed.

AFTER THE FALL

After sin came in, the first effect was the opening of Adam and Eve's eyes to their nakedness. Immediately they felt ashamed and sewed fig leaves to make themselves aprons. So the basic meaning of clothing is for covering. Clothes are used to cover nakedness. The aprons made of fig leaves could not have lasted long, for the leaves would soon dry and break into pieces. God therefore clothed Adam and Eve with the more enduring coats of skin. His purpose was to cover the body.

We should tell new believers that the meaning of clothing is for covering, not for exposure! Any dress which is not for covering is questionable; any purpose other than to cover is also wrong. *Clothing is for covering.*

REPRESENTATIVE MEANING

God uses clothes to represent both the Lord Jesus himself and the redemption we obtain from Him. We are clothed with God's salvation, we are clothed with Christ, and we are clothed with the new man. We are clothed, so much clothed that our entire beings are covered; there are no holes.

Lead new believers to understand that when they put their clothes on, they should see beyond those clothes to Christ and His salvation. "Thank God," they may muse, "I was formerly as one naked, void of any covering before God, unable to escape God's light and His judgment; but today I am clothed with the salvation of God, with the new man." From the clothes which cover them completely, new believers can see how they are fully covered in God's sight. How wonderful that we are wholly covered before God.

The rule for clothing is to cover. If it does not cover, a Christian should not wear it. Clothes which expose rather than cover should not be used. They are against the principle of covering and therefore are unsuitable for Christians.

ASK GOD

New brothers and sisters who have never had any experience in this matter should take note. You may have some doubt about some of your clothes, whether or not you can wear them. Why not bring them to the Lord? He is our High Priest. Ask Him to show you whether you may wear them. Do not think such a matter is too small. For new believers, especially for sisters, clothes are a big problem.

2. MEN'S AND WOMEN'S CLOTHING

"A woman shall not wear that which pertaineth unto a man, neither shall a man put on a woman's garment; for whosoever doeth these things is an abomination unto Jehovah thy God" (Deut. 22.5). Thus the Bible forbids a man wearing a woman's garment or a woman a man's. The tendency today is to blur the distinction between men's and women's clothing until there is none. Hence, brothers and sisters must be careful not to wear clothing indiscriminately. We must maintain God's appointed distinction—man wears man's clothing and woman wears woman's dress. Any attempt to confuse this distinction is dishonoring to the Lord. The children of God ought to learn how to dress before God; they should keep the distinction between man and woman in clothing.

3. THE SISTER'S PROBLEM

Ordinarily brothers have less of a problem with clothing than sisters have.

"In like manner, that women adorn themselves in modest apparel, with shamefastness and sobriety [modestly and with discretion]; not with braided hair, and gold or pearls or costly raiment; but [which becometh women professing godliness] through good works. Let a woman learn in quietness with all subjection" (1 Tim. 2.9-11).

God has a basic requirement for the sisters, and that is, they should possess the sense of modesty or shamefacedness. It is good for sisters to feel ashamed, for it is their natural protection. Do not wear what is against your sense of modesty. "Sobriety" is the opposite of looseness. Be sober in the way you dress; do not wear indecent clothes. We may not know exactly what "modest apparel" or "proper clothing" is, but every sister knows what will be considered modest in the area where she lives. A Christian must not be so dressed as to be thought inappropriate by the unbelievers. Our standard should not be lower than the unbelievers. We need to learn what shamefacedness is, how to be sober, and what modest dress is.

Eating

Let us now turn to eating.

The need for food existed before the fall of man. So, in Genesis 2, God gave food to man. (Clothing, however, did not become a need until Genesis 3.) Before man sinned, God already gave all kinds of fruit for man's food. God ordained that man should eat fruit.

1. THE NEED

After man sinned in Genesis 3, God gave him the herb of the field to eat, but it was only in the sweat of his face that he would eat bread. Though nothing was explicitly said about food in Genesis 4, yet the seal of God was upon Abel, not on Cain. Cain was a farmer, while Abel was a shepherd. God's seal was on Abel, because God accepted his offering. Cain offered the produce of his field to God, but he was not accepted. We do not know what God might be implying in Genesis 4, but when we come to Genesis 9 we see that God clearly gave the animals to man for food, even as formerly He had given him the fruits of the trees.

LIFE FROM DEATH

Why does God give the flesh of the beast of the earth to man for food? Because man obviously is in need of such food. The kind of food man needed before and after he sinned was not the same. Food is that which maintains life. Without eating, man cannot live. Without food he cannot

246

continue on the earth. For the sake of keeping man alive, God has ordained that man should eat the flesh of animals as well as the herbs of the field and fruits. In other words, God is showing that since sin has entered into the world, the losing of life is required to preserve life. The animals must lose their life in order to maintain our life. Before sin entered into the world life could be sustained without the shedding of blood. Hence there is a difference in the food provision for man before and after sin. Christians today, living after sin entered, should not be vegetarians; they should eat meat.

2. BLOOD FORBIDDEN

There *is* one thing a Christian should not eat, and that is, blood.

From the Old Testament to the New Testament, the teaching against eating blood is consistent. In Genesis 9 God spoke to Noah saying, "the blood thereof, shall ye not eat" (v. 4). Eating blood is forbidden by God.

In Leviticus 17.10-16 God reiterated many times, "Ye shall eat the blood of no manner of flesh; for the life of all flesh is the blood thereof: whosoever eateth it shall be cut off" (v. 14). God will not recognize as being part of His own people that soul who eats blood.

In the New Testament, at the first council in Jerusalem (Acts 15), the church was faced with a great difficulty concerning the law. James, Peter, Paul, Barnabas and other servants of God decided together that God's children should not be burdened with keeping the law; only they should abstain from things sacrificed to idols, and from blood, and from things strangled, and from fornication.

Thus the importance of the blood is evident. At the time of the patriarchs, God forbade the eating of blood through Noah; under the law, He forbade the same through Moses;

in the dispensation of grace, He forbade again through the apostles. In all three dispensations, God said no.

3. SOME PERSONAL OBSERVATIONS

Finally, I would like to express some of my opinions.

FOOD FOR NOURISHMENT

Ordinarily the principle of eating is the nourishment of the physical body. Therefore, eat what is nourishing and do not eat what does not nourish. Never make the belly your god; do not be too much occupied with food. We as God's children should know that eating is for the sake of nourishing the body and preserving physical life.

CONTENTMENT AND GOD'S ADDITION

God's children should remember that "having food and covering we shall be therewith content" (1 Tim. 6.8). "Behold the birds of the heaven, that they sow not, neither do they reap, nor gather into barns; and your heavenly Father feedeth them" (Matt. 6.26). "Consider the lilies of the field, how they grow; they toil not, neither do they spin: yet I say unto you, that even Solomon in all his glory was not arrayed like one of these" (Matt. 6.28). Verse 26 is in reference to eating, but verse 28 to clothing. All is in God's hand. "Seek ye first his kingdom, and his righteousness; and all these things shall be added unto you" (Matt. 6.33; see the whole passage of Matt. 6.25-33). I like the word "added." What does it mean? Let me ask this question, How much is three added to zero? You would remonstrate with me saying, "Three cannot be added to zero for no amount can be added to zero. This is an impossible question; there is no need to add three to zero." What, then, can be added? You can add to something already there, such as add three to one. Seek the kingdom of God and His righteousness, and all these things shall be added to you. To those who possess God's kingdom and His righteousness, He will add food and clothing. May all brothers and sisters remember well that God's kingdom and His righteousness is what we seek. All who have gained the kingdom of God are those who live in the righteousness of God. To them shall these things be added.

May God's children know how to maintain their testimony among men in these two respects of clothing and eating.

Asceticism

Scripture to Memorize:

Set your mind on the things that are above, not on the things that are upon the earth. For ye died, and your life is hid with Christ in God.

Colossians 3.2-3

Asceticism Not Found in Christianity

After one believes in the Lord, he may unconsciously carry asceticism into the church. In the past, though he might not have practiced it, he admired the ascetics. At the same time that he respected the ascetic, though, the unbeliever usually was also materialistic. So it is very easy for him to carry his admiration for asceticism into Christianity along with the thought that now he will really practice asceticism.

1. DESPISES MATERIAL THINGS AND SUPPRESSES PASSIONS

What is really meant by asceticism? To many people asceticism means the prohibition of material things. The less material things they use, the better they are. This is because they fear that these external things will fill their passions and lusts. The ascetic person acknowledges that within man there are lusts and passions. He realizes that from the lust for food to the lust for sex, all sorts of lusts are inherent in man. Each lust is shared and indulged in by the people of the world. If anyone desires to be a holy man, he must conquer these lusts and passions. Therefore, asceticism is outwardly despising material things and inwardly suppressing lusts and passions.

2. NOT ADVOCATED BY CHRISTIANITY

New believers need to be shown that Christianity never advocates asceticism. How superficial Christianity would be if this were what it stood for.

We hope that by studying a little more of the Bible, we may see what asceticism really is; nothing more than an attempt to suppress oneself in food and drink, in lusts and passions, and in other material things. This is not Christianity, nor is it the ideal Christian life. As a matter of fact, the Bible never endorses asceticism.

Dead to the Philosophy of the World

"If ye died with Christ from the rudiments of the world, why, as though living in the world, do ye subject yourselves to ordinances, Handle not, nor taste, nor touch (all which things are to perish with the using), after the precepts and doctrines of men? Which things have indeed a show of wisdom in will-worship, and humility, and severity to the body; but are not of any value against the indulgence of the flesh" (Col. 2.20-23). "Rudiments" in verse 20 should be translated as "philosophy."

1. CO-DEATH WITH CHRIST

When Paul writes to the believers at Colosse "if ye died with Christ," he takes this as a fundamental Christian fact. We who are Christians have died with Christ. The whole New Testament shows us that every Christian has died with Christ. Romans 6 informs us that "our old man was crucified with him" (v. 6). Galatians 2 states categorically that "I have been crucified with Christ" (v. 20). In the same letter, it affirms that "they that are of Christ Jesus have crucified the flesh with the passions and the lusts thereof" (5.24). The Bible teaches that we Christians were crucified with Christ. In other words, the cross of Calvary is the

Christian's cross; the cross of Christ is the Christian's cross. The starting point for a Christian is the cross, not just the cross of Christ but one's own cross too. As we receive the cross of Christ, His cross becomes our cross. He who has not accepted the fact of the cross is not a Christian. To him who has become a Christian, the cross of Christ has also become a fact — that is, he has died in Christ.

2. NOT THE PHILOSOPHY OF THE WORLD

"If ye have died with Christ from the rudiments [philosophy] of the world." No one in the grave can be a philosopher. If anyone desires to talk philosophy, he must do so while he is living. For us, however, philosophy is already dead on the cross. This matter has already been fully resolved, for the philosophy of the world postulates that holiness may be attained by abandoning material things and suppressing one's inner lusts and passions. Paul, however, says that if you have died with Christ from the philosophy of the world, you are no longer involved with such philosophical jargon.

3. NOT AS LIVING IN THE WORLD

"If ye have died with Christ from the philosophy of the world," Paul asks, "why [do you act] as though living in the world?" If death is a fact, you cannot live like the people of the world. The basic position of a Christian is death.

Ask a new believer why he was baptized if it were not that he is dead. Man must be dead before he is buried; otherwise he would be buried alive. A person is baptized because he has been crucified with Christ; therefore he is buried. Co-death is already a fact, but burial is something yet to be done. The Lord has already included the new believer in His death; now, as declared in the burial of baptism, the believer sees that he is dead. Knowing now of his death, he asks to be buried. So, having believed and been baptized, having died and been buried, how can he again be as though living in the world?

Through Paul, we can see that those who practice asceticism are still living in the world. Hence Paul says, "Why, as though living in the world, do ye subject yourselves to ordinances, Handle not, nor taste, nor touch?" According to ascetic teaching, there are things which should not be tasted or eaten, handled or even touched. Such ordinances originate from the fear of man's inward passions and lusts. At the time Paul wrote, asceticism was flourishing in Colosse. Many ordinances were practiced by the Colossians. Lest their lusts be stirred, they prohibited the use of all things which might incite the passions. There were some things they were not to handle, others they were not to touch, others they could not taste, and others they could not hear. By these strict ordinances, they hoped to keep material things separated from passions and lusts. The philosophical concept of those days was that by such separation lust was controlled.

Paul, however, remonstrates that to be subject to such ordinances is to not believe in the fact of having been crucified with Christ. If you believe you have died, should there, then, be such prohibitions? Only a person who is alive can practice the ordinances of handle not, touch not, and taste not. Asceticism has its claim only on the living, not on the dead.

Remember, all who are of Christ Jesus have crucified the flesh with its passions and lusts. If you bind yourself by the human concept of fleeing from matter and lust, you are not standing on Christian ground; you have not taken the ground of death. No one can be a Christian without death, without having died with Christ. Make no mistake on this point.

4. NOT THE PRECEPTS AND DOCTRINES OF MEN

"After the precepts and doctrines of men." All these ordinances, all these ascetic requirements, only follow the precepts of men. They are a product of the human mind. They are of man and are not related to Christ and His church. People may say, I should not eat this, I should not touch that. But let us remember, these are man's commandments, man's teachings. They are not God's.

Paul's conclusion, when he categorically states that these are the commandments and teachings of men, is serious. His conclusion is that man's ideal of life, being built on human concepts and ordinances, is totally unrelated to God. Surprisingly, the world relishes asceticism. It seems noble for one not to eat and drink what ordinary people do. Such a one must be pure to be so free of the material things which entangle others. Take note that asceticism is natural religion, not revealed Christianity. Natural religion follows the precepts and doctrines of men wherein there is neither light nor revelation, only the human reaction against passion and lust. Indeed, asceticism shows how deeply man knows that his passions and lusts are defiling.

5. ASCETICISM IS UNWORKABLE

How does Paul judge the effectiveness of asceticism? "All which things are to perish with the using." Asceticism is pleasant to listen to, and it sounds well as a philosophy to talk about. But if you try to use it, it is like a car which looks fine in the garage but always stalls on the street. Or it may be likened to a dress which looks beautiful in the closet but is found to be full of holes when put on the body. If you try asceticism, you will see it is unable to help you get rid of your evil lusts and passions.

6. SEEK THE THINGS ABOVE

"If then ye were raised together with Christ, seek the things that are above, where Christ is, seated on the right hand of God. Set your mind on the things that are above, not on the things that are upon the earth. For ye died, and your life is hid with Christ in God" (Col. 3.1-3). Paul begins with the cross and concludes with resurrection. He says that since we are a heavenly people, we should not mind the things that are upon the earth. If we stress these things (touch not, taste not, handle not), we are yet thinking of earthly things. But we are resurrected, and as resurrected people we should seek the things that arc above. By minding heavenly things, these earthly problems will automatically be solved. Let us, then, as Christians, think of the heavenly things; let us not think of such things as taste not, touch not, and handle not.

7. TRANSCENDENCE, NOT ABSTINENCE

The word of Paul in 1 Corinthians 7 is very special: "But this I say, brethren, the time is shortened, that henceforth both those that have wives may be as though they had none; and those that weep, as though they wept not; and those that rejoice, as though they rejoiced not; and those that buy, as though they possessed not; and those that use the world, as not using it to the full: for the fashion of this world passeth away" (vv. 29-31). Such is a Christian. Since the Lord who dwells in him is so great, outside things no longer matter. For people to suppress these things or abstain from them merely proves how powerful these things are. Even those who most practice asceticism are sometimes the most filled with lusts and passions. Only he who is full of Christ is free from the problem of lust. He who has a wife may be as though he had none; he who has not a wife does not seek for one. He who weeps may be as though he wept not; he who rejoices, as though he rejoiced not. He may purchase things but is as though not possessing; use, but as not using the world to the full. The Christian transcends everything. His life is not abstinence but transcendence.

BOOK SIX:
Love One Another

Sickness

Scripture to Memorize:

Himself took our infirmities, and bare our diseases.

Matthew 8.17b

1. THE RELATION BETWEEN SICKNESS AND SIN

Before the fall of mankind no infirmity of any kind existed; sickness arose only after man had sinned. One can say generally that both sickness and death resulted from sin; for by one man's trespass sin and death came into the world (see Rom. 5.12). Sickness spread to all men just as did death. Though not all sin in the same way as Adam did, yet because of his transgression, all die. Where there is sin there is also death. In between these two is what we usually call sickness. This, then, is the factor common to all disease. However, there is actually more than one cause to account for sickness coming upon people. Some sicknesses spring from sin, while others do not. So far as mankind is concerned, sickness does come from sin; but in relation to the individual it may or may not be the case. We need to distinguish between these two applications of sickness. Now it is entirely true that were there no sin there could neither be death nor sickness; for if there were no death in the world, how could there ever be sickness? Death arises through sin, and sickness through the inception of death. Even so, this cannot be specifically and indiscriminately applied to every individual, because while many do fall ill through sin there are others who become ill for reasons other than sin. In this matter of the relationship of sin to sickness we must therefore make a careful distinction between the application of this relationship to mankind as a whole and its application to individual men.

We will recall in such Old Testament books as Leviticus and Numbers that God's promise was, that if the people of Israel obeyed Him, walked in His way, rebelled not against His laws and did not sin against Him, then He would keep them from many diseases. These words plainly teach that many maladies derive from sin or rebellion against God. Yet in the New Testament we discover that some sicknesses are not caused by the person having committed any transgression at all.

The Scriptures have served sufficient notice that many (but not all) are ill because of sin. Hence the first action we must take when sick is to examine ourselves to determine whether or not we have sinned against God. By searching, many find that their illness is in fact due to sin: on a particular occasion they had rebelled against God or had disobeyed His word. They had gone astray. Just as soon as that particular sin is found out and confessed, however, the sickness will be over. Countless brothers and sisters in the Lord have encountered such experiences. Shortly after the cause is discovered before God the illness is gone. This is a phenomenon beyond the explanation of medical science.

Sickness does not necessarily issue from sin, yet much of it actually does. We acknowledge that many diseases have their natural causes, but we equally maintain that we cannot attribute all sickness to natural reasons.

2. THE LORD'S WORK AND SICKNESS

"Surely he hath borne our griefs, and carried our sorrows; yet we did esteem him stricken, smitten of God, and afflicted. But he was wounded for our transgressions, he was bruised for our iniquities" (Is. 53.4-5). Of all the Old Testament writings this 53rd chapter of Isaiah is quoted most often in the New Testament. It alludes to the

Lord Jesus Christ, especially to Him as our Savior. Verse 4 affirms that "he hath borne our griefs, and carried our sorrows" whereas Matthew 8.17 declares "that it might be fulfilled which was spoken through Isaiah the prophet, saying, Himself took our infirmities, and bare our diseases." The Holy Spirit indicates here that the Lord Jesus came to the world to take our infirmities and bear our diseases. Prior to His crucifixion He had already taken our infirmities and borne our diseases; which is to say that during His earthly ministry the Lord Jesus made healing His burden and task. He not only preached, He also healed.

There is a basic dissimilarity, however, between God's treatment of our iniquity and His treatment of our disease. Why this difference? Our Lord Jesus bore our sins in His body on the cross. Does any sin remain unforgiven? Absolutely none, for the work of God is so complete that sin is entirely destroyed. But in taking our infirmities and bearing our diseases while He lived on earth, the Lord Jesus did not eradicate all diseases and all infirmities. For note that Paul never says "when I sin, then am I sanctified," but he does declare that "when I am weak, then am I strong" (2 Cor. 12.10). Hence sin is thoroughly and unlimitedly dealt with whereas sickness is only limitedly treated.

In God's redemption the handling of sickness is unlike that of sin. With the latter, its destruction is totally uncircumscribed; with the former, this is just not so. Timothy, for instance, continued to have a weak stomach. The Lord permitted this weakness to remain with His servant. So in God's salvation sickness has not been eradicated as totally as has sin. Some maintain that the Lord Jesus deals solely with sin and not with illness too: others conceive the scope of His treatment of disease to be as broad and inclusive as His treatment of sin. Yet the Scriptures manifestly indicate to us that the Lord Jesus deals with both sin and sickness; only His dealing with sin is limitless while that with sickness is limited. We must behold the Lamb of God taking away *all* the sin of the world—He has borne the sin of each and every person. Sin's problem is therefore already solved. But meanwhile sickness still pervades God's children.

Nonetheless, we contend that since the Lord Jesus has actually borne our diseases there should not be so much sickness as there is among the children of God. While Jesus was on earth he unmistakably devoted Himself to the healing of the sick. He included healing in His work. Isaiah 53.4 is fulfilled in Matthew 8, not in Matthew 27. It is realized before Calvary. Had it been realized on the cross, healing would be unbounded. But no, the Lord Jesus bore our diseases prior to crucifixion, with the result that this aspect of His work is not as unlimited as was His bearing of our sins.

3. THE BELIEVER'S ATTITUDE TOWARD SICKNESS

Every time the believer falls ill the first thing he should do is to inquire after its cause before the Lord. He should not be overanxious in seeking healing. Paul sets a good example in showing us how he was most clear about his weakness. We must examine whether we have disobeyed the Lord, have sinned anywhere, owe anybody a debt, have violated some natural law, or have neglected some special duty. We ought to know that frequently our violation of natural law can constitute a sin against God, for God sets up these natural laws by which to govern the universe. Many are afraid to die; upon becoming sick they hurriedly seek out physicians, for they are anxious to be cured. Such ought not to be the Christian's attitude. He should first attempt to isolate the cause for his malady. Alas, how many brothers and sisters do not possess any patience. The moment they fall sick they search for a remedy.

Learn to accept whatever lesson sickness may bring to you. For if you have dealings with God many of your problems will be resolved quickly. You will find out that often your illness is due to some sin or fault of yours. Upon confessing your sin and asking for forgiveness, you may expect healing from God. Or, should you have walked further with the Lord, you may discern that involved in this is the enemy's attack. Or the matter of God's discipline may be associated with your unhealthy state. God chastises with sickness so as to render you holier, softer or more yielding. As you deal with these problems before God you will be enabled to see the exact reason for your infirmity. Sometimes God may allow you to receive a little natural or medical help, but sometimes He may heal you instantaneously without such assistance.

We should see that healing is in God's hand. Learn to trust Him Who heals. In the Old Testament God has a special name which is, "I am Jehovah that healeth thee" (Ex. 15.26). Look to Him and He will be gracious to His own in this particular regard.

4. GOD'S CHASTENING AND SICKNESS

An amazing fact is found in the Bible: that it is relatively easy for a "heathen" to be healed, but healing for a Christian is not so easy. The New Testament overwhelmingly shows us that whenever an unbeliever seeks the Lord he is cured immediately. Now the gift of healing is for the brethren as well as for the unbelievers. Yet the Bible tells of some believers who are not healed; among them are Trophimus, Timothy and Paul. And these are the best of the brethren. Paul left Trophimus ill at Miletus (see 2 Tim. 4.20). He exhorted Timothy to use a little wine for the sake of his stomach and his frequent ailments (see 1 Tim. 5.23). Paul himself experienced a thorn in his flesh from which he suffered much and was reduced to great weakness (see 2 Cor. 12.7). Whatever the nature of that thorn, be it eye trouble or some other disease, it pricked his flesh. One feels great discomfort should a little finger be pricked by a thorn. Paul's, however, was a big thorn, not a tiny one. It gave him such discomfort that he could only describe his physical condition as weakness. These three are brethren *par excellence*, yet none was healed. They had to endure sickness.

It is quite evident that sickness is different from sin in its outworking. Sin does not produce any fruit of holiness, but sickness does. The more a person sins the more corrupt he becomes; sickness, though, bears the fruit of holiness because the chastening hand of God is upon the sick. Under such circumstances it behooves a child of God to learn how to submit himself under the mighty hand of God.

If one is ill he ought to deal with every cause of his illness before the Lord. If, after all has been dealt with, the hand of God still remains upon him, then he should understand that this illness is for the purpose of restraining him from being proud or loose or for some other purpose. He should accept it and learn its lesson. To be sick is valueless if the lesson is not learned. Sickness itself does not make a man holy, but its lesson if accepted produces holiness. Some grow worse spiritually during illness; they become more self-centered. That is why one must discover the lesson in such a period. What profit or fruit can be derived from it? Is the hand of God upon me to keep me humble as He did with Paul, "to keep me from being too elated by the abundance of revelations" (2 Cor. 12.7 RSV)? Or is it because God desires to weaken my stubborn individuality? What is the use of sickness if it does not provoke me to learn the lesson of weakness? Many are sick in vain because they never accept the Lord's dealing with their particular problems.

It is always well for us to bear in mind that all sickness is in God's hand. It has been both measured and circumscribed by Him. After Job had fulfilled the course of his trial his sickness was over, for it had accomplished its purpose in him—"Ye have heard of the patience of Job, and have seen the end [purpose] of the Lord, how that the Lord is full of pity, and merciful" (James 5.11). What a shame that so many are ill without realizing its purpose or learning its lesson. All infirmities are in the Lord's hand and are measured out to us that we may learn our lessons. The sooner we learn them the quicker these infirmities pass away.

Lastly, I wish you to see before the Lord that sometimes Satan may launch a sudden attack or sometimes you unwittingly may violate some natural law. Even so, you still can bring it to the Lord. If it is the enemy's assault, rebuke it in the name of the Lord. Once a sister had a protracted fever. After discovering that it was a satanic attack, she rebuked it in the Lord's name and the fever left her. If you violate a natural law by putting your hand in the fire, you surely shall be burnt. Take good care of yourself. Do not wait until you are sick before you confess your negligence. It is important to take care of your body during the ordinary days.

Governmental Forgiveness

Scripture to Memorize:

Humble yourselves therefore under the mighty hand of God, that he may exalt you in due time.

1 Peter 5.6

There are four kinds of forgiveness in the Bible. For convenience' sake, we shall give each a name: first, eternal forgiveness; second, borrowed forgiveness; third, communional forgiveness; and fourth, governmental forgiveness. In order to walk uprightly, we need to learn what God's governmental forgiveness is. Before we touch on this, however, let us first differentiate the four kinds of forgiveness.

Eternal Forgiveness

We call the forgiveness we receive at the time we are saved eternal forgiveness. This is the forgiveness of which the Lord Jesus spoke when He said, "Repentance and remission of sins should be preached in his name unto all the nations, beginning from Jerusalem" (Lk. 24.47). This is also what Romans 4.7 refers to: "Blessed are they whose iniquities are forgiven, and whose sins are covered."

We call this kind of forgiveness eternal forgiveness because once God forgives our sins, He forgives them forever. He casts our sins into the sea, into the depths of the sea, so that He no longer sees nor remembers them. Such is the forgiveness we receive at the time of salvation. For us who believe in the Lord Jesus, He forgives all our sins and takes away all our iniquities so that before God none are left. This is eternal forgiveness.

Borrowed Forgiveness

Many times God himself says, "I forgive you!" Sometimes, though, He declares His forgiveness through the church: "God has forgiven your sins!" This kind of forgiveness we term borrowed forgiveness: "...he breathed on them, and saith unto them, Receive ye the Holy Spirit: whose soever sins ye forgive, they are forgiven unto them; whose soever sins ye retain, they are retained" (John 20.22-23). Here the Lord gives His Holy Spirit to the church so that she may represent Him on earth and be His vessel to forgive people's sins. Though we call this borrowed forgiveness, we need to exercise extreme care lest we fall into the error of the Roman Catholic Church. Notice what the Lord said. The forgiveness here is based on the Lord's breathing upon the church, saying, "Receive ye the Holy Spirit." The consequence of receiving the Holy Spirit is that the church knows whose sins are retained and whose are forgiven. Thus the church may declare whose sins are retained and whose sins are forgiven. Remember this: the church has such authority only because she herself is under the authority of the Holy Spirit. "Whose soever sins ye forgive, they are forgiven unto them; whose soever sins ye retain, they are retained"—these words come after "Receive ye the Holy Spirit." Borrowed forgiveness is God forgiving people's sins through the channel of the church.

Sometimes we meet a sinner who feels guilty after hearing the gospel. We bring him to God and he confesses that he is a sinner. He asks God to forgive his sins. He cries, he sheds tears, he repents and honestly receives the Lord Jesus. But, being a heathen, he knows nothing of the truth of salvation. If, at this moment, there is someone who can represent the church and declare to him, "God has forgiven your sins!", this would be an excellent thing to do, for it would spare him much sorrow and many doubts.

Whenever you see a person who has truly believed, you can tell him, "Today you have received the Lord; now you may thank God, for He has already forgiven your sins."

Communional Forgiveness

What is communional forgiveness? "If we walk in the light, as he is in the light, we have fellowship one with another, and the blood of Jesus his Son cleanseth us from all sin. If we say that we have no sin, we deceive ourselves, and the truth is not in us. If we confess our sins, he is faithful and righteous to forgive us our sins, and to cleanse us from all unrighteousness" (1 John 1.7-9). "My little children, these things write I unto you that ye may not sin. And if any man sin, we have an Advocate with the Father, Jesus Christ the righteous: and he is the propitiation for our sins; and not for ours only, but also for the whole world" (2.1-2). The forgiveness mentioned here is neither that which we received at the time of salvation nor that which the church extends to us. After we believe in the Lord and become God's children, we still may have need of God's forgiveness. Though we have received eternal forgiveness, we may weaken and once again sin before the Lord, thus interrupting our fellowship with God. So, once again we need forgiveness.

Governmental Forgiveness

There is still another kind of forgiveness which we call governmental forgiveness. This kind of forgiveness is seen in the following Bible passages: Matt. 9.2, 5-6; James 5.15 and Matt. 6.14-15, 18. 21-35.

What is God's governmental forgiveness? I am convinced that if I had known the government of God immediately following my salvation, I would have been spared many troubles and problems.

1. THE MEANING OF GOD'S GOVERNMENTAL HAND

There are many passages in the Bible which are related to this. For instance, "Whatsoever a man soweth, that shall he also reap" (Gal. 6.7). This is God's governmental hand. Suppose a father is always lenient with his children. Naturally his children will be wild and undisciplined. How can the house be in order if the father never rules the house? If a man often quarrels with people, the natural consequence will be that he is without any friends. You see, whatsoever a man sows, that shall he also reap. This is God's government, His appointed hand, and it cannot be changed. Be very careful, children of God, lest you stir up God's governmental hand; for, once stirred, it is hard to be removed.

2. HUMBLE YOURSELF UNDER GOD'S MIGHTY HAND

Our God is the God of government. Sometimes when He is offended, He does not immediately move His governmental hand. He just lets you get by. But once He moves His governmental hand, there is nothing you can do except to humble yourself. There is no way for you to escape; He is not like man who will easily allow you to get away. To have your sin forgiven and your fellowship with God restored is quite easy. But you cannot remove the discipline God gives you in your environment—your home, your business, or your physical body. The only thing you can do is learn to subject yourself to the mighty hand of God. The humbler we are under His mighty hand and the less we resist, the easier it will be to have the governmental hand of God removed from us. If we are not submissive and patient, if we murmur and fret within, let me tell you, it will be harder for God's governmental hand to be removed. This is a most serious matter. Twenty years ago you did something according to your own idea. Today you meet the same thing again and you have yet to eat that fruit of your earlier action. That thing has come back and found you out. What should you do when this happens? You should bow your head, saying: "Lord, it is my fault!" You should humble yourself under God's hand and not resist. The more you resist, the heavier the hand of God. So I always say that you must subject yourself to the mighty hand of God. The more you resist God's governmental hand, the more things will happen to you.

As soon as the governmental hand of God is upon you, you must humble yourself and gladly acknowledge that you deserve it, for the Lord cannot be wrong. You should be in subjection. You must not think of rebelling; you must not even murmur or fret.

God's governmental hand is truly most serious. Let us be fearful, for we do not know when the disciplinary hand of God will come upon us. God may allow some to get by all the time. Or He may overlook rebellion ten times but on the eleventh time bring His hand down. Or His hand may come down the very first time. We have no way of knowing when His disciplinary hand will descend. God's government is not something we can control. Whatever He wishes, He does.

Because of this, brethren, we must first of all try our very best to learn to be obedient to the Lord. May God be merciful and gracious to you that you may not fall into the governmental hand of God. Howbeit, if you do fall into His governmental hand, do not resist or be rash. Do not attempt to run away, but hold on to the basic principle of subjection at any cost. You cannot naturally by yourself be submissive, but you can ask the Lord to make you so. Only by the mercy of the Lord can you get through. "O Lord, be merciful to me that I may get through!" If God's governmental hand has not fallen upon you, look persistently for His mercy. If it has already fallen, if He has allowed you to be sick or to have difficulties come upon you, remember well that you should never by your fleshly hand try to resist God's government. As soon as God's government falls on you, humble yourself at once under His mighty hand. You should say, "Lord, this is Your doing, this is Your arrangement; I gladly submit, I am willing to accept it." When God's governmental hand fell on Job, the more submissive Job was, the better his condition was; but the more he boasted of his own righteousness, the worse his situation became.

Thank God, frequently God's governmental hand does not stay forever on a person. I personally believe that when God's governmental hand does fall on a person, sometimes the prayer of the church may easily remove that hand. This is what is so precious in James 5.14-16 There James tells us that the elders of the church may remove the governmental hand of God. For he says that "the prayer of faith shall save him that is sick, and the Lord shall raise him up; and if he have committed sins, it shall be forgiven him." So, when a brother finds that this is the way for him, the church may pray for him and help to remove God's governmental hand from him.

The Discipline of God

Scripture to Memorize:

Whom the Lord loveth he chasteneth, and scourgeth every son whom he receiveth.

Hebrews 12.6

The Meaning of Discipline

"Ye have not yet resisted unto blood, striving against sin" (Heb. 12.4). The apostle told the Hebrews that, though in their striving against sin they had suffered much and met with many trials and persecutions, they had not yet resisted unto blood. In this respect they fell short of what our Lord endured: "Who [the Lord Jesus] for the joy that was set before him endured the cross, despising shame, and hath sat down at the right hand of the throne of God" (v. 2b). The experience of believers can never be compared to that of the Lord. Our Lord, though despising the shame, endured the sufferings of the cross even unto blood. The believer's endurance of shame and suffering stops short of shedding of blood.

What should a Christian expect his life to be like? We must not give an improper hope to the brethren. We should show them that they will encounter many things in the future, but that in none of these things will God's purpose and meaning be lacking. Why should they have to endure many trials? Why should they brush up against many problems? What are these trials and difficulties actually for? What is the meaning of Christian suffering? Unless we are called to martyrdom, our resisting and striving against

275

sin has not reached the point of shedding of blood. Nonetheless, we still resist.

Why should these things happen? "Ye have forgotten the exhortation which reasoneth with you as with sons, My son, regard not lightly the chastening of the Lord, nor faint when thou art reproved of him; for whom the Lord loveth he chasteneth, and scourgeth every son whom he receiveth" (vv. 5-6).

The apostle quotes from Proverbs, chapter 3. He says we must not despise the chastening of the Lord, nor should we faint under His reproof. Here he tells us there are two attitudes which believers need to maintain. When a person is in the process of passing through hardship, being under the chastening of the Lord, he may easily regard it lightly and let the chastisement of the Lord slip by. Or, when he is faced with the reproach of the Lord, the hand of the Lord being heavy upon him, he may faint, considering it too difficult to be a Christian. He expects to have a prosperous road in this life—to wear a white linen garment and walk leisurely on the golden street which leads to the pearly gate. He has never dreamed that to be a Christian means he will encounter so many troubles. Since he is not mentally prepared to be a Christian under such circumstances, he feels discouraged and thinks of quitting. But the book of Proverbs indicates that neither of these reactions is correct.

The Nature of Discipline

"Whom the Lord loveth he chasteneth, and scourgeth every son whom he receiveth" (v. 6). This is quoted from Proverbs 3.12. It shows us the "why" of all chastenings.

God does not deal with everyone in the world. He only chastens those whom He loves. He chastens us because we are His beloved. He wants to make us into a suitable vessel. That is why He spends time on His children to chasten them. Chastisement, then, is love's arrangement. Love arranges these happenings. Love measures what we should meet. Love plans the details of our environment. We call this discipline because it always aims at the highest good and the ultimate intention of creation.

"And scourgeth every son whom he receiveth." Those who are chastened of the Lord are those who are assuredly accepted by God. To be scourged is not a sign of rejection, but rather the evidence of God's special approval. God does not deal with everyone; He just concentrates on dealing with those whom He loves, those who are accepted as His sons.

What we receive is not punishment but discipline. Punishment serves the purpose of repaying the wrong, but discipline has an educational purpose. Punishment deals only with the past—one is scourged because he has done wrong. Discipline has an eye toward the future though it also deals with past faults. Discipline, therefore, has these two elements—an educational purpose and training for the future. As soon as one comes to Christ and belongs to the Lord, he should be prepared to let God mold him into a vessel of honor. I can say with confidence that God wants to make every child of His glorify Him in some certain respect. All Christians shall glorify Him, but it will be in a different area for each one. Some glorify Him in one way, and some in another way. He is to be glorified in all kinds of situations that He may get a perfect glory. Each person glorifies God with his particular portion—something in his character that the Lord has formed in him. This is the outcome of the disciplinary hand of God upon him. For this reason, it is absolutely impossible for a child of God not to have God's hand upon him.

The Contents of Discipline

Some may ask, what is the discipline of God? Verses 2 through 4 mention despising shame, enduring the suffering of the cross and striving against sin, while verses 5 and 6 talk about discipline and scourging. What is the connection between these two portions? What is this discipline and scourging? What is meant by shame, suffering, and striving? Simply take note that verse 7 gathers up verses 2 to 6 by showing us that what we endure is the discipline of God. Hence, suffering is God's discipline; enduring shame is God's discipline; striving against sin though not yet unto blood is also God's discipline.

How does God discipline us? Whatever God has led you through, whatever He has permitted you to endure— this is His discipline. Do not imagine that His discipline is something special. No, the discipline of God is found in what you endure every day—a hard word, a bad face, a sharp tongue, discourteous treatment, an unreasonable criticism, an unexpected happening, various kinds of disgrace, irresponsibility on the part of family members— all the many pains and difficulties you meet, large or small. Sometimes you have to endure sicknesses, deprivations, distresses, and difficulties. All these are the discipline of God; what you endure, says the apostle, is God's discipline.

"God dealeth with you as with sons; for what son is there whom his father chasteneth not?" (v. 7). All these chastenings come upon us because God treats us as His own sons. Do remember: discipline is God's favor, not His animosity. Many have the wrong idea that when they are disciplined they are being ill-treated by God. No, God treats us like sons. Is there any son whom a father does not discipline? In disciplining you, God is favoring you! Because you have become God's children, you are disciplined. He wants to bring you to the place of blessing and of glory.

Our Attitude toward Discipline

"Furthermore, we had the fathers of our flesh to chasten us, and we gave them reverence: shall we not much rather be in subjection unto the Father of spirits, and live?" (v. 9). The apostle shows us that if we reverence our fathers in the flesh when they discipline us, acknowledging that such discipline is right and, therefore, accepting it, how much more we should be in subjection to the Father of spirits and live.

In sonship, we find discipline; and in discipline, we find subjection. Because we are sons, we will be disciplined; since we are disciplined, we must be in subjection. Remember, whatever God arranges in our environment is for the purpose of instructing and directing us in the straight path.

We must obey God. We must obey these two things He gives: first, His command; and second, His chastening. On the one hand, we obey God's word, obey His command, and obey all the precepts given us in the Bible. On the other hand, we subject ourselves to all God's arrangements in our environment; we are in subjection to all the discipline of God. Though our obedience to God's word may be sufficient, we often may yet be lacking in subjection to God's discipline. Since He has so ordered that such a thing should happen to you, you ought to be benefited by it and learn the lesson. God wants you to be benefited and to walk in the straight path. We must, therefore, learn not only to obey the Lord's command but also to obey the Lord's discipline. Although it costs us to obey the Lord's discipline, it nonetheless enables us to walk straightforwardly before God.

The Purpose of Discipline

"They indeed for a few days chastened us as seemed good to them" (v. 10a). When parents discipline their children, they reveal much deficiency, for they chasten according to their own thoughts. Consequently, the profit from such discipline is only a little. "But he for our profit, that we may be partakers of his holiness" (v. 10b). The discipline of God neither issues from temper nor is it for punishment. All the discipline of God is educational; it is given for our profit. Scourging is not administered just for pain, but the pain is meant to produce some positive value. Pain has its purpose; it is not mere punishment for some fault. If one thinks in terms of punishment, it shows that his mind is yet under the bondage of law.

What is the profit? It is that we may be partakers of His holiness. This, indeed, is most glorious. Holiness is God's nature. We may say that holiness is God's character. It is for this reason that God uses all kinds of ways to chasten His children. From the very start of our Christian life, God chastens us with persistency. He has one purpose in mind, that is, He wants us to be partakers of His holy character.

The Fruit of Discipline

"All chastening seemeth for the present to be not joyous but grievous; yet afterward it yieldeth peaceable fruit unto them that have been exercised thereby, even the fruit of righteousness" (v. 11). The apostle draws our attention to the "afterward" as well as the "present." It is a fact that for the present all discipline is not joyous but grievous. When you are faced with God's discipline, there is nothing wrong with feeling sorrowful. You should feel pained. The Bible has not said that the cross is joyous; it states instead that the cross is suffering. The cross causes us to suffer. It is true that our Lord, for the joy which was set before Him, despised the shame, but the Bible never describes the cross as joyous. The cross is not joyous, but grievous. When you are under discipline, you feel grieved. It is right for you to feel that way.

However, this is the time to learn obedience in order that you may be made partaker of God's holiness. During the period of the discipline, you cannot but feel grieved, even as our Lord felt when He passed through trials. But at the same time, you may count it as joy even as our Lord did. Does not Peter say, "Wherein ye greatly rejoice, though now for a little while, if need be, ye have been put to grief in manifold trials" (1 Pet. 1.6)? It is all right for you to feel grieved, but you also may count it as joy. To feel is one thing, to count is another thing. You do not feel joyous, but you may count it as joy.

A child of God should not always look at the present but rather at that which will follow. Notice again these words: "All chastening seemeth for the present to be not joyous but grievous; yet afterward it yieldeth peaceable fruit unto them that have been exercised thereby, even the fruit of righteousness." Do not be occupied with how much you are suffering now but rather look forward to the peaceful fruit of righteousness.

Resist the Devil

Scripture to Memorize:

Be subject therefore unto God; but resist the devil, and he will flee from you.

James 4.7

The Work of Satan

Satan's works are manifold. In order for a Christian to walk well before God, he must learn how to resist Satan. In order to do that, he must discern what is the work of Satan. According to the judgment of the Bible, many so-called natural things are actually Satanic works. From a human point of view we may consider something to be incidental, natural, or circumstantial, but the Bible distinctly labels it as the work of the devil. If we are to follow a straight course, God's children must not be ignorant of the devices of Satan—how full of wiles he is, how pretentious and deceptive. We should recognize him in order to resist him.

1. THE WORK OF SATAN IN THE HUMAN MIND

Let us now mention a few of Satan's devices so that we may resist him and overcome him before the Lord.

"The weapons of our warfare are not of the flesh, but mighty before God to the casting down of strongholds; casting down imaginations, and every high thing that is exalted against the knowledge of God, and bringing every thought into captivity to the obedience of Christ" (2 Cor. 10.4-5). Satan surrounds man with strongholds so as to prevent him from obeying Christ. The special field of his work is found in man's mind or thought life. Oftentimes man is bombarded with speculations or imaginations which are adverse to the obedience of Christ. Paul says the weapons of our warfare against these are not of the flesh. These imaginations must first be destroyed before we can bring our thoughts into captivity to the obedience of Christ.

The sphere of Satan's operation is in man's thought life. He will inject a thought, an imagination, which appears to be your own. Under this deception, you accept it and use it as if it were yours, though in actuality it is his.

Do remember that many things in the life of a Christian begin with speculations or imaginations. Many sins are first committed in the imagination of the mind. Many unpleasantnesses among brothers and sisters arise from these fancies.

Then there are those sudden thoughts. Sometimes a thought will flash into one's mind that a certain brother is wrong. Many of God's children do not recognize such thoughts as the work of Satan. A person may consider such a thought as his own and take it as true, thinking that the brother really is wrong. And yet, this is not true. It is Satan who has put the thought into his mind. How is he to resist the devil? He must say, "I do not want this thought. I return it to you, Satan." Should he accept it, it will become his own thought. It is Satan's at the start, but it will become his if he keeps it.

This is why the children of God must learn how to resist inordinate thoughts. However, they also should be careful lest they become overly attentive. Any excess in this respect will cause further confusion of the thoughts, causing them to fall further into the wiles of the enemy. If one is concentrating on his thoughts, his eyes will not be focusing on the Lord. We must, indeed, resist improper thoughts, yet we should not be wholly occupied with our thoughts.

Satanic thoughts can be quite easily withstood. There is a saying frequently quoted by many servants of the Lord that goes, "You cannot forbid a bird to fly over your head, but you certainly can forbid it to make a nest in your hair." Do remember, then, that though you cannot prohibit many thoughts from passing through your mind, you can prohibit them from nesting in you. As a thought flashes through you, you may thrust it away by simply saying, "I do not want it. I will not accept it. I reject it." Then you will see that it is thrown out.

Why are the minds of so many Christians confused? It is because they are always resisting. "Resist the devil, and he will flee from you," says the Bible. Resist him once, and he will flee. You ought to believe that he has fled away. You do not need to resist him many times. Simply believe that he has fled, for this is in accordance with God's word. Whatever then comes back is not true. You can well afford to ignore it, and, if you do, it will soon disappear.

2. THE WORK OF SATAN ON MAN'S BODY

Satan sometimes works upon the human mind and sometimes on man's body. Many sicknesses are not real sicknesses, but are actually Satanic works. Sometimes illnesses are manifestly Satanic attacks.

When Peter's mother-in-law was laid aside with a severe fever, the Lord Jesus went to the house and rebuked the fever (Lk. 4.39). Fever is simply a symptom; it has no personality. You cannot rebuke a symptom; you can only rebuke a personality. You cannot rebuke a chair or a watch, for neither of them has a personality. You only rebuke that which has a personality. But here the Lord Jesus did a surprising thing. When He saw Peter's mother-in-law ill with a fever, He rebuked the fever and it subsided. This clearly indicates that the fever was not ordinary, that it possessed a personality. In other words, it was the work of Satan. At the rebuke of the Lord, Satan retreated.

3. THE ACCUSATION OF SATAN IN THE CONSCIENCE

Satan not only attacks the mind and the body but also the conscience. This attack is what we call accusation. It causes great distress to the Christian who feels himself at fault and thus unable to rise up before God.

Accusation may weaken one's whole being. Many dare not resist for fear that it may be the reproof of the Holy Spirit. They cannot distinguish Satanic accusation from the reproach of the Holy Spirit. Hence they accept Satan's accusation as the Holy Spirit's reproach. Consequently, their lives are wasted under accusation. Do remember that Satanic accusation may cripple the most spiritual and most useful person and reduce him to naught. A weakened conscience weakens the entire person.

What is the difference between a conscience under accusation and the reproach of the Holy Spirit? It is extremely important that we know the difference. Satan's accusation is never clear and sharp, whereas the revelation from God distinctly places your sin before you. Far from being distinct, Satan's accusation is that which is continually mumbling. It is said in Proverbs that "the contentions of a wife are a continuous dropping" (Prov. 19.13b). Satanic accusation also operates somewhat like that. It comes down in two or three drops at a time, instead of a pouring out of the whole bucket of water at once. Satan's accusation babbles long like a talkative and dissatisfied woman. Her nature is such that she will not speak out clearly but she will murmur incessantly so as to leave you with a guilty feeling. So is Satanic accusation. It never comes out boldly but rather mumbles along till you feel greatly distressed. When the Holy Spirit comes, though, He enlightens you with a great light so that you distinctly see your fault.

Furthermore, the results of Satanic accusation are very different from the results of the reproach of the Holy Spirit.

If it is the reproach of the Holy Spirit, you will have joy, and at the very least, peace within you after you have confessed your sin. At the time you are reproved, you do suffer agony; but as soon as you confess your sin before God, you enjoy peace in your heart. Sometimes you will be filled with joy, for the heavy burden has been lifted. With Satanic accusation it is not so. Even at the time of prayer and confession, you are still bothered by his mumbling. He will insinuate that you are sinful and useless, that your confession before God is of no avail, that you will be just as weak after asking for forgiveness as you were before. These are sure signs that the accusation is of Satan; it is not the reproach of the Holy Spirit.

How to Resist the Devil

We need, then, to learn how to resist the devil. What are the various ways of resistance?

1. FEAR NOT

Whenever Satan works against God's children, he must first secure some ground in them. Ephesians exhorts us, "Neither give place to the devil" (4.27). Without a foothold, Satan cannot operate. Hence, his first tempting of us will be in order to secure a ground; his next will be an assault on us from the ground he has already secured. Our victory lies in not giving him any ground from the very beginning. One very large ground, perhaps the very largest, that he seeks is fear. Satan's characteristically customary work is to instill fear in the mind of God's children, a foreboding that something is going to happen.

To the question of what is meant by resistance, an elderly person once replied, "To resist means to say, 'Thank you, but I do not want it,' when something is offered to you." Whatever is offered you, you always answer, "No, thanks!" Though Satan may present you with this or that thing, your reaction is a simple refusal. Such an attitude is enough; it is all that is needed to defeat his purpose. Let us learn this lesson today: resist every thought of fear. Fear not, for fear will bring to you the very thing you are afraid of. May I remind you that no child of God should be fearful of Satan because Satan cannot overcome us. Although he is quite powerful, we have in us One who is greater than he. This is an unchangeable fact, "because greater is he that is in you than he that is in the world" (1 John 4.4b). Therefore, never accept fear. He who accepts fear is a fool. Has not the Bible clearly taught that, by resisting Satan, he will flee? What place does he have in us except to retreat!

2. KNOW THE TRUTH

The second condition of resistance is to know the truth. "Ye shall know the truth, and the truth shall make you free" (John 8.32).

What is truth? Truth is the reality of a thing. When Satan tempts or frightens or attacks people, he always comes in stealthily. He never lets you know he is there. He will not proclaim aloud that he has arrived, for that would arouse your suspicion. He lies, he counterfeits. He never does anything in the light. But if you know what the reality of the thing is, it will set you free. In other words, if you know something is of Satan, you are freed. The difficulty for many children of God is their unawareness of the enemy. They may say with their mouths that it is Satan's attack, yet they do not sense it deep down in their spirits. Though their lips pronounce it to be the work of Satan, their spirits are not as clear. But the day they see the truth, really knowing that this is Satan's work, they are instantly set free.

The power of Satan lies in his deception. If he cannot deceive, he loses his power. Hence, seeing is resisting; seeing makes resistance easy. When you are surrounded with perils in your environment, you cannot overcome if you only feel that these may be Satanic attacks. You need to know for sure that these are of Satan, and then it is easy for you to withstand. To deal with Satan takes more than opposing, for it is difficult to fight against his falsehoods. But when you meet him, you need to recognize him as such; then resist, and he will flee from you.

3. RESIST IN FAITH

Resistance must be done in faith. We must believe that the Lord has been manifested to destroy the work of the devil, that the blood of the Lord has overcome the attack of Satan, that the resurrection of the Lord has put Satan to shame, and that the ascension of the Lord transcends the power of Satan.

BELIEVE THE LORD HAS BEEN MANIFESTED TO DESTROY THE WORK OF THE DEVIL

The Son of God has manifested Himself! He has come to this earth! While here, He cast out every demon He met; He overcame every temptation from Satan. Indeed, "to this end was the Son of God manifested, that he might destroy the works of the devil" (1 John 3.8). Let us, then, believe that wherever the Lord Jesus goes, whenever He is manifested, the work of the devil cannot exist, for it is totally destroyed.

BELIEVE THE BLOOD OF THE LORD HAS OVERCOME THE ATTACK OF SATAN

How do Christians overcome Satan? "Because of the blood of the Lamb" (Rev. 12.11). Through the death of the

Lord Jesus, we are united with God into one. The primary objective of Satanic attack is to separate us from God. As long as we are one with God, Satan has absolutely no way to injure us. What, then, separates us from God? Sin alone separates us, but the blood of Jesus, God's Son, cleanses us from all our sins.

Head Covering

Scripture to Memorize:

The head of every man is Christ; and the head of the woman is the man; and the head of Christ is God.

1 Corinthians 11.3b

I would like to view this matter of head covering from far off; otherwise, it will not be easy to understand 1 Corinthians 11. To comprehend this chapter in 1 Corinthians requires that we know God and His word. First of all we need to know that God has set up two systems in the universe: the system of grace and the system of government.

1. THE SYSTEM OF GRACE

All that concerns the church, salvation, brothers and sisters, and God's children is included in God's system of grace. Everything which pertains to the Holy Spirit and to redemption belongs to this system of grace. Within the proceedings of grace, the relationship of man and woman is such that the Syro-Phoenician woman received grace from God as much as the centurion. So did Mary as much as Peter. So, too, might Martha and Mary have been raised from the dead as well as Lazarus.

2. THE SYSTEM OF GOVERNMENT

But there is another system in the Bible which we will call the government of God. This system is entirely different from that of grace. God's government is an independent system under which God does whatever pleases Him.

When God created man, He created male and female. This belongs to God's government. He created male first and female next—also a matter of His government. He does what pleases Him. He has a sovereign and independent will. When He decided that the Lord Jesus should be the seed of the woman, this too was God's government. He does not take man into His counsel.

God's government is an independent principle. From beginning to end, God brings in His governmental system. Grace only complements government. The system of grace was added because of man's insubordination and rebellion under the system of government. Grace is for the purpose of redeeming and restoring those who are insubordinate and rebellious, so that they may be subject to God's governmental system. Hence, grace actually gives an assist to God's system of government.

Head Covering and God's Government

The matter of head covering belongs to God's government. For those who do not know God's government, it is impossible to exhort them to have their heads covered. They will not be able to understand how much is involved in this matter. But those who have seen God's government in God's revealed word are able to appreciate the tremendous connection between head covering and God's government. "Now I praise you that ye remember me in all things, and hold fast the traditions, even as I delivered them to you. But I would have you know, that the head of every man is Christ; and the head of the woman is the man; and the head of Christ is God" (1 Cor. 11.2-3). What we find here concerns the government of God.

The relationship here described is not that of the Father and the Son but that of God and Christ. To use a modern expression, Christ is God's representative. The relationship between Father and Son pertains to the Godhead, but Christ sent of God touches upon God's arrangement, God's government. "This is life eternal, that they should know thee the only true God, and him whom thou didst send, even Jesus Christ" (John 17.3). God is God, and Christ is One sent by God. This is their relationship in God's government. The Son, originally equal with God, was willing to be sent by God as the Christ. God remained on high as God, but Christ was sent down to do His work. This is the first order of events in the government of God.

In God's purpose, Christ is set up to be the head of every man; therefore, all people must obey Him. He is the firstborn of all creation and its firstfruit. He is the head of every man; every man should be in subjection to Him. This is a basic principle under God's government. Christ being the head of every man is related, not to the system of grace, but to the system of God's government. Likewise, man being the head of woman also belongs to God's governmental system. God in His government establishes man as head just as He sets up Christ as head and also Himself as head. Thus the system is completed.

God is Himself the head; He sets up Christ as head; and He further makes man to be head. These are the three great principles in God's government.

For God to be Christ's head does not touch upon the matter of who is greater; rather, it is simply an arrangement in the government of God. Likewise, under God's government Christ is the head of every man, and man is the head of woman. Such are God's arrangements; such are His appointments.

Philippians 2 is clear enough: the Lord Jesus in His eternal essence is equal with God; but in God's government He became Christ, and as Christ, God became His head.

Christ himself acknowledges in the Gospel of John that: "The Son can do nothing of himself, but what he seeth the Father doing: for what things soever he doeth, these the Son also doeth in like manner" (5.19); "I am come down from heaven, not to do mine own will, but the will of him that sent me" (6.38); "I have many things to speak and to judge concerning you: howbeit he that sent me is true; and the things which I heard from him, these speak I unto the world" (8.26); and "I do nothing of myself, but as the Father taught me, I speak these things" (8.28b). Today Christ takes His place in the government of God. According to God's counsel, He is Christ and as Christ He needs to listen to God. God the Son has no need to listen to God the Father, for God the Father and God the Son are equal in honor and glory in the Godhead. But, in God's government Christ does not stand in the place of God the Son; rather, He stands in the position of Christ, the One sent of God.

Some day the whole world will know that Christ is the head of all men, for this is God's governmental decision. Today this is known only in the church; the world has no knowledge of it. But the day will come when all the people of the world will realize that Christ is the head. He will have the preeminence in all the creation. He is the firstborn of all creation and the firstfruit. Everyone must be in subjection to the authority of Christ. Likewise, God's appointment of man as head of woman is also known only in the church today. Do you get the point? Today the church alone knows that Christ is the head of man and that man is the head of woman.

We have already seen how grace can never overthrow God's government. I trust our lesson will become clearer as we learn that grace is to support God's government, not to destroy it. How can anyone be so foolish as to attempt to use grace to interfere with God's government? The government of God is inviolable; His hand always sustains it. No one, just because he has believed in the Lord, can overthrow the Father's authority, or even undermine the authority of any government. We must not say that because we are Christians we do not need to pay taxes. No, nothing of the sort! The better Christian you are, the more you will maintain the government of God.

We are here today to maintain God's testimony in the world. God has shown us that there are three different heads: God is head, Christ is head, and man is head. This is not a matter of being brothers and sisters; it is basically a governmental arrangement. Grace is concerned with brothers and sisters, but government is different. God has sovereignly willed that the head of Christ is God himself, so Christ must obey; the head of man is Christ, so man must obey; and the head of woman is man, and so woman should have the sign of obedience on her head.

The Meaning of Head Covering

"Every man praying or prophesying, having his head covered, dishonoreth his head. But every woman praying or prophesying with her head unveiled dishonoreth her head; for it is one and the same thing as if she were shaven" (1 Cor. 11.4-5).

The meaning of head covering is: I submit myself to God's government; I accept God's appointed position; I dare not nullify His government by the grace I have received; I do not even dare to think about it; on the contrary, I accept God's government. As Christ accepts God as His head, so should every man accept Christ as his head. Likewise, woman should representatively accept man as her head. In covering the head, the woman signifies that she is not head, that she is as if she has no head—for it is covered.

Let us remember that although in practice it is only the woman who has her head covered, yet, in reality, Christ has

His head covered before God and every man has his head covered before Christ. Why, then, is it that God only requires woman to have the practice of having her head covered? This indeed is marvelous, for it involves a very deep principle.

The Sisters' Responsibility

When a sister covers her head, she is standing before God on the basis of Christ's position before God and man's position before Christ. God wants the woman to cover her head in order to manifest His government on earth. This privilege falls only to woman. She does not cover her head merely for her own self; she does it representatively. For her own self, it is because she is a woman; representatively, it is because she represents man before Christ and Christ before God. So when woman covers her head before God, it is just the same as if Christ covered His head before God. Likewise, when woman covers her head before man, it is just the same as if man covered his head before Christ. Man or woman should have no head since Christ is the head. If one's head is not covered, there will be two heads. Between God and Christ one head must be covered; so too must it be between man and woman and so between Christ and every man. If one head is not covered, the result will be that there are two heads, and God's government does not allow two heads. If God is head, then Christ is not; if Christ is head, then man is not; and if man is head, then woman is not.

God calls upon the sisters to show this arrangement. It is through the sisters that God's governmental system is to be displayed. It is the sisters who are responsible to have the sign of obedience upon their heads. God specifically requires women to have their head covered when praying or prophesying. Why? Because they ought to know God's government when they come before Him. In going before God to pray for people or in going before people to prophesy for God, whether in praying or in prophesying, whether in what goes to God or in what comes from God, in whatever is related to God, head covering is demanded. The purpose is to manifest the government of God.

The Way of the Church

Scripture to Memorize:

Upon this rock I will build my church; and the gates of Hades shall not prevail against it.

Matthew 16.18b

In Revelation chapters 2 and 3, we have seven churches. At the time John wrote the book of Revelation these seven churches were local churches in Asia Minor. There were many local churches in Asia Minor, but out of these many God especially chose seven. His declared purpose in so doing was to use them as prophetic churches, for Revelation 1.3 definitely states that this is a prophecy. By choosing these seven churches as prophetic churches, God prophesies to us the way the church will go on earth.

The First Church – Ephesus

The first church is Ephesus, representing the church at the end of the first century at the time of the writing of the book of Revelation. The situation of the church at that time was like that of Ephesus.

The Second Church – Smyrna

The second church is Smyrna which stands for the church after the death of John, from the second century to the beginning of the fourth century. During this period, the church was persecuted by the Roman Empire ten times. So Smyrna describes the condition of the church under persecution from the post-apostolic period until the time Constantine accepted Christianity.

The Third Church – Pergamum

The third church is the church in Pergamum. At the beginning of the fourth century, that is, in the year of our Lord three hundred and thirteen when Constantine accepted Christianity as the state religion, the church entered into the period of Pergamum. The word "Pergamum" means "marriage," for during that period the church and the world were married and thus united together. Formerly the world persecuted the church; now the world welcomed the church. Thus, with the world coming into the church, the nature of the church was drastically changed. In Greek, gamos means "marriage." The English word "polygamy" comes from the Greek root gamos. "Pergamos" means "Behold, now is the marriage."

Of the seven churches, the first three have already passed away, but the last four continue on. When the first church passed away, the second came; with the fading of the second the third was introduced; and the ending of the third ushered in the fourth. But the fourth did not pass away when the fifth was born; the fourth and the fifth continued on together. And the sixth continued on with the fourth and fifth, and the seventh with them too. So, when the seventh church came, the fourth, the fifth, and the sixth churches still existed. Thus the seven churches in Revelation 2 and 3 are divided into two parts: the first three that have already passed away, and the last four that remain until the second coming of the Lord Jesus.

In order to know our way as children of God, we need to consider carefully the last four churches. Since there are four different kinds of churches on earth now, all of which will continue up to the second coming of the Lord Jesus, what should we do? What relationship should a child of God have to these churches? We need to choose carefully from these four lest we stay in a church that the Lord has condemned. If we do that, we will suffer great loss before the Lord. We have merely touched upon the first three in this exercise, for they have all passed away. Now we want to look closely at the last four.

The Fourth Church – Thyatira

The fourth church is Thyatira. After the Roman Caesar accepted Christianity as the state religion, it was supported by political power. In the past, political power had been employed to suppress Christianity; now it was used to support Christianity. It became a promoter. As a consequence, Christianity was not only married to the world, but was also exalted by the world. The word, "Thyatira," in the Greek means "high tower." She had now become a high tower, visible to, and respected and worshiped by, the world.

Those who study the Bible agree that the church in Thyatira points to the Roman Catholic Church, for in that system the church and the world are joined together. Consequently, the church has gained quite a position in the world. What trouble does that cause? It produces a prophetess by the name of Jezebel who teaches God's servants. The church comes under her rule and is controlled by her. The problem in the Roman Catholic Church is similar to that described by the fourth parable of Matthew 13 in which a woman hid leaven in three measures of flour. The Bible uses this woman to signify the Roman Catholic Church.

The Lord reprimands the Thyatira church not only for fornication but also for idol-worship. Is it not strange that God should reprove the church for idol-worship? Yet the fact remains that the church was worshiping idols. In the Old Testament days, people worshiped the brazen serpent. In the Roman Catholic Church, they worship the crucifix. They tell people that they have found the cross, and out of that wood they make many small crosses. They literally worship the crucifix.

The church in Thyatira represents the Roman Catholic Church. It is a church system condemned by God.

The Fifth Church – Sardis

The fifth church is Sardis. This church represents the restored church or the remnant church, that which remains. It succeeds Thyatira, though Thyatira does not cease to exist. It therefore succeeds but does not replace Thyatira.

What is the condition of Sardis? Verses 1-4 of chapter three show us that the characteristic of Sardis is that it has a name that it lives and yet is dead.

Sardis represents the Protestant Church. The Protestant Church follows the Roman Catholic Church. Though the Reformation is included in Sardis, yet it does not represent the Reformation. It represents the Protestant Church.

This is characteristic of Sardis, that it has a name that it lives and yet is dead. What marks the Protestant Church is a continuous commingling of the world and the church. Formerly, Rome ruled over the entire world; now each nation has its own church. There is therefore a great mixture of God's people with unbelievers. Such is the situation of the Protestant Church.

In the history of the Protestant Church, God has constantly raised up now and then one or two to whom He reveals His thoughts, His judgment of certain things. Those who do not or will not see often accuse those who see and obey God as being divisive. Yet, if all God's children today would judge sin and deal with things which are not of God, they would all be one with the Lord and one with each other. Therefore, judging errors and condemning sin is the true foundation of oneness.

There is another feature in the history of the Protestant Church. The first thing God does is to raise up a man.

Through the grace that man receives, great blessing is brought in. The first generation really has many glorious days. During the second generation the situation may not change much. But toward the end of the second generation, people may begin to think of how to preserve God's grace in their midst. They may conclude that they must organize in order to keep this grace. So, by the end of the second generation, organization comes in. Sometimes this organization may begin as early as at the close of the first generation; sometimes it may be as late as the third generation.

These Christians can believe God to give grace, but they cannot believe Him to keep the grace. They believe God to bestow blessing, but they do not believe Him to continue to bless. As a consequence, they devise human creeds, rules, and methods to maintain the blessing they have received. But if God's fountain is shut, the pool can only become drier, it cannot rise higher. So, in the third generation, their condition is quite dead, as dead as the church which they had originally left. Thereafter, God has to lay hold of another person or persons to whom He can give new revelation, new blessing, new separation, and new grace. This time will again become a time of revival. Again, the first generation may be full of blessing, the second generation begin to organize, and the third generation begin to decline. Thus is the history of the Protestant Church.

Both Sardis and Thyatira, the Protestant Church as well as the Roman Catholic Church, were reprimanded by the Lord. What, then, is the way for believers?

The Sixth Church – Philadelphia

Here we have the sixth church, the church of Philadelphia. "Phileo" means "to love," and "adelphos" means "brother." Philadelphia is brotherly love.

303

Of the seven churches, only two churches escape reproof and of those two, only one, Philadelphia, is wholly approved and praised. For Philadelphia alone, there is praise without reproof.

What is the characteristic of Philadelphia? "I know thy works (behold, I have set before thee a door opened, which none can shut), that thou hast a little power, and didst keep my word, and didst not deny my name" (Rev. 3.8). That which characterizes Sardis is a struggling with death. Because the church in Sardis was mingled with the world, it needed to struggle for life and to start out anew all the time. But Philadelphia is brotherly love. Here there is a return to the love of the brethren. It is no longer the world, because everyone is a brother. It has no need to struggle free from death and the things of death that tend to cling on. Philadelphia is simply a restoring to the original position of the brethren before God where all is love.

Philadelphia possesses two special features: one, they keep the word of the Lord and, two, they do not deny His name. Here is a group of people who are led by God to learn how to keep the Lord's word. God opens His word to them so that they can understand. There is no creed in their midst, only the word of God. There is no doctrine, only the word. There is no tradition, only the word. There is no opportunity for man's opinion, only the word of God. After the apostles, this is the first church which the Lord praises, for now a group of people has completely returned to the Lord's word. To them no authority other than the Lord's, no teaching, no creed is of any use.

"Thou didst not deny my name," says the Lord. This, too, is a special feature of Philadelphia. After such a long history of the church, the name of the Lord Jesus has unexpectedly become the very last name. People pay more attention to men's names—perhaps to Peter's or the other apostles. Or Christians may choose to call themselves by some other preference of theirs such as doctrine or nationality. Many take pride in saying, "I am a Lutheran," or, "I am a Wesleyan"—the names of men. Many proudly declare themselves to be Coptic or Anglican—named after a place or a country. These many names completely divide God's children! It looks as if the one name, the name of the Lord Jesus, is not sufficient to separate us from the world.

The Lord himself considers His name to be quite sufficient for His children. But only in Philadelphia is His name reckoned as sufficient. There is no need for many names, for names separate. His name is enough! Remember, the Lord is quite concerned about this matter.

The Seventh Church – Laodicea

Laodicea is a mutilated or distorted Philadelphia. Once brotherly love is lost, then immediately people's rights and opinions take over. This is the meaning of the word "Laodicea." It was the name of a city, named by a Roman prince after his wife whose name was Laodios. The prince changed the name into Laodicea, which in Greek means, "the people's rights or opinions."

When Philadelphia falls, the emphasis becomes more on "people" than on "brethren," more on "people's rights" than on "brotherly love." Love turns to rights or opinions. When brotherly love is a living thing, people's rights are a dead thing; but whenever brotherly love is waning (and the body relationship with its fellowship in life will be fading too), people's opinions begin to prevail. The Lord's mind is not sought; things are settled by the majority opinion. Philadelphia has fallen into Laodicea.

"I know thy works, that thou art neither cold nor hot: I would thou wert cold or hot" (Rev. 3.15). This is the character of Laodicea. "Because thou sayest, I am rich, and have gotten riches, and have need of nothing; and knowest not that thou art the wretched one and miserable and poor and blind and naked" (v. 17). This is what Laodicea is.

Though it is neither hot nor cold, it is full of spiritual pride before the Lord. To say, "I am rich," ought to be enough, but Laodicea emphasizes it with, "and have gotten riches"; then this is further reinforced by, "and have need of nothing"! But the Lord sees differently, for He replies, "thou art the wretched one and miserable and poor and blind and naked." From where does this spiritual pride come? Undoubtedly it is based on the past history. Once the Laodiceans were rich; so now they imagine they are still rich. Once the Lord showed mercy to them; now they remember that past history, though they are no longer in touch with the reality of it.

The Way of the Church—Our Choice

Today I hold before you these four churches. The Roman Catholic Church, the Protestant Church, Philadelphia, and Laodicea will all continue till the coming again of the Lord Jesus. Consequently, every child of God must choose today the way of the church for him. Do I want to be a Roman Catholic or do I choose to be a Protestant? Will I follow the external unity of the Roman Catholic Church or will I follow the many denominations of the Protestant Church? Or would I rather walk in the way of Philadelphia? Or was I once of Philadelphia but am now living in the past glory and boasting in my past history just as the Laodiceans do? Please remember: If people commence to be proud before God and yet depart from life, neglecting reality while remembering the past history of glory, they will soon fall into a condition of the people's rights and opinions. They sound democratic but they have no body relationship. How can they know brotherly love if they do not know the bonds of the body, the authority of the body, and the life of the body?

The way of the church as appointed by the Lord is Philadelphia. The Lord's way for us is only one—

Philadelphia. Walk in it. Be careful lest there is pride. The greatest temptation to the Philadelphian way is pride: "I am better than you! My truth is clearer and broader than yours! I have only the Lord's name—I am not like you who have another name!" Pride will plunge us into Laodicea. Those who follow the Lord have nothing of which to be proud. The Lord will spew out the proud. May the Lord be merciful. I warn you not to utter arrogant words! Live in the presence of God and refrain from saying any boastful words. By living constantly in God's presence, we will not see our riches. Therefore, we will not be proud.

Oneness

Scripture to Memorize:

I in them, and thou in me, that they may be perfected into one; that the world may know that thou didst send me, and loved them, even as thou loved me.

John 17.23

The subject before us is Christian oneness. We have already seen how the body of Christ is to be manifested on earth. Does not Paul tell the Corinthian believers that "as the body is one, and hath many members, and all the members of the body, being many, are one body; so also is Christ" (1 Cor. 12.12)? Paul does not say, "so also are Christ and His people." He merely asserts, "so also is Christ." In other words, the head is Christ, the body is Christ, the members are Christ.

In His prayer in John 17, the Lord Jesus prays for the oneness of the church on earth: "that they may all be one; even as thou, Father, art in me, and I in thee, that they also may be in us: that the world may believe that thou didst send me" (v. 21). If we omit the middle parenthetical section of this passage and read the remainder: "That they may all be one, that the world may believe that thou didst send me," we can clearly see that the oneness of the church is to induce the world to believe. Since those who are to believe are people in the world, it is evident that this oneness must be manifested before the world. The Lord expects the world to believe. This oneness, then, is present on earth today.

Oneness Is Limited to the Body

Many people try to be one with everyone who professes outwardly to be a Christian, disregarding whether such ones are really God's people and have new life, disregarding whether they really are members of the body of Christ. The oneness these people advocate exceeds the scope of the body of Christ. Their oneness includes those who are spiritually dead, and this is something foreign to the body of Christ. Such oneness is not permitted by God's word, for what the Bible promotes is the oneness of the body.

I would like to stress here that the oneness of the body is the unity of the church. The church's unity is limited to the body and cannot be extended beyond the body. The word of God never sanctions oneness with nominal Christians.

Oneness Includes All the Body

The scope of Christian oneness is very precisely defined. It includes all children of God. The measure of the body of Christ is the measure of Christian oneness. Christian fellowship is as comprehensive as the body of Christ.

We wish to draw the attention of all brothers and sisters to this thing: God wishes His children to be one in the Holy Spirit. God does not say that just any oneness will do; He insists that oneness must be in the Holy Spirit. Only this is called Christian oneness. It is a oneness in Christ. To keep Christian oneness, we must keep in Christ, in the body, in the oneness of the Holy Spirit. So, the scope of Christian oneness is as inclusive as the body.

Oneness Is Not Association

Once people see the destructiveness of sects and God's condemnation of them, they begin to realize the need for Christian oneness. They become conscious of the inappropriateness of having fellowship with any group smaller than the body of Christ and, at the same time, they become aware of the need to have fellowship with all the children of God. In this day, such an awakening is quite extensive among Christians. Some time ago, a Christian leader wrote me a letter in which he stated, "Although we do not approve of the teaching against sects, we nevertheless agree that Christian oneness is a must." Indeed, Christian leaders today do know they should stress Christian oneness rather than sectarian unity.

I acknowledge that over the past few decades many have stressed oneness. Nonetheless, the fruit of this has not been the oneness of the body but the oneness of association. This latter type of oneness is a human production. It is what is called the ecumenical movement or an interdenominational work. I personally feel this is a midway expediency; it falls short of either end.

Oneness Needs to Be Maintained

How, then, should we maintain oneness? We have to reject any organization which includes unbelievers, for it is not a church. We must leave all sects, for they divide the body of Christ. And we should repudiate all associations of sects, for this is a work of the flesh.

If there is to be a church in a locality, its scope must be as comprehensive as the body of Christ: it must include all God's children in that locality—nothing more, nothing less. Whether the people of God are willing to take this stand or not is their own responsibility. But those who wish to follow the Lord must be faithful. They must take this non-

311

sectarian ground. The basic rule of the church is that the church neither includes any unbelievers nor allows any sort of association to substitute for the body. We stand on the ground of the body of Christ, for this is the scope of the church. And this is the one and only course God's children must take everywhere.

God has put us on this pure ground of oneness on which all children of God must meet. What if some do not gather together? We dare not make any false claim; we only maintain that we do stand on the ground of the body of Christ.

Without hesitation, we concede that there are many brothers and sisters in the sects, in national churches, and in various associations. If they are faithful to the Lord, they ought to return home and stand with us on this body ground. The door is always open to them. But, as for us, we cannot but stand on body ground.

Love the Brethren

Scripture to Memorize:

Hereby know we love, because he laid down his life for us: and we ought to lay down our lives for the brethren.

1 John 3.16

1. THE CONSCIOUSNESS OF LOVE

There are only two places in the Bible where the phrase "passed out of death into life" is used. Let us compare these two places:

"Verily, verily, I say unto you, He that heareth my word, and believeth him that sent me, hath eternal life, and cometh not into judgment, but hath passed out of death into life" (John 5.24). He who believes has passed out of death into life.

"We know that we have passed out of death into life, because we love the brethren" (1 John 3.14a). Love of the brethren is evidence of having passed out of death into life.

It may be quite difficult to distinguish on the basis of faith whether a person has truly believed in the Lord or is merely pretending to believe; whether he believes with his heart or just with his mind; whether he has really met the Lord or has only gone through a formula. But to discern on the basis of love is quite easy. Even John, who wrote so much about faith, found it hard to differentiate between true and false faith. He therefore used love to divide the true and the false. Whoever has the consciousness of love is a child of God; whoever lacks this consciousness is not a child of God. Every child of God will naturally have an unspeakable sensation toward another believer—as if he is closer than a brother. He who possesses this consciousness is a true believer.

Something in you witnesses to the truthfulness of your faith. Out of the faith that you have issues an unspeakable love. This brotherly love is unique, for it has no cause other than the fact that someone is a brother. You do not love him because he agrees with you. It is natural for people who have the same interest or the same outlook to love one another. But the one you love is different from you in education, temperament, background, and viewpoint. You love him simply because he is a believer even as you are. You are brethren; therefore you have fellowship. There is an indescribable feeling, an unexplainable sensation toward each other. This consciousness is the evidence of your having passed out of death into life. If I love the brethren, I know I have passed out of death into life.

2. THE LIFE OF LOVE

By faith you meet God, pass out of death into life, and become a member of God's house. You are born again and have become a part of God's family. Faith draws you to the brethren as well as to the Father. It gives you the knowledge of God that you may believe in Him and receive life from Him. Soon after you receive life, you discover that there are many others who have also received this life. Instinctively, this life within you pulls you to those who possess the same life as you. You like to be near them, and you delight in having fellowship with them. You love them spontaneously.

John's gospel tells us that by believing we may pass out of death into life; his epistle shows us that those who have passed out of death into life love the brethren. God has so ordained that by faith we come out of death into life, and that by passing out of death into life we love. By our loving the brethren, we ourselves are assured that we have indeed passed out of death into life. This, therefore, becomes the acid test for God's children. The brethren must love one another; only if we love one another are we truly brethren. If we do not love one another, we are not brethren. If we do not love the brethren, we are not begotten of God. One may confess with his mouth that he believes, but before God his faith is not real since he does not have love toward the brethren.

If you have truly believed in God and have life in you, you will naturally be attracted to the brethren. Your love for Christians will be spontaneous; you will feel they are closer to you than your brethren in the flesh, more intimate than the best of your friends. This brotherly affinity is ingrained. You find an inscrutable sensation surge within you which makes you love your brother and love to be with him. Thus do you know you have passed out of death into life. You have the witness within you as well as in the word of God.

3. THE THOUGHT OF LOVE

"He that saith he is in the light and hateth his brother, is in the darkness even until now. He that loveth his brother abideth in the light, and there is no occasion of stumbling in him. But he that hateth his brother is in the darkness, and walketh in the darkness, and knoweth not whither he goeth, because the darkness hath blinded his eyes" (1 John 2.9-11). Is it not very clear that whether or not one is a brother, whether he is in the light or in the darkness, can be determined by how he treats his brother?

If there is a brother here—and you know he is a brother—yet you hate him in your heart, this sufficiently proves that you are not a Christian. Suppose there are five brothers here. Of these, you confess that you love four but hate one. Let me tell you, you are not a brother. The love of the brethren does not mean loving the lovable or loving those whom you prefer. It means loving a person simply because he is a brother. That is the sole reason for loving him.

4. THE CHARGE OF LOVE

"This is the message which ye heard from the beginning, that we should love one another . . . We know that we have passed out of death into life, because we love the brethren. He that loveth not abideth in death" (1 John 3.11, 14).

The love we are talking about is not ordinary love but the love of the brethren. He who lacks this love, as the Bible indicates, yet abides in death. If I am cold to a person, void of any feeling toward him, I know he is a stranger who has no relationship to me. But if I sense an affinity within me, I know he is my brother. Before I trusted in the Lord, I did not have the slightest feeling or attraction toward believers. Today if I still have no inward sense of affinity toward them, I am afraid my faith is faulty, for he who loves not abides in death. I was dead, and now I am still in death. Faith, therefore, is evidenced by love. The reality of faith is judged by the proof of love. Whoever believes in God has love for the brethren. If love is not evident, that person is proven to be yet in death and thus no different from unbelievers.

Let us now consider what is meant by hating one's brother. There are certain things that may be permissible to God's children, but hatred is not one of them. If a brother displays an unpleasant temperament, I may dislike him in my heart. If he commits a sin deserving excommunication, I may perhaps deal angrily with his case. I may severely reprimand a brother who has done something nasty. But how can I be a saved person if I hate another brother? Just to hate one person is proof enough that one is not of God.

The life within all children of God is so rich that they can love every brother and every sister. Such love is spontaneous in all who belong to God. There is no difference between loving one brother and loving all the brethren. The same love is shown to the one as to the other. He is loved because he is a brother. The number of persons has no bearing here. Brotherly love is love of all the brethren. If a person hates one brother sufficiently, it shows that brotherly love is not in him.

5. THE REALITY OF LOVE

"Beloved, let us love one another: for love is of God; and every one that loveth is begotten of God, and knoweth God. He that loveth not knoweth not God; for God is love" (1 John 4.7-8).

Why should we love one another? Because love is of God. Whoever loves is begotten of God, and whoever does not love, does not know God. God is love, and love comes from God. When He begat us, He implanted love in us. We did not have this love in the past, but now we possess it. It is from God. And it is given to all who are begotten of God that we may love one another.

6. THE ABSOLUTENESS OF LOVE

"Whosoever believeth that Jesus is the Christ is begotten of God: and whosoever loveth him that begat loveth him also that is begotten of him" (1 John 5.1). How very precious this word is. It is so natural to love those who are begotten of God if you love Him who begets you. There is absolutely no possibility that you can love God without having the slightest consciousness of love toward your brethren.

317

Priesthood

Scripture to Memorize:

Ye are an elect race, a royal priesthood, a holy nation, a people for God's own possession, that ye may show forth the excellencies of him who called you out of darkness into his marvelous light.

1 Peter 2.9

There is an office mentioned in the Bible called the priesthood. The priesthood is a group of people wholly separated from the world in order to serve God. They have no profession or duty other than the task of serving God. They are priests.

The History of the Priests

From the book of Genesis onward, God has had His priests. Melchizedek was God's first priest. During the time of Abraham, Melchizedek had already separated himself for the service of God. From Melchizedek till after the nation of Israel was established, there were always priests.

When the Lord Jesus was on earth and even after His departure, the priesthood continued. And after His ascension, the Bible shows us that the Lord Jesus became a priest before God. In other words, He is in heaven ministering fully unto God.

The priesthood continues on throughout the dispensation of the church. After that, those who have part in the first resurrection will be priests of God and of Christ and shall reign with Him for a thousand years (Rev. 20.6). Thus, in the millennial kingdom, God's children will continue being priests of God and of Christ. They will be kings to the world and priests to God. The nature of the priesthood will remain unchanged, for the priests will still serve God.

Even when the new heavens and the new earth come, the priesthood will not fade away. In New Jerusalem all God's children and all God's servants will do nothing but serve Him.

Here is a most wonderful thing: the priesthood commenced with Melchizedek—who is without father, without mother, without genealogy, having neither beginning of days nor end of life—and it continues on through the millennium. Its service extends to the eternity to come.

The Kingdom of Priests

Although at first only Melchizedek was priest, the purpose of God is for all His people to be priests—not just a few of them.

After the Israelites came out of Egypt and to Mount Sinai, God spoke to them through Moses, saying, "Ye shall be unto me a kingdom of priests, and a holy nation" (Ex. 19.6a). Why does it say a kingdom of priests? For one reason only: that the whole nation should be priests. Not one person in the country was to be just an ordinary person; all were priests. This is God's purpose.

Let us take special note here: After this incident of the golden calf (see Ex. 32), God immediately informed Moses that hereafter the nation of Israel could not be a kingdom of priests. Though this was not explicitly stated, yet it was implicitly understood, for henceforth God gave the privilege of being priests to the tribe of Levi alone. What was originally intended for the whole nation of Israel was now given to the house of Aaron of the tribe of Levi.

The Priesthood Changed

For about fifteen hundred years, from Moses till Christ, the people of God were not able to present themselves directly to God. Only one family was chosen to be priests. In order to approach God, every person must pass through them. If anyone dared to draw near to God by himself, he would be smitten to death. During that period the function of the priest was of tremendous importance. How noble the priesthood was! How great! But then, suddenly, the New Covenant came and under it men could be saved and redeemed directly. Suddenly we hear the word, "Ye also, as living stones, are built up a spiritual house, to be a holy priesthood, to offer up spiritual sacrifices, acceptable to God through Jesus Christ" (1 Pet. 2.5).

Peter tells us that Christ is the foundation of the church. He is the stone rejected by the builders that has become the head of the corner. Through Him, we too have become living stones to be joined and built together to be both a spiritual temple and God's holy priesthood. The voice from heaven informs us that all saved ones are God's priests. All who have become living stones and are related to the spiritual temple are the priests of God.

All of a sudden, the promise which had been laid aside for fifteen hundred years was again taken up by God. What the Israelites lost, the church gained. Universal priesthood was lost to Israel, but today, with the New Covenant, the voice from heaven comes to tell us that all saved ones are priests.

"He made us to be a kingdom, to be priests unto his God and Father" (Rev. 1.6). Originally, the whole nation of Israel were priests but they soon disqualified themselves. The church, however, is today a kingdom of priests. What the Israelites lost after worshiping the golden calf is now fully gained by the church through the Lord Jesus. All who are in the church are priests. God's destined kingdom of priests is thus wholly realized.

What is meant by the church being a kingdom of priests or by all in the church being priests? This simply implies that the occupation of all who have received God's grace is one: to serve God. As I have said before to the young people, the occupation of a medical doctor who has believed in the Lord is not medicine, of a nurse is not nursing, of a teacher is not teaching, of a farmer is not farming, of a businessman is not business. Remember, when you became a Christian, your profession underwent a complete change. All Christians have only one profession and that is, to serve God. From now on I am God's priest. Outwardly I may be busily occupied in various things, but inwardly I am before God, serving Him. Everything is done with this as the spiritual objective.

The Service of the Priests

To be a Christian is to be a priest. Do not expect anyone to be a priest for you. You yourself are to so function. Since we have no intermediary class among us, no one will substitute himself for you in spiritual things. Let there not be a special class of such workers created in our midst.

If God is gracious to us, we will naturally find all brothers and sisters functioning in the church. All will preach the gospel, all will serve God. The more prevailing the priesthood is, the better the church. If the priesthood is not universal, we have failed God; we have not walked uprightly.

For such as we—who are poor, weak, blind, and crippled—to be accepted by the Lord to be priests is unquestionably our glory. In the Old Testament times such people could not function as priests. All who were disabled, lame, or with blemishes were barred from service. But today we—the base, the unclean, the dark, and the disabled—are called by God to be priests. Oh, He is Lord! As I have said, I only want to crawl to Him and kneel before Him and tell Him, "Lord, I am happy to serve You, I am glad to be Your servant. That I may come to You is evidence that You have lifted me." Let me tell you, to be a priest is to draw near to God. To be a priest is to have no distance between you and God. To be a priest is to be able to enter directly into His presence. To be a priest means you do not need to wait for help. To be a priest means you can touch God.

If some day the brothers and sisters in every place are found serving God, then in truth will the kingdom of God have come. It will be a kingdom of priests, for all the people will be priests. I look toward this event as a most glorious thing. May we pay whatever price is needed for us to serve God. May we deal with all idols.

The Body of Christ

Scripture to Memorize:

There is one body, and one Spirit, even as also ye were called in one hope of your calling.

Ephesians 4.4

There are quite a few things we would like to mention in regard to the body of Christ.

Christ, the Church, and the Body

"No man ever hated his own flesh; but nourisheth and cherisheth it, even as Christ also the church; because we are members of his body" (Eph. 5.29-30. Darby's version adds in brackets, "We are of his flesh and of his bones").

In the Old Testament God shows us how He took a rib out of Adam and built Eve. Eve came out of Adam. Or, to use another expression, Eve was Adam. Similarly, if we ask, "What is the church?" the reply is that the church comes out of Christ. As God built Eve with that which He took out of Adam, so He builds the church with that which is taken out of Christ. Christ has given us not only His power, grace, nature, and will, but also His own body. He has given us His bones and His flesh. He has given Himself to us, just as Adam gave his bone to Eve.

The Bible tells us that Christ is the head of the church, and the church is the body of Christ. Individually, every Christian is a member of the body of Christ, for every one comes out of Him.

One thing to especially notice is that the body of Christ is on earth. It is on earth, though it does not belong to the earth. It is heavenly, yet it is on earth. Do not think that the

325

body of Christ is in heaven. When Paul persecuted the church, the Lord Jesus challenged him on the road to Damascus, saying, "Saul, Saul, why persecutest thou me?" (Acts 9.4). The word of the Lord here is really wonderful. He did not say, "Saul, Saul, why persecutest thou my disciples?" but He said, "Saul, Saul, why persecutest thou me?" He did not ask, "Saul, Saul, why persecutest thou my people?" or "Why persecutest thou my church?" He simply said, "Saul, Saul, why persecutest thou me?" Thus it was revealed to Paul that the church and Christ are one. The oneness of the church and Christ is of such a nature that to persecute the church is to persecute Christ. Moreover, the incident on the Damascus road indicates that the body of Christ is something on earth. If it were in heaven, it would not be persecuted nor could it be persecuted. But today the church on earth is the body of Christ. Thus Saul could persecute the church.

According to the Bible the church of Christ is the body of Christ, and the body of Christ is the church of Christ. Not even a doctrine can be used as justification for founding a church. Holiness is important, for without holiness no one can see God. Faith is very necessary, for by faith we are justified. However, neither holiness nor faith may serve as the reason for establishing a church, for the church is the body of Christ. It is not the gathering of those who believe in the doctrine of holiness, nor is it an assembly of those who advocate justification by faith.

Certainly, nationality cannot be the ground of the church, such as the Lutheran Church in Germany or the Anglican Church in England. After God revealed to Martin Luther the truth of justification by faith, he was instrumental in spreading the Protestant movement. But this did not give him or his followers the right to establish a national church. If there are but ten Christians today standing on the ground of the body of Christ, they have the right to form a church. But Germany with her twenty million Christians cannot organize a church. Just because she has so many people is not sufficient cause for the establishment of a national church.

The ground of the church, therefore, is the body of Christ in a locality. It is not based on doctrine or nation, or on spiritual food or Biblical interpretation. Wherever we go, we must be clear of this one position: that the church is the body of Christ. If a local church is formed on this basis, it is not sectarian.

Church Unity in the Holy Spirit

"As the body is one, and hath many members, and all the members of the body, being many, are one body; so also is Christ. For in one Spirit were we all baptized into one body, whether Jews or Greeks, whether bond or free; and were all made to drink of one Spirit" (1 Cor. 12.12-13).

To say that the church comes out of Christ touches upon the matter of the source of the church. All Christians have new life. The one life of Christ has been multiplied into tens of thousands, and thousands of thousands of Christians. Chapter 12 of John shows us how a grain of wheat falls into the ground, dies, and bears many grains. All the grains partake of the life of the first grain. One grain becomes many grains, and the many all come from the one grain.

We have seen how one grain can become many grains, but how can many grains again become one? Scripture shows us that the formation of the body of Christ is the work of the Holy Spirit. How does the Holy Spirit accomplish this work? He does it by baptizing many grains into one. From one Christ come the tens of thousands and thousands of thousands of Christians. These thousands of thousands of Christians are baptized into one body in one Spirit. Such is the basic teaching of 1 Corinthians 12.12-13. To use a different metaphor, we may say that all of us are stones hewn out of the same rock and then cemented together into one whole by the Holy Spirit.

The body of Christ, then, has two basic principles: first, unless it comes out of Christ, it is not the body of Christ; second, unless there is the work of the Holy Spirit, it is not the body of Christ. We must be baptized in the Holy Spirit and be filled with the Holy Spirit so as to be joined into one. To say that the church begins at Pentecost is correct; to say it begins at the house of Cornelius is also correct; for both Jews and Gentiles have been baptized into one body. We first receive life from the Lord and this life is in the Holy Spirit in order to make us one body. Everyone who knows the Lord knows this body. Everyone who knows the Holy Spirit knows this body. If people walk according to the Holy Spirit, they are naturally aware of God's children being one body. The physical body has many members, but the head, through the nervous system, controls all the members. Likewise, the head of the church joins the many members together into one body through the Holy Spirit.

The Body the Basis of Fellowship

Let us reread 1 Corinthians 12.12: "As the body is one, and hath many members, and all the members of the body, being many, are one body; so also is Christ."

The church comes out of Christ, and, through the operation of the Holy Spirit, becomes one body. All the members are fitted together and coordinated with one another in the Holy Spirit. Thus, the fellowship or communication of Christians falls within the body. In other words, the basis for Christian fellowship is the body.

We are members one of another and we are one body. Naturally our fellowship is based on the body of Christ. There is no other relationship for fellowship except that we are all members of the body of Christ. We are neither all Jews nor all Greeks, all freemen nor all bondmen. We cannot base our fellowship on any of these relationships. Hence, the body is the one and only basis of our fellowship.

The Ministry of the Body

The body is not one member, but many. If the foot shall say, Because I am not the hand, I am not of the body; it is not therefore not of the body. And if the ear shall say, Because I am not the eye, I am not of the body; it is not therefore not of the body. If the whole body were an eye, where were the hearing? If the whole were hearing, where were the smelling? But now hath God set the members each one of them in the body, even as it pleased him. And if they were all one member, where were the body? . . . And God hath set some in the church, first apostles, secondly prophets, thirdly teachers, then miracles, then gifts of healings, helps, governments, divers kinds of tongues. Are all apostles? are all prophets? are all teachers? are all workers of miracles? have all gifts of healings? do all speak with tongues? do all interpret?

1 Cor. 12.14-19, 28-30

The Holy Spirit gives diverse gifts to the members of the body of Christ according to the individual needs of the body. The Lord's purpose in appointing the members to different ministrations is to supply the needs of the body. Thus He gives diversities of ministrations. He would never make the body all eyes or ears or feet. The church needs many different kinds of ministries in order to fulfill its spiritual service. It needs the ministries of the word, and it needs the working of miracles. Both the ministry of the word and supernatural ministry are present in the body.

329

A church must have room for all the ministers (that is, all the members) to serve the body. The church includes all brothers and sisters, comely and uncomely. All have their respective spiritual usefulness and all are engaged in the Lord's service. The body should not have many useless members. As everyone in the body is a member and each member has his function, so every member ought to render his service before God. This is how the church is manifested.

The Testimony of the Body

The cup of blessing which we bless, is it not a communion of the blood of Christ? The bread which we break, is it not a communion of the body of Christ? seeing that we, who are many, are one bread, one body: for we all partake of the one bread.

1 Cor. 10.16-17

The church is the body of Christ. Her main task on earth is to manifest this body and the oneness of this body. She does not need to wait till she reaches heaven to manifest the oneness of the body. It is here on earth that she ought to manifest the oneness. Those who confine the manifestation of the oneness of the body to heaven are those who seek to maintain and strengthen sects and divisions.

"Seeing that we, who are many, are one bread, one body." The New Testament pays great attention to this matter of the breaking of bread. It is mentioned in Acts 20.7: "And upon the first day of the week, when we were gathered together to break bread," showing how God's children break bread in remembrance of the Lord every Lord's day. This act shows forth, on the one hand, how the

Lord's body was broken for us, and, on the other hand, how this body is one. The breaking speaks of our Lord's laying down His life on the cross for love of us, and the oneness tells of all God's children being one today.

The Authority of the Church

Scripture to Memorize:

Let every soul be subject to the authorities that are above him. For there is no authority except from God; and those that exist are set up by God.

Romans 13.1 (Darby)

We will now consider the matter of the authority of the church.

The Governing Principle of the Universe

Before God created the universe He established a principle by which to govern it—the principle of authority. He Himself would be the highest authority and, at the same time, the source of all authority. Under Him would be several archangels, and under them would be many angels. On the earth would be other living creatures. That is how God arranged to govern the universe, and that is how it is. He upholds all things by the word of His power—the stars, the earth, and all the living creatures. He has established laws to regulate every living creature and every natural phenomenon. Therefore, authority is of paramount importance in the universe. If any living or non-living thing disobeys its law, it will bring chaos to the universe.

The Principle of Obedience

Not until the Lord Jesus was born did God find His chosen One. The Lord himself told us, "The Son can do nothing of himself, but what he seeth the Father doing; for what things soever he doeth, these the Son also doeth in like manner" (John 5.19); "I do nothing of myself, but as the Father taught me, I speak these things" (John 8.28b); "I seek not mine own will, but the will of him that sent me" (John 5.30b). Here we find a Man who yielded absolutely to God's authority.

The Lord Jesus was himself God and yet He did not count being on an equality with God a thing to be grasped; rather, He submitted Himself wholly to the authority of God. After He died on the cross God raised Him from among the dead and highly exalted Him. He was made Lord and Christ, and was given "the name which is above every name; that in the name of Jesus every knee should bow, of things in heaven and things on earth and things under the earth, and that every tongue should confess that Jesus Christ is Lord, to the glory of God the Father" (Phil. 2.9b-11).

After the ascension of the Lord, His church was formed. He did not establish His church as an organization or institution according to the expectation of men. This Lord who arose from the dead and ascended on high is to be the head of the church, and the whole church is to be His body. In other words, as He lived a life of obedience on earth, so He wishes His church to once again manifest an obedient life today.

In the Bible the gospel itself is also a command. We are exhorted not only to believe the gospel but also to obey. The Holy Spirit is given to those who obey God, that is, to those who obey the word which is preached. Remember, obedience is involved in the very acceptance of the Lord Jesus. It is God's command that men everywhere should believe. Believing, therefore, is obeying. From the very start, those who are in the church ought to learn how to obey the Lord, how to obey God's authority.

The Authority Upheld

The church is a corporate body having the special characteristic that its members, as long as they live in this world, live in obedience. We take obedience as our principle of daily life.

The church today needs to be brought to the place where she can declare that what God did not obtain at the time of Adam He now has obtained in her. What God failed to get from the nation of Israel is today found in the church. What the world—the men of every tribe and tongue and people and nation—does not have, the church does have. In other words, on this huge earth there is at least one group of people which upholds the authority of God. Though the people in this wide, wide world are rebellious, the church is the one body that is obedient to authority. She should be able to lift up her head and say, "Lord, what You did not get from Satan and his rebellious followers You now have in the church."

Thus, unto the principalities and the powers in the heavenly places God's authority is now made manifest through the church. The church today is on the earth not only to preach the gospel and to build herself up but also to manifest the authority of God. Everywhere else God's authority is rejected, but here in the church His authority is upheld. People in the world do not seek the will of God, but the church is here seeking His will. In other words, the church is an obedient body. If you are unsaved and therefore not in the church, you are excepted; otherwise, once you come into the church you must before God uphold this one basic principle of enabling God's authority to be accomplished in the church. God's will cannot get through anywhere in the world, but His will should be able to prevail in the church. You and I must uphold God's authority in the church.

For this reason, the brothers and sisters in the church must all learn to be obedient. Please bear in mind that no sin is more serious than that of disobedience, for it contradicts the very reason for the church's existence. What mattered with the Lord Jesus on earth was not whether He lived well but whether He was obedient. As a matter of fact, if the Son had done anything on His own, it could only have been good. But He insisted that He could do nothing by Himself, for He did not come to do His own will but to do the will of the Father who sent Him. Remember that there is one authority in the universe that must be upheld, and the Lord did uphold it. Today, may the church do the same.

Obedience is the life of the church. It is her very nature and therefore her basic principle. She exists for the purpose of upholding obedience. She is the precise opposite of the condition of the surrounding nations. While the nations of the earth take counsel together against God and against His anointed, saying, "Let us break their bonds asunder, and cast away their cords from us" (see Ps. 2.1-3), while they struggle to be free of the law of the Son of God, the church declares with joy, "I most gladly put myself under His bonds and His cords in order to learn obedience." This is the church. She becomes not only a body which obeys the direct authority of God but also an organ for the testimony of obedience. She upholds on earth God's indirect, delegated authority as well as God's direct authority.

The Authority of the Church

In the Bible much is said about obedience.

1. THE LAW OF THE BODY

The church is the body of Christ. Within the body is an inherent law. Every member has his use, and every member is governed by a strange and mysterious law of function. It is imperative for the members to learn how to be subject to the law of the body. If any member should act independently, out of his own idea, it betrays a sickness. The characteristic of the body is oneness. When that oneness is wrecked, the body most surely is sick.

For this reason, no child of God should violate the law of the body of Christ and act independently. Independent actions always speak of rebellion. Rebellion is expressed by independent action. To act independently is to not be in subjection to the authority of the head, to the principle of oneness which God has ordained for the body, or to the law of oneness prescribed in the Bible. Independent action is both a matter of disobedience to the Lord and of insubjection to the body.

2. SUBJECTION TO CHURCH AUTHORITY

Matthew 18 shows us that if two or three brothers fail to convince you, they should bring the matter to the church. The whole church then should deliberate before God. If the decision still is against you, what will you say then? Will you say, "Though the body judges me to be wrong, the head reckons me right; though my parents forsake me, the Lord keeps me; though my brethren reject me, the Lord receives me. I will bear the cross here"? No, such an attitude would show that you are outside the church. How can you consider yourself persecuted and ill-treated, suffering at the hands of your brethren? My advice to you is to humble yourself and say, "Whatever the church says is right, for there can be no further judgment. If all the brothers and sisters say I am wrong, I am wrong, in spite of my own feeling." We need to learn how to be in subjection to the authority of the church.

There is the authority of God in the church. Do not be so hardened as to refute the decision of the fraternity. A proud person has no place in the church, for he knows neither obedience nor the church. Let us learn to be gentle, humble, and submissive. The church has authority before God. What the church rejects, God rejects.

3. REPRESENTATIVE AUTHORITY IN THE CHURCH

THE RESPONSIBLE BROTHERS – THE ELDERS

The Bible shows us that those who are responsible brothers before the Lord, those who are overseers or elders, represent God's authority in the church in a special way. The other brethren should learn how to stand in a position of subjection to them before God. The work of those whom God appoints to authority in the church is to oversee all the affairs of the church. Hence, the brethren should learn to accept their decisions and to be in subjection to them.

Everyone among us ought to learn obedience. It is most pitiful if a person never in his life learns subjection. We must be obedient to the church, God's ordained authority on earth, as well as to God himself. We must also obey the authority which God establishes in the church—the responsible brothers.

ELDERLY AND ADVANCED BRETHREN

"Now I beseech you, brethren (ye know the house of Stephanas, that it is the firstfruits of Achaia, and that they have set themselves to minister unto the saints), that ye also be in subjection unto such, and to every one that helpeth in the work and laboreth" (1 Cor. 16.15-16). Those of the house of Stephanas had no thought but to serve the saints in the church at Corinth. Paul exhorted the saints to be in subjection to them. Whoever is appointed of God to be authority in the church is to be obeyed. The Corinthian believers must be in subjection to the house of Stephanas and to those who labored with Stephanas. We too must respect those who are older than us, who have been in Christ longer as firstfruits and who have set themselves to minister to us. Never think that you can reject them. No, they should be obeyed.

LEADERS

"Obey them that have the rule over you, and submit to them: for they watch in behalf of your souls, as they that shall give account" (Heb. 13.17a). The word of God is quite clear that we must obey those who watch over our own souls. There is no such thing as our choosing whom to obey. It would create great difficulty if we were to listen to one brother and not to another. Do remember that there is nothing unusual in hearkening to what a brother says. We all must learn to obey those who are ahead of us as well as those who are above us. We must learn to obey those who lead us as well as those who are especially gifted and greatly used of the Lord. We should always seek to find out who those ahead of us are.

Why must we obey those who lead us? "They watch in behalf of your souls, as they that shall give account; that they may do this with joy, and not with grief: for this were unprofitable for you." (v.19). Whoever is ahead of you and watches over your soul in order to give an account before God, that is the person to whom you must render your submission.

LABORERS AMONG US

"We beseech you, brethren, to know them that labor among you, and are over you in the Lord, and admonish you; and to esteem them exceeding highly in love for their work's sake" (1 Thess. 5.12-13). Some are used of the Lord to lead, to admonish, and to rule over you. To them you should give respect and honor. To them you should give obedience. If a Christian can find no one on earth to obey, he will be the strangest person in the world. A Christian ought to be able to see people everywhere who are ahead of him, who carry more spiritual weight, and who watch over his soul. It is to them that he should subject himself.

This being the case, the church must uphold this one principle—a principle which God cannot find in Satan, in the world, or in the universe. This principle is obedience. It is the basic lesson of the church. What the world rejects, the church gains. The basic principle of the church is obedience.

The Kingdom

Scripture to Memorize:

Who [God] delivered us out of the power of darkness, and translated us into the kingdom of the Son of his love

Colossians 1.13

According to prophecies recorded in the Bible, the condition of the kingdom or nation will become increasingly serious. For nation shall rise against nation, and kingdom against kingdom. The structure of the government will become tighter and tighter. And as the book of Revelation predicts, it will be found that with the manifestation of the Antichrist, "no man [shall] be able to buy or to sell, save he that hath the mark, even the name of the beast or the number of his name" (13.17). This too will constitute a most serious affair. Hence we need to talk somewhat concerning the matter of the kingdom or nation.

1. GOD HAS CALLED US TO ENTER THE KINGDOM OF HIS SON

Whatever the Lord fared while on earth, that is what we too will fare on earth. And whatever He will have on earth in the future, we shall also share with Him. The psalmist declares: "Jehovah saith unto my Lord, Sit thou at my right hand, until I make thine enemies thy footstool" (Ps. 110.1). The Lord Jesus is now waiting for God to give Him the kingdoms of the world to be His footstool. He is above all politics. He is to set up another kingdom, even the kingdom of the heavens. All who are called out of the nations and kingdoms of this world are destined to be the citizens of

His kingdom to come. We believers have a share in that kingdom because of the life which God has given to us. This is the Christian's position toward that kingdom.

The course which God has chosen for Christ is our course too. Just as the Lord does not assume management over any kingdom today, so this is to be our attitude as well. One day He shall rule the nations with an iron rod; thus will His kingdom come. And at that time we too shall have our kingdom.

The Lord tells us to bless the nations, not to curse them (1 Tim. 2.1-4). Only at the opening of the fifth seal (as recorded in Revelation) will the souls underneath the altar ask for vengeance and not for blessing. When the Lord was asked to divide the inheritance for some people, His answer was: "Man, who made me a judge or a divider over you?" (Luke 12.14). That was a civil case, it was not what a Christian today should do. On another occasion, when a woman taken in adultery was brought to the Lord, instead of her being condemned by the Lord, she was set free with these words: "Neither do I condemn thee: go thy way; from henceforth sin no more" (John 8.11b). This was a criminal case, and our Lord would not lift up His hand at all; rather, He wrote on the ground with His finger and let the dust be blown away. That was the Lord's way for handling the situation, and it is to be as well the way for us who have fellowship with Him. "I think," said Paul, that "God hath set forth us the apostles last of all, as men doomed to death" (1 Cor. 4.9a). It would therefore be highly abnormal for the Corinthian or any other believers to reign today in this world (cf. v.8).

2. CONCERNING THE BELIEVER'S ATTITUDE TOWARD POLITICS

"Let every soul be in subjection to the higher powers: for there is no power but of God; and the powers that be are ordained of God" (Rom. 13.1). God has set on earth two institutions: one is the state or kingdom, the other is the church. The government has authority, but so does the church have authority. God is the source of all governmental powers. All the powers on earth are ordained of God for good. If these powers or authorities should rebel and resist Him, they will sooner or later be removed. They are all under the control of God's authority. Even a policeman is ordained of God. So that the Lord has commanded us to be in subjection, though He has not charged us to be powers in the world. We must be in subjection to all state authorities. And likewise in the church, we submit ourselves as well to all spiritual authorities there.

God so sets up powers on earth that Christians should have no reason to fear them. We believe in government; we reject anarchy. The powers which are ordained of God are done so in order to punish the evil and to approve the good (see Rom. 13.3). And even though such powers may go wrong, the principles of punishing the evil and approving the good can never be wrong. Those who execute the law must themselves keep the law. Governing authorities dare not openly declare that they will punish the lawful.

For the sake of conscience, Christians should be in subjection to the government which God has set up on earth: "Render to all their dues: tribute to whom tribute is due; custom to whom custom; fear to whom fear; honor to whom honor" (Rom. 13.7). It is a Christian duty to learn to pay the tax. "Be subject," said Peter, "to every ordinance of man for the Lord's sake: whether to the king, as supreme; or unto governors, as sent by him for vengeance on evil-doers and for praise to them that do well" (1 Pet. 2.13-14).

3. Concerning the Limits of Obedience

God alone deserves unlimited obedience; all others who

exceed the measure of authority which God has given are not worthy of obedience. The obedience which a Christian renders to his country is not absolute. Obedience is a matter of action, whereas submission is one of attitude. From the book of Exodus we learn that the Hebrew midwives did not do what Pharaoh of Egypt commanded them—to kill all male children born to Hebrew women; and neither did Moses' mother obey this same decree of Pharaoh. Because the command of Pharaoh was contradictory to the law of God, it need not and should not be obeyed. Again, Daniel's three friends disobeyed the king's order, and they were commended by God. Daniel himself refused to follow the king's decree and was thrown into the lions' den; he too was approved of God. When Herod ordered to be killed all the male children in Bethlehem and its borders from two years old and under, Joseph took the baby Jesus and departed into Egypt.

Unless the order of the country's authorities contradicts God's laws or commands, we should learn to obey such authorities. Yet Peter and John said to the ruling authorities of their day who had forbade them to speak or teach in the name of Jesus, "Whether it is right in the sight of God to hearken unto you rather than unto God, judge ye: for we cannot but speak the things which we saw and heard" (Acts 4.19-20). If any nation's ruling powers take the step of persecuting us for religious reasons, we need not obey, but should submit ourselves even to the extent of our being put in jail.

4. CONCERNING WAR

In the Old Testament period we find that God is a God who goes to war. He is called "Jehovah of hosts." Many of the battles which Israel fought were ordained of God. In the future at Har-Magedon (i.e., Armageddon; see Rev. 16.14,16; also, Zech. 14.2), God will gather the nations to war. So we cannot say that war is totally unjustified. However, during this period of grace, the Lord Jesus announces to his followers: "Blessed are the peacemakers: for they shall be called sons of God" (Matt. 5.9). He also declares this: "My kingdom is not of this world" (John 18.36a). Hence He wants us to preach the gospel of grace to men during this period of time. His word to Peter was: "Put up the sword into the sheath" (John 18.11a). Now is the time to put up the sword into the sheath. If this matter of war is left to our choice, no Christian may approve of war nor engage in it; but if we are forced into it, we as Christians will not bear arms but will be prepared to suffer the consequences for not doing so. It is good for the Christian not to be forced upon with respect to carrying arms. May we ask God to deliver us from it. Though war is permitted to happen by God, we as Christians must not take part in it[*].

---

[*]Concerning politics and war, Christians hold very different views. Each must therefore follow the dictate of his or her conscience.— *Translator.*

The Second Coming of the Lord

Scripture to Memorize:

He who testifieth these things saith, Yea: I come quickly. Amen: come, Lord Jesus.

Revelation 22.20

This last verse of the last chapter in the last book of the Bible was written about sixty years after the ascension of the Lord. The Holy Spirit has already come, and of the original twelve apostles only one was still alive. The Lord is coming soon.

We must not only look back to the cross but also look forward to the Lord's return. The grace of God which has brought salvation to us is to enable us to wait for the glorious appearing of the Lord. We should therefore serve the living God on the one hand and wait for the Lord's return on the other. Though we yet live on this earth, we break bread to remember the Lord till He comes. Though we lay stress on service as to how we need to fulfill the priestly ministry, we nevertheless know that such service on earth will not continue forever. One day we shall become the bride of the Lamb. All the objectives of the believers are not earthly. However much we may emphasize the local church, even that will not last on earth. We are looking and waiting for the Lord's return. The calling of God for us is not earthly, but heavenly. In sum, God has not called us to build permanently on earth.

According to the signs of the times given in the Bible, the coming of the Lord is undoubtedly near. Let us therefore wait, which means that whatever we do is for the sake of awaiting His return. Miss Margaret E. Barber was one who awaited the coming of the Lord with a single mind. Nothing about her had any permanent note. "I may suddenly meet the Lord," she once said, "at the next turn."

Since ours is a heavenly calling, there is nothing permanent or timeless on earth. As soon as we come to the Lord, we become the people who wait for the Lord's return. We are waiting for His coming, and not simply knowing that He will return. Not all who study the book of Revelation necessarily wait for the Lord's coming. Some people are well acquainted with the great white throne, the new heaven and the new earth, and other prophecies, but they may not be waiting for the coming of the Lord.

We are not out to change the world; rather, we are called out to be those who are unto the Lord. We entertain no hope of this earth, nor do we anticipate anything from the world. At His first coming, the Lord delivers us from sin and grants us the life of God that we may commune with God. This, however, is only half of the work. Though the question of sin is solved, the problem of death yet remains. The dominion of sin in man's life is over, but the kingdom of Satan still lingers. The power of death is broken, nevertheless our mortal bodies may yet die. Although we are saved, we continue to live in this corrupt environment. The holier the life, the deeper the feeling over the defilement of this world. The salvation which we now experience is but half the story, because the Lord Jesus— though He has saved us—has not yet changed the world.

The World

The second coming of the Lord is to change the world. He will not only give us enjoyment within but also allow us to enjoy the environment without because He will change the environment on earth. Many people are interested in social problems. They argue: "The salvation of the Lord saves only individuals but leaves the world full of inequality. Even the lower animals suffer so much. All the things in the world serve as enticements to men to sin. Though individuals may be saved, what about all these negative social conditions?"

As to this matter of waiting for the Lord's second coming, there appear to be two different concepts held among Christians. On the one hand, some believers are set on improving the world, but unfortunately they end up being defiled by it instead. On the other hand, others say that our responsibility is to rescue people out, and that the improvement of this world must wait till the Lord's return.

The Bible is not lax with respect to these matters. God has not said that so long as sinners are saved and are assured of going to heaven that that is enough. The Bible entertains no such thought. For heaven is not a matter of individual salvation; there is also the matter of the new heaven and new earth, which comes when—and only when—all who are ordained to eternal life have believed in the Lord. The Bible does have the salvation of society or the salvation of the world in view, but this work will be completed only with the second coming of the Lord. Today the church is commissioned to preach the gospel that individuals within the world may be saved, and yet the Lord has not forgotten the world. We are called today to rescue people out of the world, and not to change the world itself. This world has absolutely no hope whatsoever. All the problems on earth will only be solved at the Lord's return.

Some Basic Problems

On the earth there are a number of basic problems:

1. INJUSTICE

God has said that only when His Son comes again shall

righteousness be manifested: "With righteousness shall he judge the poor, and decide with equity for the meek of the earth; and he shall smite the earth with the rod of his mouth; and with the breath of his lips shall he slay the wicked" (see Is. 11.4).

2. WAR

There has always been the slaughtering of mankind on this earth. What the world needs most is peace. At the coming of the Lord, war shall be put to an end: "He will judge between the nations, and will decide concerning many peoples; and they shall beat their swords into plowshares, and their spears into pruning-hooks; nation shall not lift up sword against nation, neither shall they learn war any more" (Is. 2.4). Peace comes from the Lord and from no one else.

3. PUBLIC HEALTH

We have no absolute control over pestilences. According to Jeremiah and Ezekiel, they are fully controlled only by God. At the return of our Lord, all these shall pass away: "the inhabitant shall not say, I am sick: the people that dwell therein shall be forgiven their iniquity" (Is. 33.24). People will also live long too: "There shall be no more thence an infant of days, nor an old man that hath not filled his days; for the child shall die a hundred years old, and the sinner being a hundred years old shall be accursed" (Is. 65.20).

4. HUNGER

This is a major problem. Farm produce does not meet the world's needs. The whole world looks most attentively at this problem. A strange phenomenon prevails on earth, which is, that farm produce is difficult to grow whereas weeds grow quite easily and quite profusely. It is the weeds which squeeze out the wheat, not the wheat the weeds. A little carelessness in pulling out the weeds may at the same time destroy the wheat and ultimately hurt the harvest (see Matt. 13.28-30). This confirms that the curse on earth as told of in Genesis 3.17b,18 is indeed a fact ("Cursed is the ground for thy sake; in toil shalt thou eat of it all the days of thy life; thorns also and thistles shall it bring forth to thee; and thou shalt eat the herb of the field").

It awaits the return of the Lord to solve this problem completely: "Behold, I will do a new thing; now shall it spring forth; shall ye not know it? I will even make a way in the wilderness, and rivers in the desert. The beasts of the field shall honor me, the jackals and the ostriches; because I give waters in the wilderness, and rivers in the desert, to give drink to my people, my chosen" (Is. 43.19,20)—"The wilderness and the dry land shall be glad; and the desert shall rejoice, and blossom as the rose" (Is. 35.1)—"Jehovah hath comforted Zion; he hath comforted all her waste places, and hath made her wilderness like Eden, and her desert like the garden of Jehovah; joy and gladness shall be found therein, thanksgiving, and the voice of melody" (Is. 51.3).

5. EDUCATION

This surely is a basic need for society. Man should be instructed to know good and evil. But at the return of Christ, the knowledge of the Lord shall fill the earth completely: "They shall not hurt nor destroy in all my holy mountain; for the earth shall be full of the knowledge of Jehovah, as the waters cover the sea" (Is. 11.9)—"This is the covenant that I will make with the house of Israel after those days, saith Jehovah: I will put my law in their inward parts, and in their heart will I write it; and I will be their God, and they shall be my people. And they shall teach no more every man his neighbor, and every man his brother, saying, Know Jehovah; for they shall all know me, from the least of them unto the greatest of them, saith Jehovah: for I will forgive their iniquity, and their sin will I remember no more" (Jer. 31.33-34).

6. POLITICS

The whole world, whether at the international or at the domestic level, is engaged in striving for political power. Yet at the coming of the Lord, the seventh angel shall sound the trumpet and great voices in heaven shall declare: "The kingdom of the world is become the kingdom of our Lord, and of his Christ: and he shall reign for ever and ever" (Rev. 11.15).

At His first coming, the Lord's gospel solves my personal problem of sin; but at His second coming, He shall solve all the problems on earth. What the Lord Jesus does today is mainly on a personal basis, not on institutional ground. It awaits His second coming for all the problems on earth to be solved by means of His government. Today we are men of unclean lips dwelling in the midst of a people of unclean lips (see Is. 6.5); but in the future we shall be clean men standing among a clean people. It is absolutely impossible for man to establish love through hatred. Any human attempts to establish peace and prosperity today are subject to human error and can possibly lead to indescribable sufferings of mankind as a consequence. But when the Lord shall come, all will be perfectly established. How significant indeed is the second coming of the Lord.

The Lord Is Coming

Our calling is heavenly, and it is not for the purpose of changing this piece of earth. Nothing is permanent with us, nothing is indispensable. According to the Lord's arrangement, it is equally good for us to have or not to have. Everything will be fine if He comes. We live for His sake, and we wait for His return. At His coming our salvation shall be completed. Not only I personally shall be changed, even the environment shall be changed. Today we speak of coming out of the world and being not of the world; at that day, we need not say such words anymore. Nothing really matters much today, even the most spiritual work for the Lord is not permanently needed. Our one and only hope is to await the Lord's return. How can we be deeply rooted on earth? Does not the word of God test us all the time? The Lord is at the doors (see Matt. 24.33). Let us wait for His coming.